POLITICS, RELIGION, AND CULTURE IN AN ANXIOUS AGE

Previous Publications

Democracy by Other Means: The Politics of Work, Leisure, and Environment

Sustainable Democracy: Individuality and the Politics of the Environment (with Tom DeLuca)

The End of Homework: How Homework Disrupts Families, Overburdens Children, and Limits Learning (with Etta Kralovec)

Closing the Book on Homework: Enhancing public Education and Freeing Family Time

Liars, Cheaters, Evil Doers: Demonization and the End of Civil Discourse in American Politics (with Tom DeLuca)

POLITICS, RELIGION, AND CULTURE IN AN ANXIOUS AGE

JOHN BUELL

palgrave
macmillan

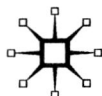

First published in 2011 by
PALGRAVE MACMILLAN®
in the United States—a division of St. Martin's Press LLC,
175 Fifth Avenue, New York, NY 10010.

Where this book is distributed in the UK, Europe and the rest of the
world, this is by Palgrave Macmillan, a division of Macmillan Publishers
Limited, registered in England, company number 785998, of
Houndmills, Basingstoke, Hampshire RG21 6XS.

Palgrave Macmillan is the global academic imprint of the above
companies and has companies and representatives throughout the
world.

Palgrave® and Macmillan® are registered trademarks in the United
States, the United Kingdom, Europe and other countries.

ISBN: 978–0–230–11772–3

Library of Congress Cataloging-in-Publication Data

Buell, John.
    Politics, religion, and culture in an anxious age / by John Buell.
        p. cm.
    ISBN 978–0–230–11772–3 (hardcover)
    1. Political culture—United States. 2. Rhetoric—Political
aspects—United States. 3. Religion and politics—United States.
4. United States—Politics and government—2001–2009.
5. United States—Politics and government—2009– I. Title.

JK275.B835 2011
306.20973—dc22   2011005453

A catalogue record of the book is available from the British Library.

Design by Newgen Imaging Systems (P) Ltd., Chennai, India.

First edition: August 2011

10 9 8 7 6 5 4 3 2 1

Printed in the United States of America.

CONTENTS

Preface: A Hair Trigger Nation?

In December 2005 a US air marshal killed Rigoberto Alpizar, a passenger aboard an American Airlines plane in Miami. The victim was carrying no explosives. Suffering from bipolar disorder and off his medication, he had issued threats. Taking no chances, the air marshal shot him. Days afterward, *Boston Globe* columnist James Carroll wondered if we have not become a hair trigger nation so obsessed with risks that we have turned our guardians into our potential killers. Carroll also asked if the Miami incident "isn't the domestic equivalent of this nation's hair trigger foreign policy?"[1]

That tragic incident, however, soon passed from media attention. Yet the incident left a set of important questions in the minds of some. One Maine psychiatrist, writing two years after the event, commented:

> How quickly this all passed from public consciousness! I was reminded of the tragedy by a patient who is now doing well but who had not long ago descended into his own psychosis, and in that confused and terrifying state had faced his own moment of truth with the law. The Maine State Police had subdued him with non-lethal means, but he recognized in the tragedy of Mr. Alpizar that his fate might have been horribly different.
>
> Perhaps Mr. Alpizar disappeared so quickly from the public eye because his story too painfully highlights a national tragedy: we are frightened and divided—beset by fears of terrorists, of evil-doers, of people who do not share our beliefs and values, of people who look and act different. We seek comfort, circle the wagons if you will, in the company of those who are like us, who do not set off the warning bells of oddness or deviance. At our worst, we find comfort in making scapegoats of those who frighten us with their difference. We find solace in the fiction that ours is the better country, the better God.
>
> Much of our political discourse reinforces the drift toward fear and division. And while we can usually count on religion to lift us up and appeal to our better nature, much of the church has fallen into the broader cultural morass. The Protestant Right has hardened its heart against those who fail to toe the doctrinal line. The Vatican has found its bete noire in homosexuality. The excesses committed in the names of Judaism and Islam in the Middle East and elsewhere are nothing less than horrific.[2]

Americans are fond of the phrase better safe than sorry. And fear plays an important role in our physical and cultural survival. If we are not literally hardwired to perceive and respond with intense physical reactions to incidents or events that might threaten our survival, such instincts are at least deeply embedded in our preconscious awareness of the world. Fight or flight is an all too human—and often necessary—response to many of the events and challenges of our world. Nonetheless, human beings can become so intellectually and emotionally preoccupied with fear of death even when they face no immediate risk and of their own physical and intellectual limits that they cannot act in the world and may even increase their own immediate risks. They crawl into intellectual or emotional cocoons.

More broadly, a climate of fear of death often occasions or is intensified by fear of those who are different from us. Fear of cultural outsiders often peaks during periods of mass pandemics, as hatred of Jews and Gypsies reached intense levels during the Plague and SARS became an occasion for discrimination against Asian travelers and residents showing no visible signs of the disease. Conversely, fear of outsiders can in turn increase our expectations for and fears of "natural catastrophe." Thus diseases associated with certain minorities or lifestyles may be more feared than other equally fatal conditions. The rapidity and intensity of cross-border migrations of people and ideas have intensified nationalistic, racist, and fundamentalist currents not only in the United States but in much of the world. These currents have in turn added to a general climate of fear.

It is one thing to take reasonable precautions in the event of clear or likely danger. Yet death is a part of the human condition and fear of death too easily morphs into or is colored by a resentment of human finitude, that is, our (often premature or unpredictable) deaths and our limited knowledge of ourselves and our world. Non-Western philosophy, especially that indebted to some currents of Buddhism, has captured this phenomenon well. Eckhart Tolle, asked by a questioner if a certain amount of fear isn't healthy self-protection and if without fear he wouldn't go sticking his hands in fires, responded:

> The reason why you don't put your hand in the fire is not because of fear, it is because you know you'll get burned. You don't need fear to avoid unnecessary danger—just a minimum of intelligence and common sense. For such practical matters it is useful to apply the lessons learned in the past. Now if someone *threatened* you with fire or physical violence, you might experience something like fear. This is an instinctive shrinking back from danger but not the psychological condition of fear we are talking about here. The psychological condition of fear is divorced from any clear and immediate danger. It comes in many forms: unease, worry, anxiety, nervousness, tension, dread, phobia, and so on. This kind of psychological

fear is always of something that *might* happen, not of something that is happening now. You are in the here and now while your mind is in the future. This creates an anxiety gap. And if you are identified with your mind and have lost touch with the power and simplicity of the Now, that anxiety gap will be your constant companion. You can always cope with the present moment, but you cannot cope with something that is only a mind projection—you cannot cope with the future. Moreover, as long as you are identified with your mind, the ego runs your life. ... Because of its phantom nature and despite elaborate defense mechanisms the ego is very vulnerable and insecure, and it sees itself as constantly under threat ... What message is the body continually receiving from the ego, the false, mind-made self? Danger, I am under threat. And what is the emotion generated by this continuous message? Fear, of course. Fear seems to have many causes. Fear of loss, fear of failure, fear of being hurt and so on, but ultimately all fear is the ego's fear of death, of annihilation. To the ego, death is always just around the corner. In this mind-identified state, fear of death affects every aspect of your life. For example, even such a seemingly trivial and "normal" thing as the compulsive need to be right in an argument and make the other person wrong—defending the mental position with which you have identified—is due to the fear of death. If you identify with a mental position, then if you are wrong, your mind-based sense of self is seriously threatened with annihilation. So you as the ego cannot afford to be wrong. To be wrong is to die. Wars have been fought over this ... [3]

In modern Western societies, life expectancy has reached new highs, but in some ways this development only intensifies resentment of death and the quest for permanent mastery or denial of it. These resentments in turn often lead to quests for final moral standard, dogmatic certainties about our role in and governance of nature, and the conviction that without widespread acceptance of universal, fundamental moral and intellectual standards, anarchy or social collapse will result.

This is not a uniquely fearful time. Many medieval Christians eagerly or fearfully awaited the end of the world at the turn of the first millennium. Yet fear and the related quest for existential certainty do wax and wane. Arguably they are on the rise today. In the face of a world becoming increasingly fearful and divided along lines of nationality, race, and ideology, there are religious and philosophical traditions that can issue in both more acceptance of the fact of death without falling back on dreams of heaven or harsh scenarios of divine punishment for those left behind by a vengeful god.

Those who are most gripped by fears today are also often devotees of logics of divine punishment or hatred of those who stand outside the privileged circle. They maintain that failure to draw strict moral lines or affirm an omnipotent God leaves the world trapped in a swamp of relativism and headed for anarchy and destruction.

Such arguments are not limited to the economic and cultural right in US politics. Some have also charged that current weather patterns and disease outbreaks are necessary and inevitable consequences of capitalist overreach. Others see in the current economic difficulties the nearing collapse of the US empire, a fitting end to its overreach. Yet, though current technologies may and do run substantial risks and modern capitalism's ambitions may exceed its grasp, consequences of that overreach may themselves be inherently unpredictable. Sometimes, stuff does not happen. In addition, events such as blackouts or the tragedy of New Orleans are seldom reducible to the actions of a few "greedy" individuals or even to a simple set of institutions.

Just as basically, those who worry about the role that doomsday scenarios, whether of the left or right or so-called postmodern variety, play in shaping politics must be on guard that they do not become enveloped in their own doomsday scenarios. I see an ineliminable element of uncertainty, indeterminacy, and unpredictability in life. I worry that widespread failure on the part of political and cultural elites to acknowledge these limits and a related proclivity even to embrace deeply opposed apocalyptic worldviews increases the risk of catastrophe. Nonetheless, I must fight the temptation to believe that their moral absolutes will necessarily foster apocalypse or that even broad acceptance of some variant of my perspective will assure salvation. And I must fight the temptation to view those who resist this perspective as blind or ill-willed. Nonetheless, there is a strong case for examining the role of apocalyptic perspectives across the political and philosophical spectrum and for articulation of possible alternatives.

In this work, I examine the ways several doomsday scenarios now interact with and often reinforce each other. These, in turn, may have adverse consequences for our political freedom. Merely highlighting the excesses of these movements is not, however, adequate. Existential anxieties, modes of social and community interaction, cultural history, and past policy choices have made our nation especially vulnerable to these tendencies. Demands for a more "fact- based" or scientific politics do not constitute an adequate response. "Facts" and "values" within the social sciences are not simple dichotomies. Our understanding of how the world works helps shape our actions and aspirations. In addition, science itself raises some fundamental value questions of its own. Even within the natural sciences, there are important disputes as to the predictability and law-like nature of the natural world. These philosophical disputers have moral implications.

A book that both explores alternative approaches to contemporary existential anxieties and relates these alternatives to some of our most contentious issues can advance moral discourse while serving a constructive political purpose by encouraging the emergence of coalitions to resist the

worst excesses of the culture wars and class conflict. How issues are resolved or handled depends, as George Lakoff argues, on how they are
framed.[4] In this book, the framing that I advance includes not merely
word choice but historical narratives, core assumptions, tone and style of
argument, and even aesthetic representations.

I do not categorically reject all versions of apocalyptic scenarios. I cannot prove them wrong, and more basically I accept the possibility—even
the likelihood—of major ecological or economic collapse. What I reject is
the certainty of such events, especially the ability to predict when tipping
points will occur. Nor do I see such events as inherently redemptive or the
last word in evil. Finally, I reject the notion that apocalyptic narratives
are likely to do full justice to unfolding events or that by themselves they
can be a sufficient incentive to constructive action. Risks can and must be
assessed and addressed, but with attentiveness to the limits of our predictive powers and the fears and values we bring to the task.

In seeking to get beyond fear-driven politics, I present alternative modes
of thinking about the human condition both within Christianity itself as
well as in some currents of contemporary philosophical discourse. These
alternatives differ among themselves in important ways, but they allow
us to confront and accept the fact of death, the limits of our perspectives,
and the inherent unpredictability of both human action and the natural world. I discuss the prophetic Christianity of mid-twentieth-century
theologian Reinhold Niebuhr, more recent scholarship on the historical
Jesus by Stephen Mitchell, Mennonite theologian John Howard Yoder,
John Sanders's open theism, the process theology of Catherine Keller, and
the immanent naturalism of Jane Bennett and William Connolly. Though
such alternatives differ from each other, they contribute to a broader dialogue that can help build a movement to resist the most dangerous forms of
apocalyptic politics. It may even paradoxically reduce some of our immediate political and natural threats.

Though much indebted to the theological and philosophical works
mentioned earlier, I depart from this literature in two regards. First, I strive
to be accessible to a wider readership than that of professional political
theorists and theologians. Second, the book continually moves back and
forth between highly publicized political issues and the underlying religious and ethical concerns implied in the debates. An understanding of
the philosophical issues involved can be advanced not merely by abstract
analysis but also by attending to the particular political controversies in
which they are embedded.

The book is organized around a series of policy-based case studies
of major media crises or natural catastrophes portrayed as potentially
destroying our civilization. Each "crisis" received lazer-like attention from

the media for a period of time. Even though one crisis often gives way to the next, earlier crises often recur years later in slightly altered guises.

All these crises do, however, share an uneasy and shifting mix of widely felt social concerns and scientific and philosophical understandings of the natural and social worlds. Each resonates with and often intensifies the others. A range of alternative ethical, religious, and philosophical perspectives and concomitant policy agendas might counter these destructive trends. That hope informs my work.

Acknowledgments

Throughout my high-school years, my mother and grandmother took my brother, sister, and me on train trips from our Grosse Pointe, Michigan, home to Miami Beach. Reluctant to fly, we rode a train from Detroit to New York City and from NYC to Florida every spring vacation. Even as a child, the trip served as an unsettling educational experience. Trains often travel through messy social scenes that planes glide over easily. During my ninth grade year, our sleeper car stopped for nearly an hour in Northern Florida. On the tracks next to ours, eight or ten shirtless African Americans were engaged in vigorous activity. Each was throwing large blocks of ice from the ground to fellow workers perched on top of the passenger cars. The men on top of the car were then dumping the ice into a compartment on the train. Puzzled by this scene, I asked my grandmother what they were doing. "Filling the ice chest that refrigerates the cars," she replied. All I could think was: "what an awful job." Since I had seen my father load ice blocks into the ice chest of his sailboat, I realized the ice blocks were about fifty pounds apiece. I could hardly imagine throwing them anywhere.

I felt vaguely uneasy, but soon moved on to fantasizing about what we were gong to do in Florida. Later that spring, I found another tonic that helped put aside any residual anxieties. A friend lent me Barry Goldwater's *Conscience of a Conservative*. Though I was not especially interested in the Cold War politics, I was very taken by the libertarian economics. The view of a market society and decentralized government with its prospects of autonomy and progress for all was compelling. It conveyed a message of political freedom and opportunity for all if government would just get out of the way. As one who grew up the son of a surgeon and grandson of a successful department store executive, emphasis on free markets and personal initiative made sense to me.

On the next trip to Florida, my assumptions started to unwind. Required to spend a night in NYC en route this time, I suggested to my mother a cab ride through Harlem, about which I had read during a civics class. Somewhat reluctantly, my mother obliged. I was stunned and a bit scared when our cab stopped at a red light, only to have two men jump out from the curb and begin to wash our windshield. They asked for money, but the cab driver simply cursed and drove off immediately as the light changed. My most indelible Harlem memory was of a child, perhaps four, sitting on the broken porch of a thoroughly dilapidated house. I wondered how much of a difference "personal initiative" would make in his life.

Enter senior year. As a senior, I had the opportunity of taking a non-graded elective. I chose a theology course being offered by a young assistant Presbyterian minister. Lyman Stookey (a distant relative of Noel Paul Stookey) had recently graduated from Union Theological Seminary, where he had been a student of Reinhold Niebuhr. Stookey plunged us into a set of complex moral issues, including the poverty and unemployment in Detroit's inner city. Were these examples of the injustices once attacked by the biblical prophets, who spoke a truth to the limits of all human powers and institutions? I felt obliged to take up a defense of Detroit's major employers and corporate interests and to invoke my knowledge of market theory. Stookey responded respectfully that this was a powerful system of thought that could surely not be disproven, though a number of countervailing arguments could be advanced. More telling for me was his further suggestion that our theoretical understanding of how the world works can also act as affirmations of our own core identities and values. Were not grand theories, including even Marxism, implicated in some form of self-justification? Did we not owe it to ourselves, at least periodically, to try on other modes of thinking about and relating to the plight of the poor and the excluded? Where were their voices in my calculus? That spring, on my Florida vacation, I borrowed Stookey's well-underlined copy of Niebuhr's *Nature and Destiny of Man* (1941). Stookey had changed my life and I owe him one of my greatest debts. He did not stay long in Grosse Pointe and I lost all contact with him. In preparing this book, I learned that he passed away a few years ago after a life of activism and community service. I regret never having conveyed my appreciation to him.

The conversation I began senior year in high school I continued with friends at Amherst College. With George McNeil and Don Sackheim in particular I have had debates and e-mail exchanges about the nature and origins of morality. Their friendship and encouragement has been as important to this project as the intellectual stimulation.

As will be apparent from the very first pages, my debt to William Connolly is immense and continuing. But beyond the obvious scholarly connections, I can say that I would never have been a political theorist but for my encounter with him and his work. From college on I had an interest in politics, but my early encounters with the field left me with the impression that political science had little to do with politics. It seemed an abstract world of formal model building. Though I found notions of "free will" implausible, political science's faith in laws struck me as just that—a faith unwilling to admit its own status and allow any other competitors into the ring.

My first encounter with Bill was a chance meeting when a mutual friend invited him to speak at the prep school where I had been teaching. Bill placed the politics of political explanation at the heart of his work. And equally important to me was the playfulness and generosity of his mind. At the time I had been working on a rather naïve attempt to recruit and revise Republicans' (stated) faith in decentralization as a tool of social justice and a more egalitarian vision of community. While disagreeing with my thesis, he offered many constructive suggestions and challenges. And to this day he can be counted on periodically to rib my naivete. He has been generous with his time and his thoughtfulness to me and my family over four decades now. And though he periodically denigrates my feeble jump shot, I take great pride in having bested him on the Amherst squash courts.

While in graduate school I met Tom DeLuca. His continuing work on democratic theory and political equality has been an inspiration to me. His book on nonvoting deepened my understanding of working-class resistance to aspects of the liberal agenda. He and I coauthored two books. I endured his compulsive fine-tuning and he suffered through my obsessive punctuality. I know I am the better for this encounter. Tom's many comments on this work have sharpened its focus and helped me clarify my own ideas. Most important has been his friendship. He has encouraged me to persist in the face of the many ups and downs the review process often occasions.

I am also fortunate that Peter Bachrach, one of the preeminent democratic theorists of his era, retired to my small Maine community. In our conversations, Peter persuasively championed the idea that democratic politics is more than voting. It included the active formulation of goals and policies within our schools and especially our workplaces. He worried about the power gap between the ruler and the ruled. Years before the Tea Party emerged he speculated that the masses might become alienated, disaffected, and mean. Democracy could become vulnerable to attack by an antidemocratic mass movement.

Conversations with former College of the Atlantic colleagues have also been a continuing source of inspiration. Zoologist John Anderson has discussed themes ranging from evolutionary biology to climate science. Philosophy professor John Visvader has shared reflections on everyone from Kant to Foucault and has invited me to the college for early versions of several chapters of this work.

I owe another great debt to Jane Bennett, a debt that also taps a connection to my high-school years. My senior-year Latin course included poetry by Ovid and Lucretius's De RerumNatura. The latter's materialism with its description of the odd behavior of atoms in the void struck me as a primitive notion that had been voided by modern science. Neither my college physics nor my reading of contemporary theology suggested any connection between our pictures of nonhuman nature and political values. Jane's continuing work long since disabused me of this notion. The shape of the built environment and of human institutions both reflects and is shaped by our encounters with and interpretations of nature, both organic and inorganic. Jane has redeemed the Lucretian swerve for me. Equally important, she has read and provided thoughtful critique of several chapters and has been unwavering in her encouragement.

George Price, priest at St. John (Episcopal) Church for over a quarter century, and Harriet Price, historian and longtime activist, provided a compelling example of humble but telling activism in the world. Both also read large sections of the manuscript and offered many constructive suggestions.

David Wagner, professor of sociology and social work at the University of Southern Maine, has been equally helpful. His award-winning book on the drug war made me much more aware of the ways in which US society constructs threats and of the deeper existential and economic needs served by these "dangers." More recent work on the role of philanthropy in sustaining elites has also added to my understanding of the difficulties of social change. Dave read the entire manuscript and made numerous helpful comments.

Finally, a project that has involved so much of my life would have been impossible without support at home. In my case, the support has gone beyond much valued encouragement and the time to be alone with my thoughts. My wife Susan Covino Buell has been a meticulous editor of almost every page of this work, demanding greater clarity, providing examples and anecdotes, and calling my attention to relevant media and print stories. Her participation in local antiwar and social justice causes has given her insights that have been vital to my work. Had I possessed the time and ability to follow all of her suggestions, the manuscript would have been better. Our three children have been equally supportive. From an early age my youngest son Tim has made me more aware of the role of intuition in our thought processes. He has also made me more attuned to body language as a form of communication. Elisabeth has provided not only steady support for the project but has also asked provocative economic and theological questions. And Todd, the oldest, was for many years the family's only staunch conservative Republican. And despite many temptations, we still fed him. He now lives in Germany and has even admitted that some features of social democratic Europe are worthy of consideration. May wonders never cease.

INTRODUCTION
LISTENING TO TALK RADIO

On a dull Sunday afternoon last Fall I tuned in to a talk radio program on one of Eastern Maine's few remaining locally owned radio stations. Talk radio generally pains me, not so much because of the content, as the tone. Tone and content are not fully separable, but talk radio often conveys less a consistent position than diffuse anger and dogmatic certainty, and contempt for those of differing views and ways of living. Nonetheless, I was curious about what topics and issues were disturbing my neighbors.

Instead, the station was playing a nationally syndicated program featuring an upcoming media star. In an agitated, tone Glenn Beck blasted a school in Texas for grading students solely on the basis of the effort expended. Beck raised relevant objections not only with regard to social standards but also with regard to students' self-esteem. He then, however, went on to a broad indictment of US public education as dominated by a squishy sentimentalism. An ill-defined "they" had abandoned all rigorous evaluation. He conveyed an image of a school system near collapse.

When Beck accused schools of rampant sentimentalism, I was left wondering where he had been for the last eight years. Parents, school boards, political and business leaders have been pushing for stronger, objective, and uniform standards by which schools and teachers are to be judged. High stakes testing has become the norm in many states. Schools and even students that fail to meet the standards are to be sanctioned severely. "No Child Left Behind" (NCLB) might be President Bush's only enduringly popular initiative. Yes, a few figures and a few schools and teachers had publicly opposed these harsh policies, but they were a clear minority. Just as importantly, neither did most of the opponents of NCLB advocate the elimination of standards nor were they suggesting that effort should be the only standard. They argued for broader and more diverse modes of assessment. What evidence is there that effort grading had become predominant or that effort should not be one criterion?

Beck's mantra that day was hardly unusual for him. *The New York Times* recently ran a front-page analysis and interview that highlighted his broader political sensibilities. Beck has been a star player in Fox News's generally successful efforts to regain viewer share after suffering some declines in the run up to Barack Obama's victory. The *Times* interviewer characterized Beck as follows:

> He says that America is "on the road to socialism" and that "God and religion are under attack in the U.S." He recently wondered aloud whether FEMA was setting up concentration camps, calling it a rumor that he was unable to debunk. Mr. Beck has used phrases like "we surround them," invoked while speaking vaguely about people who do not share his discomfort with the "direction America is being taken in." With a mix of moral lessons, outrage and an apocalyptic view of the future, Mr. Beck...is capturing the feelings of an alienated class of Americans...
> Tapping into fear about the future, Mr. Beck also lingers over doomsday situations; in a series called "The War Room" last month he talked to experts about the possibility of global financial panic and widespread outbreaks of violence. He challenged viewers to '"think the unthinkable' so that they would be prepared in case of emergency. 'The truth is—that you are the defender of liberty,' he said. 'It's not the government. It's not an army or anybody else. It's you. This is your country.'"[1]

Beck has his Left counterparts. Some on the Left treat all opposition to new government regulation as corporate inspired or a product of other "special interests." Some attribute the failings and injustices of US capitalism to tiny bankers' conspiracies, regardless of the evidence. Or, today the unspecified greed of a few is blamed for our economic travails, with little evidence to suggest that individual greed is any more pervasive now than at other points in our history, or that there is too little effort to examine the factors and forces allowing greed more free play.

The Human Predicament

Fear, anger, and dismissive contempt know no political boundaries and may be seen as symptoms of deep predicaments that grip all of us. Part of our predicament is difficulty in articulating or defending the exact nature of our situation. A conference on religion and politics during the spring of 2009 at the New School for Social Research featuring Templeton Prize winner Charles Taylor and William Connolly, author of *Capitalism and Christianity American Style*, helped me clarify my own contestable thoughts on this.[2]

To be human is to be finite in two senses of this term. It is first to be mortal and to know that one is mortal. To be human is, in Connolly's words, to "run the risk of resenting severely the obdurate fact of mortality." Finitude also refers to the limits of our knowledge. We construct our understandings of our lives and our fellow human beings with and against a background of intuitions, instincts, and ideas that we can never fully capture. We can always stand outside of and critique any of our current certainties. Anxiety, both about our mortality and about the persistently incomplete and contestable interpretations of our mortality, can cause us to construct totalizing worldviews and moral systems and claim these as final truths. These truths will live on, even if we do not.

These existential anxieties also often lead us to see those opposed to our worldviews as irredeemably stupid, perverse, or evil. Some further cement their sense that they are especially worthy by viewing themselves as a minority under siege, even if the only threat to their position lies in the disagreement that others (often even only a few) have to that position. The final vindication of their position, however, lies in the outcome of an ultimate battle between good and evil, in which the chosen few triumph and eliminate their opponents.

These destructive and exclusionary tendencies and warlike outcomes are not absolutes. They are risks within the human condition that can be intensified or restrained by life circumstances, broader economic conditions, work upon ourselves, and the shape of the religious and philosophical discourse we encounter and develop. Exclusionary stances seem strongest in a world of rapid change, poverty, hardship, and global insecurities. Older readers might compare William Buckley's intellectually playful *Firing Line* with the O'Reilly Factor's bombastic and hostile tone.

Religion's Many Voices

Some secular thinkers have cited Christianity, or more broadly religion, as the primary cause of such exclusionary excesses. Yet comprehensive and absolutist theories are not confined to religion. Wholly secular conceptions of socialist morality or of the fatherland have fueled some of history's worst purges and excesses. "Religion" includes many voices that have opposed both secular and religious excesses.

Even in the United States, where fundamentalist strands of Christianity have assumed such cultural and political prominence, Christianity includes important strands that address the human predicament in ways intended to chasten the worst outcomes of existential fears. Some of these voices are dissenters within the evangelical movement itself.

Consider how different Christians deal with the meaning of Jesus's famous answer to the question of when the kingdom of God will come.[3]

He answers: "the kingdom will not come if you watch for it, nor will anyone be able to say it is here or it is there. For the kingdom of God is within you." For some Christians this luminous phrase suggests that if one lives by the precepts of God, one will be able to enter a real kingdom of eternal life.

For others, the kingdom of God is an inner spiritual experience to be shared with our fellow human beings rather than a place to go to after death. Since the sharing is vital to the experience itself, it is important to cultivate a spirituality of care for life and the world.

Both interpretations can still the fear of death for some sets of the population, but their very contests can also evoke anxieties and retribution. Much depends on how proponents of each advance their cause. Do they acknowledge the contestable nature of their own foundations even as they advance and live out their doctrines? Much also depends on other aspects of religious discourse itself. Must contested interpretations of the kingdom of God be set in a narrative of revenge and counter-revenge? Is the Bible about religious war on behalf of a final truth, the celebration of a God who imposes his order and whose truths we know? Or is it a celebration of a God of mystery, whose will we can never fully know and who speaks to us through the diverse and pluralizing voices of the human and material worlds—through the whirlwind—as process theologian Catherine Keller would suggest. God's ever-unfolding mystery challenges us to be ever open to new surprises in ourselves and others.

Pat Robertson is pretty sure he knows the answer to this question. Following a decision by the Dover, Pennsylvania, school board to ban the teaching of intelligent design in their classrooms, Robertson thundered:

> I'd like to say to the good citizens of Dover: if there is disaster in your area don't turn to God, you just rejected him from your city. And don't wonder why he hasn't helped you when problems begin, if they begin. I'm not saying they will, but if they do, just remember, you just voted God out of your city. And if that's the case, don't ask for his help because he might not be there.

There is no doubt that Robertson can claim biblical warrant for his posture. Listen to the book of Revelation. Its author, and some passages in the Gospels themselves, embraces faith in resurrection, the Second Coming, and the day of final judgment. Revelation, however, is more distinctive in situating those doctrines in a universal revenge story that is vitriolic. Christ is envisioned as returning to inaugurate a thousand-year reign of peace against the devil and his innumerable consorts:

> Then I saw heaven opened, and there was a white horse! Its rider is called Faithful and True, and in righteousness he judges and makes war...He

is clothed in a robe dipped in blood and his name is called The Word of God... From his mouth comes a sharp sword with which to strike down the nations... Then I saw the beast and the kings of the earth with their armies gathered to make war against the rider and the horse and his army. And the beast was captured and with it the false prophet who had performed in its presence the signs by which he deceived those who had received the mark of the beast... These two were thrown alive into the lake of fire that burns with sulfur. And the rest were killed by the sword of the rider on the horse.

At the end of this thousand-year period, Satan, somehow, is released again; and the divine war starts over. Christ again speaks directly to John in his vision:

Those who conquer will inherit these things and I will be their God and they will be my children. But as for the cowardly, the faithless, the polluted, the murderers, the fornicators, the sorcerers, the idolaters, and all liars, their place will be in the lake that burns with fire and sulfur, which is the second death.

John closes his vision with a fateful statement, "I, John, am the one who heard and saw these things." And John conveys the message Christ said directly to him. "I warn everyone who hears the words of the prophecy of this book, if anyone adds to them, God will add to that person the plagues described in this book; if anyone takes away from the words of the book..., God will take away that person's share in the tree of life."

Like the John of Revelation, Pat Robertson is very confident in representing the detailed will of the vengeful God who inspires him. He addresses existential anxieties, but at the price of not only potentially greater violence but even of increasing the fear of death, violence, and pain that accompany it. These believers may become inclined to cling all the more fiercely to his message and his campaigns. Whether this is a viscous or virtuous circle depends on one's perspective.

Calling for a "fact-based" politics is no satisfactory answer to these webs of exclusivity. Such a politics fails to address the question of motive. Why should one be inspired to pursue the facts? Why do some disregard in some areas of life the kind of evidence they find persuasive in others? In addition, our knowledge of the world is not independent of the frames we employ in viewing the world. And our understanding of how the world works enters into our behavior. How we deal with individuals who are gripped by differing facts and values cannot be resolved simply by the facts.

There are, however, other religious voices worth considering. James Carroll recently pointed out in an article titled "The End is Near" in the *Boston Globe* that Revelation—along with Daniel—are the only two books of the Bible that highlight these revenge scenarios and a view of life as a battle to impose a final truth. These books emerge from circumstances that shed some light on their dangers and appeal to some. Carroll points out:

> Apocalyptic thinking itself is anti-human. Though it comes to us out of...the Bible, and though it is a staple of Hollywood disaster films (see the new "Transformers" movie), the readiness to see catastrophe as looming has itself produced catastrophic consequences down through the centuries. Even more destructive has been the religion-sponsored (and Hollywood-advanced) inclination to see catastrophe itself as a good thing, for what is the biblical Apocalypse if not God's destroying of the world in order to restore it?

> The apocalyptic tradition

> attempted to make sense of merciless violence by imagining a cosmic conflict between forces of good and evil. To be faithful to God was to be on God's side in the great final struggle against Satan. This idea helped a besieged and frightened people to stand fast—against the Seleucid tyranny in the 2nd century BCE and against Rome in the late 1st century CE. Even apparent defeat (represented by the destruction of the Temple in 70 CE) could in this way be perceived as an ultimate victory, even if in another realm. The otherness of that realm became the point. The apocalyptic imagination, unlike the broader biblical view, was bifurcated, not only setting God against an evil nemesis but also dividing the temporal order (time against eternity) and space (earth against heaven). The present life is not what matters. The next life (millennium, afterlife) is everything. This cosmic dualism seized, especially, the Christian mind, and its elements are regarded as essential to the religion.[4]

I would add that those Christian minds locked in broad and debilitating struggles that emerged from and helped define a strong sense of group or national identity would be most receptive to this worldview. And even for those not engaged in such struggles but in whom the existential dread of death or finitude of knowledge rings strongest, such a worldview has powerful appeal. Those whose theologies treat unexpected or premature death as the punishment of an all-powerful God or for whom the death of a loved one has evoked excruciating pain would be especially vulnerable. Yet the very appeal of such a perspective, while easing existential anxiety through its self-righteous certitudes, does so at the price of increasing collective vulnerability. As Carroll puts it, "a worldview informed by such contempt for earthly existence will be hard put to take the slow-motion violence of environmental degradation as problematic."

Carroll goes on to point out that the Bible in large measure rejects Revelation. Jesus's "message in no way devalued the present world in favor of a future heaven, any more than the author of Genesis denigrated the created world when God saw it as 'good . . . very good.'" Uncriticized theological assumptions, in other words, both foster exaggerated rejection of what is different and

> inhibits the human capacity to respond appropriately to Earth's new vulnerability. The overwhelming message of the Bible, read critically, is that this world is the world that counts. Any notion of afterlife that suggests otherwise, undercutting care for the home planet, must be discarded, along with the habits that have put us at this precipice.

One message critics of apocalyptic and bifurcated versions of Christianity might emphasize is found in the work on the historical Jesus project. Stephen Mitchell in *The Gospel According to Jesus* collects sayings that at least 80 percent of the biblical scholars who participated in "The Jesus Project" conclude were spoken by Jesus himself. I am most taken by these classics from the Beatitudes:

> Blessed are the poor in spirit, for theirs is the kingdom of God.
> Blessed are those who grieve for they will become comforted.
> Blessed are the merciful, for they will receive mercy.
> Blessed are the peacemakers, for they will be called sons of God.[5]

These are clearly not the message of one who wishes to impose a totalizing worldview. There is no loud and angry rhetoric of punishment and prophecy of doom if we do not live up to these standards. The Beatitudes, however, seem to run a different risk. Does the notion of a God of love imply passivity in the face of evil? Equally important, what other religious and philosophical perspectives might contribute to our understanding of injustice and our willingness to address it? I will address both questions in the context of issues already deeply infused with apocalyptic distress. But first one more brief comment on talk radio and the contemporary political landscape.

Politics and Passion

Politics will never be a songfest. Ideas and passions are not easily separated. It is hard to advance an idea without some commitment to the argument and without thereby risking anger toward those who don't see our line of thought.

Passions, however, can be reconfigured. As I wrote the first draft of this chapter, a sharp debate surrounded the nomination of Sonia Sotomayor to the Supreme Court of the United States. Neuroscientist George Lakoff pointed out that the conservative attack on her "empathy" was an attempt to derail the entire inclusive Democratic agenda by redefining the "empathy" for which President Obama nominated her. Lakoff argued:

> Empathy is the capacity to care, to feel what others feel, to understand what others are facing and what their lives are like. Empathy extends well beyond feeling to understanding, and it extends beyond individuals to groups, communities, peoples, even species. Empathy is at the heart of real rationality, because it goes to the heart of our values, which are the basis of our sense of justice.

Lakoff points out that against this view cultural conservatives posit a different definition of empathy. Their "empathy" is "idiosyncratic, personal feeling for an individual, or one ethnicity or even the defendant in a legal case."

Because empathy is so narrow and dangerous a feeling in their eyes, judges need to put it aside and rely on strict and narrowly defined traditions or in the same vein, original constitutional intent.[6]

Such a view of the judiciary tends to lock in the status quo by blinding the Courts to current patterns of exclusion or the emerging claims of new rights. Original intent is no objective standard and even practitioners of this method cannot always agree. Its only real purpose is to shut down debate and provide cover for currently powerful groups or coalitions.

Fighting to restore the earlier and, in Lakoff's view, more defensible concept of empathy is thus vital. Democrats did manage to confirm Sotomayor but they still face the task of reclaiming the concept of empathy.

Lakoff is surely right here. Discussions over the shape of empathy and its role in our political life help frame a whole range of issues in ways that will open or constrict the political landscape. But one must enter this debate at more than a political level.

The diffuse and variegated nature of our passions is being used by today's conservatives, as by theorists as far back as Hobbes, as an occasion to buttress a strong imposition of traditional order. But if humans do contain multitudes, as Whitman argued, and are capable of attentiveness and receptivity to the diverse and pluralizing voices of their fellows, order can't and shouldn't be based on narrow and imposed truths. Cultural conservatives are engaged in a tortured rationalization for the powerful and the well-positioned.

These debates around "empathy" resonate with and are influenced by primal concerns about death and deep religious and ethical perspectives about the role of difference in our lives and societies. Modern Hobbesian narratives do not merely draw on the fear of death; they even intensify that fear.

Fear of death and finitude can be curbed in part through doctrinal work. Anxiety about the finitude of our knowledge can be eased to the extent opponents across a field of issues can acknowledge mutually the limits of their own positions and foundations.

More direct work on death itself can also help. The hospice and right-to-die movements have reshaped the experience of death both for the dying and for their loved ones. The right to die movement is especially significant and sensitive not merely because it challenges some Christians' belief that only God should control the time of death but also, because, to the extent it does alleviate extreme concerns about death, it can curb the existential pressures that shape and are reflected in the exclusionary worldviews and tactics in which so many are implicated.

Empathy is not a trait one has or does not have. It is potentially an expansive and deepening trait. The experience of many in the civil rights movement enhanced their own empathy. Martin Luther King confronted and tamed his own fear of death. He risked martyrdom, and his willingness to accept that fate both enlarged the scope of his efforts and concerns and advanced his cause by changing others through his example. King's reading of prophetic Christianity encouraged his challenge to the powerful and the well-positioned who abuse their power. His broad analysis, evocative metaphors, and style led many others to see and connect injustices in their lives and those of others.

But as Romand Coles points out, preaching on behalf of the poor and dispossessed must be accompanied by willingness to listen to and encourage the voices on behalf of whom one purports to speak. This was at times a point of friction even within the civil rights movement, with some criticizing King's top-down leadership style.[7]

In their best moments and incarnations, however, some antiwar and civil rights movements of the 1960s embraced forms of grassroots democracy and nonviolence that were inspired by and enhanced an appreciation of the many ways of life and thought humanity can embrace. They sought to speak through the example of listening and cultivating responsiveness in others. They elicited more generosity and intellectual openness among their allies and even some of their adversaries. They achieved some surprising victories.

Coles suggests that at times, nonetheless, their very reluctance to engage in or support broader ideological critique of the status quo, their willingness to protest primarily by example, as practiced by such organizations as the Student Nonviolent Coordinating Committee (SNCC),

> left much too (or much too persistently) inaudible the distinctive modes of ethical and political being that SNCC sought to cultivate. In a world

of selves born and overwritten with a plethora of governing political discourses (and with accompanying dominant practices), one result of giving
SNCC's practices too little expressive deliberation and development was
that the practices were increasingly misunderstood and assimilated to more
established modes of ruling.[8]

Ideally, critical discourses of various persuasions can both speak among
themselves and speak to—and listen to—the community voices and ongoing troubles on whose behalf they purport to strive. Through such a difficult dialogical process there is some hope that both theory and democracy
can remain vital. Absent such dialogue, talk radio is unlikely to become
worthy of the name.

CHAPTER ONE
EVIL AND IDENTITY

My work on this project has been bookended by two tragedies, the devastation of New Orleans by hurricane Katrina and the horrific Haitian earthquake. They were natural tragedies, what some have called acts of God. Both, however, have had a startling if underplayed lesson. Individual responses and social policies both before and after these natural cataclysms did more damage than nature itself. And on occasion, invoking God only added to the tragedies.

Reports on Katrina and Haiti—and numerous earlier tragedies—might make it easy to conclude that violence is inescapable. Violence even in modern liberal democracies hardly surprises us any more, but at one time a range of democratic and liberal theorists viewed democracy or representative government as ways to blunt antagonism and violence. Nonetheless, before concluding that violence is intrinsic to the human condition, we might consider possible theoretical and practical antidotes to the reflexive resort to violence.

These acknowledge the reality of, even the propensity toward, evil without decreeing it to be an inevitable aspect of human nature. And they suggest alternative discourses and practices. These thinkers are often dismissively labeled postmodern or "deconstructionists." And by postmodern, their critics have deceptively characterized them as celebrants of a dilettant-ish, undisciplined flitting among ideas and lifestyles. Rather than being "deconstructive," a range of discourses loosely indebted to Nietzsche and, more recently, to Derrida, Foucault, and DeLeuze and Guattari can help encourage narratives and policy agendas that do the difficult and challenging work of highlighting and redressing the violence toward difference. They counter the apocalyptic narratives that sustain and are sustained by such violence. And rather than being foreign, these ethical and political narratives at their best are both aided by and already fruitfully challenging a range of contemporary domestic theological and philosophical traditions, including Catholic and Protestant versions of the social gospel, prophetic Judaeo Christianity, Buddhism, and forms of green spirituality and nature worship. Some have called themselves radical democrats or late modern thinkers.[1] I will call them deep pluralists, a term I hope to further elaborate as this work proceeds. Their depth lies not in any claim to final, self-validating foundations. Their pluralism goes all the way down. It includes a willingness to acknowledge and explore multiple competing foundations for pluralizing rights claims and ways of being.

Democracy and the Paradox of Politics

Even Rousseau, the most profound and committed of radical democrats, identified a core problem with democracy, albeit one for which he proclaimed "mission accomplished" prematurely. In the *Social Contract*, Rousseau comments: "For a general will to be brought into being, effect (social spirit) would have to become cause, and cause (good laws) would have to become effect. The problem is how to establish either condition without the previous attainment of the other on which it depends" (86). In a recent essay Bonnie Honig points out that Rousseau locates this problem only at the foundation of the republic. From Honig's critical vantage point, Rousseau is wishing the whole problem away through the myth of a wise, benevolent, and disinterested founding father. If one is attentive to this paradox, then even Rousseau's less apparently mythic resort to a general will, if examined hard enough, reveals the presence of impurities. Commenting on the same paradox, William Connolly says:

> Rousseau's artful efforts to legitimate the subordination of women can be seen, first, to express the necessity of subordination (of either men or women) within the family so that the will of a unified family can contribute a single [undifferentiated] will to the public quest for a general will, and, second, to conceal the violence lodged within the practices of male authority in the family by treating subordination as suitable for women as such. So Rousseau both exposes the paradox in the founding of the general will and conceals it in his presentations of that will once it is founded.[2]

In this regard he succumbed to one of modernity's deepest problems, the propensity to establish and secure one's own identity by marginalizing difference, whether ideas or modes of living that challenge our own often merely even by their presence.

Deep pluralists are fascinated with the issue of identity. This is the frame that they use to interpret world events. James Der Derian reminds us that "we" make war on "them," but just who we and them are and come to be defined as such is the vital question.[3]

Human beings need individual and collective identities in order to function and even to be ethical human beings. Connolly points out that "identity is relational and collective. My personal identity is defined through the collective constituencies with which I identify or am identified with by others (as white, male, American, a sports fan) it is further specified by comparison to a variety of things I am not."[4]

Identity in short depends not only on who we are but also on who we are not. But the need for identity coupled with its dependence on that which is different often occasions a certain degree of anxiety.

This very need for identity, grounded in the human incompleteness without any social form, in our need to reduce common life to easily absorbed rules and rituals, in the need to coordinate our activities, can often impel us to describe the differences on which we depend in a way that gives privilege or priority to us.[5]

One way to diminish the validity and strength of difference and therefore to buttress the sense of the finality and self-sufficiency of our own identity is to construct that which is different as a danger to ourselves. Thus Tocqueville characterized the Americans of his day as a Christian nation, contrasting this core identity with that of atheists, who were deemed to be restless, egoistic, and amoral by virtue of lacking the source on which morality depended.

Deep pluralists do not deny there is a "real world" with real dangers. But as David Campbell points out, there are many dangers, so many we can hardly even enumerate them.[6] We respond and act on the raw world only through the concepts that guide us to certain ones rather than others. Many of the most discussed, feared, and targeted grow not out of the harm that our usual and widely accepted statistical measures identify but out of a need to confirm/reconfirm our sense of who we are. Thus, as Campbell points out, such diseases as pneumonia and chronic liver disease have killed far more people than HIV, but the latter was deemed a public health emergency. Heterosexuality constituted a large part of mainstream identity and thus public attention was drawn to a disease widely associated with different sexual practice and with a population already deemed sick, deviant, or even subversive by virtue of that practice.

In addition, the role of interpretation in emphasizing dangers does not stop at this point. Since the statistical case for the intensity and frequency of any threat may be murky or even dubious, other interpretive strategies become vital. There is a focus and emphasis on the connection of this practice and the disease to other characteristics generally reviled in the community. Thus reports of HIV as associated with lurid sexual practices (such as anonymous sex in bathhouses etc.) that undermine public morality are given widespread play. And the use of terms such as epidemic, more often applied to AIDS than to tuberculosis, a disease spread more easily than HIV, reinforced the fear both of the disease and of its primary symbol.

Thus, treating HIV as especially dangerous and connected with socially destructive practices reinforces the sense of deviance connected with particular sexual behaviors, solidifies disdain for the group that practices these behaviors, and thus further validates mainstream sexual identity. During a period when conventional understandings of gender and sexuality were under great stress, the politics of HIV played a key role in efforts to sustain the validity of that conventional identity.

Now consider crack. Media reports of crack use among inner city blacks sparked talk of a health emergency and push for a war on illegal drugs. Many epidemiological studies, however, have shown that legal drugs, smoking and alcohol, have always killed far more Americans. And illegal drug use, including crack and different forms of cocaine, were also consumed by large percentages of white, middle-class Americans. Crack, however, was associated with many poor African Americans, some of whom were dependent on welfare. The concern for illicit drug use among inner city blacks as a major health emergency itself reflects an understanding of the world through the lens of one who identifies himself as white, hard working, independent, and rational. Inner city blacks and their purported behaviors were already stigmatized by large segments of the community. Tales of crack's dangers and potency further diminished this group.

Campbell points out that as with AIDS, another related aspect of the stigmatization process lay in connecting crack to other indicators of risk to the community. Crack addiction was associated with violent criminality that threatened the community even though government statistics and crime reports attribute violence primarily to turf wars over its sale of an illegal substance rather than its direct pharmacological effect on addicts.[7] In a final twist, crack has been connected to the terror war, with discussions of the way crack purchases presumably fund terrorist sources abroad, even though some of these terrorists have been shown to be right wing paramilitary groups often supported by the United States. Emphasizing crack as a crime and terrorism promoter concentrated in the black community cast further doubt on this group and its purported lifestyle, lent more urgency to the war on both drugs and terror, and strengthened mainstream culture's sense of its own worth and virtue.

And again if we think back to the context of the crack wars, the late 1980s and early 1990s especially, the white working class saw much of its hard work failing to produce good wages and its jobs increasingly insecure. Self-worth was at a premium.

Deep pluralists arguing along the lines I have sketched earlier would not claim to have proven that AIDS and crack were not real health issues deserving of some sort of public policy intervention. They can and some do engage in efforts to assess the relative health risks of many behaviors, and becoming more attentive to the role that identity politics plays in this area can make us more aware of risks. The statistical battles, however, can seldom be won conclusively. The deep pluralist perspective itself suggests there may be very real questions about the accuracy of reports as to the cause of death in cases of socially stigmatized diseases. Their intent is to point to the ways in which some of the crack discourse reflect blanket disdain for statistics that government elites produce and rely on in other contexts and that cast doubt on claims of a health and public safety emergency. And their goal, rather than to advance a truth claim about AIDS or crack, is an ethical one, a world of more openness to different ways of being in the world.

Deep Pluralist Truths

Critics of these scholars accuse them of saying in essence there is no real world, nothing outside the text. This is a distortion and a caricature. Deep pluralists surely know there is a world beyond texts, but that world can be given no fixed or clear form outside of our concepts.

They then use this inability as the basis of fashioning a new, positive understanding of truth governing our sense of the necessary relation of identity to difference. The truth lies in our attunement to that which exceeds the text. Within the text itself one can discern traces of that which exceeds the text, gaps, concerns, anxieties, murkiness, either conscious or unconscious, on the part of the text's authors. These gaps are suggestive of efforts to diminish or degrade difference.

But were gays and inner city African Americans and atheists not really a threat to the future of civilization? We can't establish any means outside our own concepts to answer this question. But drawing on the deep pluralist perspective, we can provoke the texts in some ways.

The threat these groups posed was conveyed merely through rhetorical style and conventional generalizations used in many other contexts and unsupported by specific evidence. Thus Tocqueville described atheists in language reminiscent of ways Native Americans were described. And both atheists and modern "crack heads" were described as a "disease" on the body politic, two metaphors that push a sense of a natural, coherent entity beset by some deep and dark pathology, the evidence for which is not provided. Tales of wild orgies are presented and even if counterevidence is provided later, it receives little or no attention. What is evaded or disregarded speaks volumes.

The tendency to privilege one's own sense of identity is further buttressed by the larger philosophical claim that order or even knowledge itself depends on one unitary standard of truth or protocol for establishing truth that is an inescapable basis of our work. James Der Derian quotes Derrida's famous line that the entire history of Western metaphysics can be seen "as a series of substitutions of center for center" in a perpetual search for "the transcendental signified," that is, a standard beyond question. Der Derian adds:

> From God to Rational Man, from Empire to Republic, from King to the People—and on occasion in the reverse direction as well, for history is never so linear, never so neat as we would write it—the security of the center has been the shifting sight from which the forces of authority, order, and identity philosophically defined and physically kept at bay anarchy, chaos, and difference.[8]

Thinkers across a range of disciplines and ideologies maintain that such a standard has been established, whereas deep pluralists point to the ways in which previous claims of final standards have broken down. The very breakdown of each of these efforts to center truth suggests a new orientation to truth.

The related tendencies both to sanctify our own identity and to regard order as dependent on a unitary standard are reinforced by one other characteristic of identity. Identity is inscribed not merely at a conscious, intellectual level. Our sense of who we are is developed through nonverbal interactions with parents and intimate others, through film and mass media, through rituals within churches, and through practices in school and work. These all entrench identity in complex if not fully consistent ways.

Other deep pluralists get at the gap between the world and our knowledge of it in different but related ways. They interrogate our faith in an orderly, predictable world, trying to suggest that it is in fact a faith with unacknowledged ties to earlier, religious views of the world. Der Derian puts this point quite powerfully:

Originating in the paradoxical relationship of a contingent life and a certain death, the history of security reads for Nietzsche as an abnegation, a resentment, and finally, a transcendence of this paradox... The desire for security is manifested as a collective resentment of difference: that which is not us, not certain, not predictable... The fear of the unknown and the desire for certainty combine to produce a domesticated life, in which *causality and rationality* become the highest form of a sovereign self, the surest protection against contingent forces.[9]

What if nature or reality is inherently bumpy, not smoothly textured all the way down or through or is subject to periodic disruptions as some neuroscience and even much physics now suggests? In such a case the quest for simple, linear laws of society and nature, reflecting the human fear of finitude and quest for a secure identity, can itself be dangerous. Life does give and require of us simple linear patterns and calculable regularities, but that we need them does not mean that they are always appropriate in all domains and circumstances.

If there is a gap between the world and our knowledge of it, what is the status of our claims regarding the nature of identity formation and the diminution of difference in the process or the related notion that nature is bumpy, that any order, necessary as it is, will encounter periods or areas of resistance? Isn't it self-contradictory to deny we know the world in itself and then suggest we know the world engenders resistance to human formations?

In the first place, most deep pluralists do not advance such positions as final truth claims but rather as interpretations that should be put on the field of play. And they suspect that continual efforts by conventional moralists to trap them in logical fallacies (what is the truth status of your claim that human truths are in part limited or exclusionary?) reflect faith in a logical world and antipathy to a world that may be paradoxical at its core. Second, they present considerations at least as powerful as those advanced on behalf of other worldviews. Connolly's defense of a bumpy nature has three sources:

> The first is in Nietzsche's effort to become alert to the ways in which human life has been lived and organized. If the variety is great and if each form seems to express somewhere in their organization a measure of estrangement from their own forms..., then perhaps each encounters resistance because no actual form of life speaks to every drive and tendency in the species... The second source flows from Nietzsche's review of how providential interpretations of the world and its Creator have tended to defeat themselves in western history as they tried to perfect their understandings. These defeats call the idea of a world Creator with a grand design into question. But if the self and the world are not predesigned by a master designer, then it would be surprising if any historical form of self and society cohered smoothly with everything residing in the material from which it is formed...

Connolly goes on to add that "the very possibility of such dissonance in nature can transform discourse and life. It can expose familiar forms and unities as more artificial and strange as it identifies elements of power in their being. The notion of resistance in nature is a presumption, no more or less defensible than that of a Creator or eternal life."[10]

The aim shared by all these thinkers is not to abolish identity or standards or to disavow any quest for orderly understanding of social and natural phenomena but to encourage ways of holding these that are as open as possible to difference. In the famous term used by the late French philosopher Jacques Derrida, they seek to keep alive the play of differance, a pun that plays on the dual meaning of this term as both to differ and to defer. Final meaning is indefinitely postponed in the interest of openness to the ever-proliferating differences on which it depends. Thus to return to the example of Tocqueville and the atheists, one attuned to the propensity of identity to demean difference can open up reconsideration of what one means by atheist or the significance of restlessness. If a restless mind is framed against a lethargic or passive one, is restlessness so bad in our current context of profound and continuing change? With regard to atheism one might ask if atheism is rejection of all forms of theism or merely of conventional Christian notions of an all-powerful God. If we open up the latter possibility, it can inaugurate discussions of other sources of moral behavior.[11]

From the perspective of one who sees nature as bumpy and history as nonlinear, one can't predict the outcome of such discussions. Whatever that outcome, it is unlikely to reach any final resting point. Indeed one must suspect claims to such a resting point as one more effort to secure and center identity. Over time new understandings of theism will likely open other fissures and questions. In fact, the very success of certain reforms and reconceptualizations in addressing current problems can lead to overly inflated claims on behalf of the reforms and new identities and squeezes on the other forms of difference through which formerly rebel identities now establish themselves.

Keeping the play of differance alive does not, however, mean rejection of all established identities, rules, or regularities. Politics strives to establish the rules and modes of common life without which established patterns of diversity could not exist. But politics also serves to alert us to the damage in claims of finality for any currently existing pattern.[12] Disorder and disruption are often required to promote orders that are more just and sustainable. In a wider-ranging interview with David Campbell and Morton Schoolman, Connolly suggests that too many theorists are overly worried by the disruptive moment in democratic thought and practice: "If you think of human beings as essentially embodied and always already entangled in social life, you don't fear *too much* that a specific genealogy will reduce a collective identity to shambles."[13]

Contemplation of the potential bumpiness of nature and of the gaps in our discourse of identity can inspire more openness to difference, clearly an ethical task. Deep pluralists counter their mainstream critics' claim that order requires fixed standards by reminding them that they have hardly proven beyond reasonable doubt the assumption that the world is perfectly orderly. And if the world is not perfectly orderly and if the quest for some order may entail repression of poorly articulated difference, then enhanced sensitivity to such currents is in fact both a practical and an ethical task.

Contemporary liberals, social conservatives, and communitarians all accuse deep pluralists of having no morals, of letting anything go. The accused reply that they do draw lines and have ethical standards. Murder is murder and not to be excused, not because God or some transcendent standard of reason says so but because violence stands in the way of the flourishing of different forms of life, which they have come to value. Another difference between a deep pluralist morality and conventional norms is that punishing violence, as an example, may need to be changed over time, both in terms of the forms of punishment deemed appropriate and in terms of just what counts as violence as our knowledge changes and as the implementation of law itself changes social relations and understandings. Refusing to examine the standards we hold can itself be a form of violence.

We reject the idea that our only alternative to anarchy is a community, nation, or world united around one or a few core philosophical principles from which most social codes and laws are derived. Today's world has become violently fractured by faiths and political movements proclaiming the need for a fixed and unitary standard of truth.

Efforts to solve the paradox of politics may be seen as a central manifestation of identity's efforts to marginalize difference. Rousseau's conditions for the formation of a general will (the small size of the state, self-sufficient rural economy, a common heritage, a state religion) are so restrictive as to be hardly applicable to modern conditions even as the symbolism encourages repression of difference by positing the possibility of the ideal. In the contemporary era, this paradox is solved through notions of time, progress, scientific method, and laws that govern nature and the economy.

We can strive to resolve the paradox, for example, Rousseau, or we can negotiate it. Since efforts to resolve it seem to have issued not in peace and harmony, perhaps we are better off with a strategy that acknowledges and strives to build on the persistence of paradox

Multidimensional Pluralism

In response to this perspective on the human predicament some deep pluralists have sought to build a new constructive ethos and democratic political theory that places paradox and the dual moments of democracy at its center. In an effort to negotiate the twin, related paradox of identity and politics, they propose a multidimensional pluralism. Connolly, who has been at the forefront in developing this aspect of the theory, adopts an orientation to other moral and theoretical perspectives sensitive to identity's propensity to marginalize difference.

This approach has several prongs and has been spelled out in slightly different ways in several works by Connolly. I will synthesize the strands that most move me.

Connolly's pluralism encourages each faith and moral community to bring aspects of its faith relevant to specific issues into the public realm. It thereby eliminates the impossible requirement that one bracket fundamental concerns, a requirement that has enraged many who feel excluded and see hypocrisy on the part of liberals who issue such requirements. Second, to support the possibility of such a process faith amplifies awareness of the elements of mystery and undecidedness in its own position. Connolly has certainly done that by admitting elements of speculation inside his core positions on identity and nature. And as a part of and result of these two conditions, it seeks to build an element of forbearance toward elements of mystery in other creeds comparable to those in its own doctrine. And finally, if the sources of moral action are plural and contestable, so too are the dimensions of human life. Multidimensional pluralism seeks to expand the number of dimensions on which society can become more diverse, including marriage forms, gender relations, linguistic use, work and household organization, among a list that would and should grow. Each of these prongs builds on and supports the others. As diversity becomes installed in various facets of the common life, more constituencies acquire the leverage and the incentive to push their faiths from within to honor new rights claims. And the emergence and success of such claims lend intellectual plausibility and visceral support to forms of identity that do not depend on complete marginalization of difference.[14]

This does not mean that everything is tolerated. Deep pluralists have a moral agenda that goes well beyond sanctioning the most ruthless forms of violence.

> A generous ethos of engagement between partisans honoring different moral sources expands room for diversity to be even as it engenders its own limits . . . It limits the prerogatives of . . . religious, gender, sexual, ethnic, and national constituencies who feel aggrieved unless the culture in which they participate sanctifies as imperative for everyone the particular organization of being they embody; . . . it does not stop such constituencies from living within the orbit of such assumptions; it does stop them from placing such assumptions at the authoritative center of political culture.[15]

Connolly's last point here is vital to his multidimensional pluralism, not merely as an embodiment of it but also in that its openness to what groups do on their own and to their rights to present their own exclusive worldview constitutes a possible catalyst for a less divisive politics.

Connolly acknowledges that such a pluralism is hardly inevitable. As we have seen, from the perspective of deep pluralism identity is established not merely at the highest abstract level but through related, not fully consistent devotional practices, gut feelings, pictorial images, and complex emotional and cognitive connections. This may make rapid swings in identity unlikely, but the very complexity introduces a moment of unpredictability and volatility even in core identities. Connolly's great worry is not that a politics of becoming will produce inevitable anarchy. One can imagine a situation in which multidimensional pluralism itself or other cultural changes or human tragedies so agitated and threatened core identity that extreme fundamentalist reactions occurred. In the interview alluded to earlier, he suggests:

> We must be cautious about seeking too much too soon in this domain, because of the fascist reactions the quest for a wholesale shift can trigger. Nonetheless, in a culture of democratic pluralism it is important to engage in genealogical practice from time to time. The acceleration of speed heightens this need. It means that we often encounter modes of suffering and possibility for which the established banisters of judgment have not adequately prepared us. Democratic pluralism would die on the vine, or devolve into a mere celebration of past achievements, if the experimental temper were dropped from it.[16]

Were cultural crisis or deep pluralism to push too far and engender fascist reaction, the most important task would be to form "a militant assemblage of pluralists, with each party drawing on modes of inspiration that do not coincide with that of others" to resist authoritarian incursions.[17]

Fortunately, multidimensional pluralism already has some presence today in some advanced democracies and though never fully attainable it can serve as a worthy regulative ideal for these democracies. In any case, the ideal need not be fully shared by all parties in order to have a positive impact. The example in tone, narratives, and content can affect others who do not share the worldview and thereby alter political patterns. In a world fractured by fundamentalisms of various sorts it is worth a try.

Multidimensional pluralism as theory and practice can't be fully vindicated through a discourse that all can come to accept. It forgoes notions of unity that some find precious, while defenders such as Honig often point to the abuses implicit in most robust notions of patriotism, constitutionalism, and the common good.[18] Ultimately on an individual level one can simply live these varying faiths and frame judgments accordingly, but any cost-benefit analysis will reflect in part, even at the level of perception of evidence let alone how it is weighed, the theoretical orientation and lived experience one has adopted.

Public Policy and Plural Resources

But rather than attempt further abstract analysis of this perspective, I will examine a number of dimensions of public policy. I seek to explicate the role that a multidimensional pluralist discourse and practice geared to negotiate the paradoxes of politics and identity might play in illuminating these issues and encouraging a less destructive politics. A deep pluralist perspective true to its own ethos will engage, energize, and learn from a range of social justice perspectives and help constitute a powerful rejoinder to current exclusionary and apocalyptic narratives and agendas. And in this process of engagement, I hope to give nonspecialists a better understanding of and appreciation for deep pluralist discourse.

Versions of deep pluralism inspired by Derrida, with its emphasis on the gaps and fissures in identity and our premature claims on its behalf, differ from others such as Bennett's inspired in part by Nietzsche, with its celebrations of a bounteous nature. And of course both have important differences from the prophetic Christian and process theology discussed in this book.

There are, however, important overlaps and an increasing willingness to engage in fruitful dialogue, one to which all these traditions at their best are committed. In my own case I feel that I have learned and profited from this conversation. For me, however, the conversation cannot be merely abstract. It grows out of and in turn enlarges my perception of the political and philosophical issues in play. Furthermore, as I have explored particular issues, certain strands and debates seem more pertinent—or at least move me more—depending on the issue at hand. Put simply, however much their tensions at the abstract level, differing traditions move me, though in disproportionate degrees depending on the issue. When I confront racial, ethnic, and class injustice, I am moved more by (my reading of) Niebuhr and by the modern devotees of Derrida. Their conversation and their sensitivity to possible exclusions that Catholic natural law theology may evade seem most compelling. A conversation among these three strands seems best suited to address the tangled issues of race and class.

On ecological politics pride of place goes to the neo-Nietzscheans, the immanent naturalists, and their conversation with Christian process theology. This conversation, of course, has implications for our understanding of responsibility for evil and thus for social justice issues but at least for me evokes them less directly. All of these discourses come into play for me as I consider the exclusions, injustices, and rigid fundamentalisms that are magnified by our volatile, crisis-ridden economy. Nonetheless, I intend no walls here. All of these strands can contribute to and in turn be developed and elaborated through any of these issues as well as others I have not considered. I only hope to add to a conversation that will grow in depth and breadth.

In the next chapter I will focus on the charged racial and class rhetoric growing out of Katrina and suggest the role that a deep pluralist perspective on these events in conversation with voices in both prophetic Christianity and process theology can play in revealing racism's several faces and encouraging a more inclusive politics.

Immigration politics is also a central challenge to those who would seek to bury the paradox of politics and sustain a secure core identity. The very fact and perception of immigration is enough by itself to challenge any confidence that the paradox of politics has been resolved at the founding. Or put in other terms, foundations are a constant process. Bonnie Honig comments: "Every day—through birth, immigration, and maturation to adulthood new citizens are received by established regimes and every day established citizens are reinterpellated into laws, norms, and expectations of their regimes such that the paradox of politics is replayed rather than overcome in time."[19] Following Honig, I will examine the love/hate affair of US citizens with immigrants and the role that has played in securing identity and attempts to resolve the paradox of politics. Discourses, including those inspired by various strands of Christian as well as deep pluralist practices and proposals that might frame an orientation outside of the assimilation/exclusion duo, are examined.

As Honig indicates, intrinsic to the effort to confine the paradox of politics to a foundational moment is the notion of linear time: "the first thing to go, when we confront the chicken-and-egg paradox of politics, is our confidence in linear time, its normativity, and its form of causality."[20]

A deep pluralist focus on the way identity discourse frames and solidifies identity is revealing in the case of auto culture. In addition, prophetic discourse can expose the role of power in sustaining consumer society. But in this area, I would emphasize our understandings of nature and causality. Throughout much of modern times two views of nature have predominated. Many secular theorists have sought to counter an understanding of a natural chain of being or more modern green notions of a natural harmony between man and the planet with an understanding of a nature that is law-like and accessible to full explanation. The Catholic social gospel was largely wedded to the older view of nature and it contributed mightily to initiatives to curb economic growth. Yet both perspectives share more than they acknowledge and can be barriers to the inclusiveness of an environmental agenda. They may limit as well the terms on which nature is understood and enjoyed. Jane Bennett's *Vibrant Matter* (2009) draws creatively on Epicurus, Lucretius, and Nietzsche among others to move beyond discussions of the ways we look at nature. She offers speculation on the vital dynamism of nature in itself. I will examine differing conceptions of nature in itself, including both complexity theory and Bennett's immanent naturalism and the status of those conceptions. Debates about energy and climate policy might be reshaped through wider consideration of these concepts. These concepts may reshape our interests and moral commitments.

The discussion of laws and nature also informs an inquiry into the question of whether modern capitalist economies are governed by "laws," and if not into how reformers can intervene in ongoing crises. These questions are not merely economic as our answers to them help undergird one's sense of the legitimacy of the social order. As I will argue in the final chapter, capitalism's current crisis is enfolded in complex ways with severe cultural tensions and environmental crises. Confidence in the magic of the market or technical fine-tuning may blind us to elements of abundance as well as to risks that we best consider.

Finally, struggles over identity and the injustices they can entail are no longer restricted to cities, states, or nations. These "domestic" conflicts interact in complex ways with relations among nation states. Can a multidimensional pluralism find expression at the level of relations among nation states and if so how would it connect to domestic struggle? Drawing especially on the work of David Campbell and James Der Derian, I will examine the ways in which contemporary debates between foreign policy realists and idealists serve to obscure other alternatives informed by prophetic and deep pluralist perspectives and the contributions these latter perspectives might make to issues in foreign policy.

Conventional IR schools, liberal idealism on the one hand and realism on the other, different on some dimensions, may share one characteristic. They treat the nation state as a given. Confidence in the solidity of the nation state both grows out of and helps sustain faith in a clear, stable identity. Reading IR through the lens of deep pluralism encourages collaboration across national boundaries and moral and religious lines to increase the dimensions of diversity within nation states. One of its great strengths is to reduce the role that national conflict has in sustaining fixed and dogmatic forms of identity. To the extent they are successful, such struggles can undermine the belief that sustainable society depends on one central ethnic, national, or philosophical core. And domestic and international struggles can go in tandem. To the extent that domestic struggle reduces the commitment to or need for exclusive identity, there is less existential pressure to buttress identity by invocation of a foreign threat.

CHAPTER TWO

KATRINA, ROSA PARKS, AND THE COLOR OF GOOD AND EVIL

The role that dominant cultural themes play in our understanding of danger becomes clearer as we look back on Katrina and the public discourse that followed it. A natural catastrophe, the discourse that followed it emphasized the Bush administration's lack of preparedness for catastrophe and the role that FEMA played. Some brief consideration was given to the racial injustices Katrina exposed, but these themes soon disappeared from the mainstream media, which themselves became complicit in a subtle form of racism. In a broader sense, the role that a messianic vision of America—even on the part of some on the left—may have played in both the lack of preparation and the rescue efforts following the storm was neglected.

It is easy to condemn George W. Bush for the callous treatment of Katrina's victims and surely he merits much blame. But a long pattern of racism, sustained by and in turn reinforcing fundamentalist discourse, created the preconditions for tragedy. Even the Christian Social Gospel, which has played an admirable role in redressing poverty and must be part of any constructive conversation regarding social justice, may have not only harbored blind spots but also a worldview that dimmed its sensitivity to a range of social issues. Several strands within prophetic Christianity and deep pluralist discourse can highlight injustices, challenge fundamentalist ethical and religious discourse, and constructively engage the social gospel tradition. I will weave together historical interpretation and strands of deep pluralist and prophetic discourse as part of an effort to draw lessons from Katrina.

Reflections on the Superdome: Whose and Which Crimes Count?

How ironic that just two months after thousands of poor and minority residents of New Orleans were forced to sleep in the Superdome, Rosa

Parks became the first woman—and a black woman no less—to lie in state in the Capitol Rotunda. The mother of the modern civil rights movement could rest in state in the Capitol, but the children of that movement spent a week in utter desperation and have since undergone a painful diaspora. Worse still, this pretentiously named stadium was funded by public taxes, but with tickets costing ninety dollars and up, its games were priced well beyond the reach of the poor. For most it was probably their first and last visit to the dome. Rosa Parks's stay in the Rotunda has been used to cleanse the class and racial wounds Katrina exposed, but it has also inadvertently opened up uncomfortable questions about her legacy.

Let's start with Katrina. In its wake, even President Bush made a brief, albeit highly veiled, reference to the role of race in the tragedy. In his 2006 State of the Union message, he remarked:

> We're providing business loans and housing assistance. Yet as we meet these immediate needs, we must also address deeper challenges that existed before the storm arrived. In New Orleans and in other places, many of our fellow citizens have felt excluded from the promise of our country. The answer is not only temporary relief, but schools that teach every child, and job skills that bring upward mobility, and more opportunities to own a home and start a business. As we recover from a disaster, let us also work for the day when all Americans are protected by justice, equal in hope, and rich in opportunity.[1]

Nonetheless, Katrina never became an occasion to reshape either policy or even the tone of national political debate. What opportunities for housing were advanced were done so through deregulation of housing finance in ways that ended up encouraging more exploitation of the most vulnerable.

Some Christian conservatives were criticized after earlier catastrophes for bringing God, religion, and philosophy into debates about natural catastrophes. Yet unexpected deaths of apparently random individuals inevitably invite profound religious and philosophical questions. More importantly, individuals' readings of tragedy subtly infiltrate the content and tone of their political dialogue. Social conservatives have a right to their say, though I am troubled by the dogmatism with which they express their claims. My own faith suggests that other religious interpretations, expressed with more sensitivity to their own limits, could yield tangible changes in the direction of our policy.

Katrina, like other natural disasters, leads many to wonder why some die and others are spared, a question Job raised. Katrina, however, also exposes another modern evil, the forms of exclusion and discrimination that leave the poor and racial and ethnic minorities even within advanced societies so vulnerable. These are distinct forms of evil, but they can interact.[2] From my perspective, anxieties raised by nature's sheer unpredictability and human finitude (our mortality and our limited knowledge) often lead to destructive policy debates. These debates go beyond exploring a legitimate range of questions about how best to understand and prepare for catastrophe. They become in effect quests for revenge against the human condition. The nature of these connections and the toll they take both on suspect minorities and even on those who stigmatize these minorities will be one continuing theme of this work.

In the immediate aftermath of hurricane Katrina, even most major social conservative organizations shied away from attributing the disaster to abortion or other "sinful" practices in the city. Nonetheless, an air of moral certainty and condemnation colors many perspectives on this tragedy. Some have a racist tinge. The cruel politics of race has a way of trumping the most generous hopes of social democrats. Shortly after the hurricane struck, Jonathan Freedland, a columnist for the *Guardian* (London), commented:

> Privately, conservatives also wonder how much sympathy white, suburban America—the crucial middle ground all politicians covet—will feel for Katrina's victims. One close-up observer describes what he suspects is a widely-held—if rarely articulated—view of those left behind in New Orleans: "They lived in a silly place, they didn't get out when they should, they stole, they shot at each other and they shot at rescue workers." If that's the view, then Bush won't suffer too badly.[3]

Bush in fact suffered very little from Katrina, even as he broke promises to the city to help it rebuild. Many of its victims still live hundreds of miles from their homes. Only as the war dragged on and as the economic prospects of middle-class Americans deteriorated did his popularity sink. The ugly politics of race did in fact trump brief concerns about FEMA responsiveness.

Violence is inexcusable, but some media and political leaders failed to distinguish between acts of brutality and thefts intended to save one's family from starvation. In addition, in the weeks following the hurricane, it became obvious that many media had taken anecdotal reports of violence, such as the rape in the Superdome, as facts without bothering to examine the evidence.[4] Weeks after the hurricane hit, the New Orleans coroner admitted that there was no evidence at all of extraordinary violence in the Superdome or the convention center, which had been widely portrayed as jungles of disorder and lawless violence.

That sketchy and poor documented reports of violence were so firmly believed may reflect not only racism but efforts to ease a guilty conscience about the fate of those left behind. Surely the violence and unpredictability of the hurricane and reports of violence functioned to strengthen calls for harsh forms of political order. Unconfirmed reports of mindless violence in the Superdome functioned not only to reinforce the worst stereotypes about the minority poor but also to lend support to traditional concepts of order. Those who don't accept prevailing property norms or aren't well-to-do are seen as always on the brink of anarchy and violent death. The only alternative to complete social breakdown is order strictly enforced by a clear, unitary authority. Such a view is then reinforced by a picture of death itself in the most grisly forms. As with Hobbes, it is not simply the contention that life without a clear fixed code to govern most areas of social life will break down into anarchy. The fear of death itself is intensified by portrayals of the brutal form in which it comes.

The deleterious role of race in our national dialogue was highlighted for all to see in the weeks following Katrina by Bill Bennett's comment on race and crime. Bennett gained notoriety for suggesting that one way to reduce the crime rate would be to abort all black male fetuses. He argued that black males commit a disproportionate amount of the crime and that reducing the number of black males would therefore reduce crime.

Yet the very media portrayal of Katrina should lead us to cast doubt on Bennett's logic. At the height of the tragedy, as victims were portrayed in a desperate quest for survival, the media captioned pictures of black families wandering through stores with the title "looting." Pictures of identical activities by white families were captioned as families in desperate quest of food.[5]

Such disparities, along with Bennett's remark, invite a question. How does race itself affect the ways in which we frame and report crime? Drug use, from casual marijuana all the way up to the more serious hard drugs, is widespread among all sectors of the population, but minorities caught using drugs are more likely to be cited for violations of law and to receive the stiffest sentences and least likely to have access to rehabilitation programs. Crack and powder cocaine are treated differentially even though both have similar pharmacological effects, with powder, a favorite of the middle-class stock broker set, treated more leniently than crack.

Media portrayal of Katrina and discussions of African American crime also invite a broader look at the category of theft. Polly Toynbee, a columnist for the UK-based *Guardian*, recently commented that the best way to reduce the rate of domestic violence, violent crime, and child support violations in Great Britain would be to abort all male fetuses. This suggested to me an analogous examination of crime in the United States. The media dwelled on talk of minority looters, but said little about a far grander theft. Congress has enacted a law requiring the Department of Labor to notify

Wal-Mart before investigating it for violations of hours and overtime regulations. When a company forces its employees to lie about the hours they work or locks them in its premises, at best it is subject to civil penalties, though in fact it has robbed them. When many of these employees are illegal immigrants to begin with, the company in effect holds over their head the threat of deportation. It might as well be saving your money or your life. Yet these actions are not a part of official crime statistics, and if the government is now going to notify Wal-Mart before conducting further investigations, what chance is there of even becoming aware of the impropriety?

Just as importantly, several studies of urban police departments show that the frequency and severity of racial profiling have continued unabated in recent years despite the publicity and attention to these concerns. *Boston Globe* columnist Derrick Jackson remarked:

> There is no evidence that anyone is seriously getting rid of it on a nationwide scale. The Globe became the latest newspaper to report that despite the rhetoric, the silent terrorism of everyday citizens continues at home even as we decry terrorism abroad. A Globe analysis of more than 750,000 traffic tickets found that Massachusetts is no different from any other state or city that has studied its policing patterns.[6]
>
> Statewide, African-American and Latino drivers get double the traffic tickets than their share of the population would predict. Then, even before tickets cool in the palms of their hands, African-American and Latino motorists face a 50 percent greater chance than white drivers to have their cars searched. That is despite the fact that drugs were found more often on white drivers who were searched. (*Boston Globe*, January 8, 2003)

Nor have most media explored the long history of police violence directed against many African American residents of New Orleans. It is hardly surprising that as the crisis dragged on many residents still refused to leave. Many heard credible stories of individuals being relocated and then denied the right to leave their new sanctuaries.

The interlocking questions of race and poverty are equally complex and defy easy attributions of blame. Americans well outside the circle of the Bush administration regard poverty as a reflection of moral character. President Clinton, who gained praise among some liberal commentators for his willingness to begin a dialogue on race, was notably silent on class. And Clinton's well-publicized denunciation of rap stars was a none-too-subtle attempt to suggest that African American lifestyles had much to do with their poverty. Worse still, his welfare reform program, ending "welfare as we know it," though formally race neutral, could not fail to have a disproportionate effect on African Americans, who had suffered from a long history of inadequate schools and limited opportunities. His trade programs then systematically reduced the number of good manufacturing jobs that had eased earlier minorities out of poverty. Where jobs have grown, as in the service sector where most New Orleans residents worked, wages have been stagnant or declining even as worker productivity has increased.

Even in the wake of Katrina and the ugly racial neglect it exposed, the rebuilding of the city has been carried out in a manner that has potentially racist implications. Many of the contracts for replacement housing and schools were granted on a no-bid basis, while rules setting minimum wage standards were initially waived. Protests eventually forced the Bush administration to pay prevailing union wages, but its continuing reliance on no-bid contracts not only in New Orleans but also in Iraq suspends market competition in ways that serve established, predominantly white corporate interests.

Yet even in the face of such acts, the perception that African Americans are to blame for their conditions continues. It even goes well beyond conventional conservatives. Several years ago the comedian Bill Cosby evoked praise from most of the media when he suggested that African American males, through their sexual profligacy, their consumerism, and their abandonment of their children, were a major cause of African American poverty. Cosby paid little attention to the ways in which divorce and drug use permeate all sectors of this society. Worse still, he failed to address the ways in which the mainstream and white-controlled media celebrate a life of sexual excess both through their commercials and their programming. Unbridled capitalism imposes long work days, but to market products to an increasingly affluent upper class and to ease the psychic burdens of the long work day, its major media promote beer, cars, and fashions as a way up the social ladder and as forms of escape from the incessant grind.

The Long Legacy of Race

Cosby is part of a long line of commentators with a familiar litany of complaints singling out African Americans for uniquely harsh criticism. These critics have argued in effect that Irish and Italian Americans came to this country in difficult circumstances and made it out of poverty. If African Americans are failing in that endeavor, there must be something wrong with their culture. Yet there are critical differences here. African Americans were brought over as slaves. Slavery may have ended in 1865, but it would take another full century for most to gain the political rights that earlier waves of immigrants routinely enjoyed within a few years of their arrival on these shores.

When Deval Patrick, the first African American governor of Massachusetts, took the oath of office in January of 2007 on the Bible of a slave, it was an occasion for celebration and self-congratulation, a precursor of the national pride that would follow Barack Obama's victory a year later. The celebration, however, hid a deeper question: Nearly a century and a half after the end of slavery, why does the politics of race remain so charged? From the Willie Horton ads in the 1988 campaign to controversies surrounding Howard Dean's comments about drivers of pickup trucks with Confederate decals, one could infer that the Civil War was a recent memory.

The ideals of individual liberty that inspired the American Revolution led even many prominent Southern slaveholders to believe that slavery was an anachronism that would soon end voluntarily in the South. In a famous letter to her husband, Abigail Adams commented on the irony of Southerners fighting so hard for liberty from England at the same time as they enslaved other human beings.[7]

For John Adams, however, the greater concern was that if emancipation were pushed, unity in ongoing struggles with Britain would be damaged. John Adams's views prevailed. The Constitution sanctioned continuing importation of slaves and infamously treated them as three-fifths persons, thereby increasing the power of slaveholders. Slavery was never as economically significant in the North and was abolished in the first three decades after the Revolution. Nonetheless, it became even more entrenched in the South. The cotton gin made cotton an ever more valuable export, and the mills of the industrializing North enabled a growing market for textiles.

But North and South were locked in increasingly bitter battles over economic issues. Southerners favored free trade to aid their export crops and the North demanded tariffs to help emerging manufacturing. Northerners fought the expansion of slavery to the territories in order to blunt Southern political power. Slavery became identified with the Southern way of life and was increasingly defended by all Southerners. Although nonslaveholding whites did not have a direct stake in slavery, they increasingly defined themselves by reference to black slaves. After the Revolution, Southern states enacted laws limiting the property, marriage, and political rights of blacks. Small farmers and working-class whites could feel that if they weren't rich, at least they weren't blacks. They enjoyed the political and social privileges of the white aristocracy and often identified with it.

War and defeat of the South pushed the country to abolish slavery. Emancipation, however, left many slaves wondering what freedom really meant. The war also devastated most of the South. Freed slaves were given no land and many soon became disappointed. As Felix Haywood, a freed slave interviewed in the 1930s at age eighty-eight, suggested: "we thought we were going to get richer than the white folks because we knew how to work, but it did not turn out that way. Freedom made us proud, but it did not make us rich."[8]

The war was bitterly unpopular among many Irish Catholic immigrants in Northern cities. Subjected to fierce discrimination themselves, they feared competition from newly freed slaves for the few unskilled jobs on which they depended. The antidraft riots in New York City in 1863 still stand as among the most violent in our history. Ironically, war and abolition of slavery even intensified racism in the South, as lower-class whites were also thrown into competition with newly freed blacks.

The Social Gospel and its Critics

Freeing blacks was a major gain, but it did not resolve deeply entrenched racial animosities. As a prolonged agricultural decline hit the South and depression and labor troubles dominated Northern politics, the country lost interest in Reconstruction. Southern whites imposed harsh black codes limiting the movements of blacks and systematically stripped them of political rights. Lynching became far more commonplace. The mutually reinforcing patterns of racial animosity and economic dislocation remain major themes in our history and are in turn often fed by Manichean religious and moral perspectives. Even the Social Gospel and the New Deal liberalism with which it was connected played an inadvertent role here.

Like the United States of 2010, our country a hundred years ago faced pools of urban poverty and unemployment, dramatic changes in technology, the expanding reach of corporate markets, and the mobility of the men and women who staff our factories, hospitals, and offices. We brought together differing lifestyles, cultural expectations, and religious rituals. Hear Edward A. Ross, a mentor to TR, as quoted in James Morone's *Hellfire Nation* (2004):

> That the Mediterranean peoples are morally below the races of northern Europe is as certain as any social fact... William does not have as many children as Tonio because he will not huddle his family in one room or eat macaroni off a bare board... Millions of immigrants are bred in the coarse peasant philosophy of sex. They deprave native tastes and lower the intelligence of the community.[9]

Morone characterizes American history as an evolving conflict between two distinctive moral visions. Early Puritanism spawned both of these moral visions. It emphasized personal godliness and a community that took responsibility for the godliness of its members. The first tradition, the one most commentators associate with the Puritans, portrays an unending struggle between good and bad individuals. Our national strength depends on the personal moral integrity of individuals. If all Americans work hard, lead disciplined, monogamous lives, avoid the perils of consciousness-distorting substances, all will enjoy at least a modicum of prosperity. The task of the community as a whole is simply to enforce these personal norms.

Against this moral vision Morone recounts another moral tradition— the Social Gospel. It portrays the moral distinctiveness and greatness of this society as its willingness to provide both ample opportunities and a generous safety net for all. Within such a framework, individuals are far more capable of rising to the level of responsible citizenship and attentiveness to the needs of family. It is the ideal of inclusiveness that defines national greatness.

Morone emphasizes the differences between these two different off-shoots of the Puritan experience—we might call it Ken Starr versus Teddy Kennedy. There are big differences between these perspectives and in my estimation, much more to be said for the Social Gospel version. Nonetheless, problems lurk in the assumptions both perspectives share.

These twin traditions were related to a single experience. Early Puritans came to a new world to escape the persecution of the Old World, to build a church and society in direct contact with God. Yet paradoxically in a land where all save the Native Americans were from far away and where no one was persecuted, it became hard to build and sustain a coherent identity. Persecution in England also had left the Puritans all the more determined to establish a direct relationship with and dependence on their God and to regard all that differed from that mindset as not merely different but evil. "The Puritans groped back to the tried and true—they found terrible new enemies to define them. The saints constructed their us against a vivid series of immoral them: heretics, Indians, witches. Each enemy clarified the Puritan identity."[10]

The rise of public primary education, Social Security, the New Deal, and eventually the GI Bill after World War II reflect the Social Gospel tradition. Morone celebrates the achievements of an inclusive politics. He comments on a 1935 picture of his Italian grandfather after lunch at a Staten Island restaurant. He is seated dressed in formal business attire along with other New York branch managers of the Metropolitan Life Insurance Company. The group includes an Irishman, two Jews, three Italians, and their Bulgarian boss. Just one generation after Ross wrote, the dangerous animals had mysteriously morphed into successful business leaders in formal attire.

To his great credit, Morone is not, however, an unqualified defender of the Social Gospel tradition. He recognizes that advocates of that tradition, like FDR, made compromises with older forms of moralistic and exclusionary politics in order to enact some of their visions. Southern segregationists were accommodated in the interests of enacting Social Security, the Wagner Act, and other key New Deal statutes.

Possible limits of the Social Gospel, however, lie not merely in the inevitable compromises advocates must make to enact it, but also in the claims to the universality in even the original proposals and agendas. Advocates of the social gospel differed in their emphasis from the conventional personal moralists but were not above making strong moral demands of their own. Like Ross, many condemned particular ethnic habits or their stereotype of these. Prohibition found strong support among many. Social Gospel advocates may have seen bad behavior as more rooted in social circumstances than did their traditional "Puritan" brethren, but both were quite sure they knew what constituted bad behavior.

Morone does point out that such pivotal Democratic intellectuals as the radical Protestant Reinhold Niebuhr advocated an alternative to both the Social Gospel and moralistic Puritanism. At the heart of Niebuhr's theology lay a "demanding existentialism reverberating with irony, paradox, and historical contingency."[11]

Human beings respond both to the fact of their own mortality and to the inevitable gaps and yawning limits that seem to stand outside every claim with efforts to build more complete and comprehensive moral visions to give purpose to their lives and their deaths. Yet those very anxieties and the problems and the difficulties encountered in building comprehensive truths predispose us to claim finality for our partial truths.[12]

In the context of mid-twentieth-century America, Niebuhr found most objectionable a kind of Calvinism that took prosperity or material success as proof of God's approval. Commenting on the significance of Niebuhr's work, theologian Catherine Keller comments:

> This most public US theologian of the twentieth century warned half a century ago that we must "unmask our pretensions of innocency" or face the apocalyptic consequences of our messianic imperialism... Far from constraining human power drives, the construct of an all-controlling omnipotence, to the contrary, seems to have fired them up.[13]

Reading Keller and Niebuhr together deepens our understanding of both and can shed light on some of the anxieties and worldviews that have contributed to the injustices Katrina highlighted.

Against American Calvinism's reading of God's grace as a reward for and sanctification of marketplace or imperial success, Niebuhr and process theologians such as Keller propose an ethic inspired by Christian agape, the complete self-giving, life-sacrificing love that Jesus displayed on the Cross. For both, the power of God lies in HIS challenging example. The significance of the Atonement lies not in Christ's death so much as in the willingness to take on fleshly form and accept the risk of death in order to break down barriers and open oneself and the larger society to broader possibilities. Through HIS actions and HIS example, HE transforms both HIMSELF and the people around HIM. God enters history, gives it meaning by suggesting that a world with death and suffering is not therefore worthless. God is strong in the acceptance of HIS own vulnerability. As Keller puts it,

> the vulnerability of the flesh—whether to an unwanted temptation or to an agonizing death—cannot be wished away. But an honest embrace of our vulnerabilities may turn them into sources of empowerment. For those weaknesses seem to lie close to our strengths: our disorganization lies close to our creativity...our insensitivity close to our decisiveness.[14]

Death is no punishment for sin inflicted by an all-controlling God.

Niebuhr views the Crucifixion in a slightly different but related way. In Niebuhr's interpretation, God enters, gives meaning to and transforms history by the example of HIS sacrifice, but the very fact that He dies within history shows that His wisdom can never be fully embodied within history even as that wisdom remains a perpetual challenge.

For neither Keller nor Niebuhr does the celebration of agape lead to a denial of the need for law or passivity in the face of violence. Keller describes a victim of spousal physical abuse visiting her new pastor. She mentioned that her previous pastor of twenty years had told her she should rejoice in her suffering because it brought her closer to the life and example of Jesus. She has tried but is finding it more difficult as the husband is now turning on the kids.

The young pastor has a different message: "It isn't true. God does not want you to accept being beaten by your husband. God wants you to have your life, not to give it up. God wants you to protect your life and your children's life."[15] Yet many forces are arrayed against changing the ingrained habits of mind and broader ideologies that enable exploitation. Too much privilege or too much violence or habit or even a sense of woundedness can shut down one's willingness to revise such practices.[16] In ways analogous to Niebuhr's views, this shutting down is sin in its proper sense, for our attitude toward those we live with is a test and trial of our attitude to the source of all creation.

Nonetheless, there are forces at play in the world that make change possible. Process theology speaks of two aspects of divine reality in the world:

> The divine Eros is felt in each creature as the "initial aim" or the "lure." It is a lure to our own becoming, a call to actualize the possibilities for greater beauty and intensity in our own lives. The responsive love, by contrast, can be called the divine Agape. The Eros attracts, it calls: it is the invitation. The Agape responds to whatever we have become; in com/passion, it feels our feelings: it is the reception. They are different gestures of divine relationality—yet their motions are in spirit inseparable, in constant oscillation.[17]

Seen in this light, Love thy neighbor as thyself does not mean that one stop loving oneself. It does entail that I develop greater awareness of the ways my Eros, my desire to clarify and assert my own distinctive individuality, depends on what Keller terms com/passion—a willingness to accept what is different in others. As Keller point out, even in the more narrow (sexual) erotic relations, without com/passion for the differences and limitations of the other I turn him/her into an idol, a mere projection of myself, who will soon disappear.

> Passion is only sustainable in as much as it modulates into com/passion. It does not cease to be passion. It does not therefore lose the element of self-love: love the other like you love yourself! Not because the other is like you—not even because you like the other! If agape sacrifices the fullness of ourselves, it is a false agape, lacking self-esteem and therefore lacking, precisely, the power of persistence. It does not offer cheap grace to the violator but a chance of transformation: forgiveness is not an excuse to continue to violate but a chance to interrupt the cycle of violence. If Christian love enables violators to continue to violate, it violates the gospel law of love.[18]

We are called to such an openness. The "we" here includes persons, animals, and plants. Among persons, a tinge of consciousness of this lure allows us to choose to grasp fresh possibilities or not. We are not ordered or driven, but this is no reflection on the limits of God. Were we so ordered, the universe would lose its element of becoming and mystery that so enhances our lives. Part of the mystery of life is whether we will accept the call and the kind of world that would emerge if more of us accept it.

To enable Eros and agape to flourish together and reinforce each other, however, demands intervention more than personal transformations. In order to maintain any civilized life, some behaviors must be punished. Some order must be maintained even to be able to grasp the will of God.

Even in the smallest communities, many desires come into contradiction and there must be structures of coordination. These structures allow us to express and coordinate our differences. But these structures and standards can themselves become rigid barriers to emergent currents of life and thought.[19]

Nonetheless, as Keller argues, the story of the Crucifixion is one of how acceptance of our vulnerability can also encourage our creativity and a deepening sense of our growth through interaction with difference. For Niebuhr, the Crucifixion and the Resurrection remind us that however damaged and inadequate any attempt to realize agape in history will be, that example remains perpetually relevant. It challenges us to look at the injustices occasioned by our most thoughtful efforts to achieve justice. As Keller puts it in language Niebuhr would probably also endorse, "The law becomes legalism when it freezes into the absolute; when in fear of the dissolute it loses the porous flexibility of an open system. When it merely stifles desire rather than stirring life-affirming desire."[20]

Yes indeed laws affecting spousal abuse must be enacted and police often called in. But how these will change the perpetrators and the broader mindset about men and women in such situations remains an open question and the sense that one can fully and with full justice solve such problems can inflict its own damage and injustice. Human beings, inspired by the Christian narrative of an ideal that touches and gives meaning to history but can never be fully redeemed within it, can become more attuned to their own limits. Richard Wightman Fox sums up these central themes:

God's self-disclosure in Christ, Niebuhr argued, gave new meaning to history. The essence of that self-disclosure was the Atonement, Christ's suffering love that led inexorably to the Cross. Perfect love must be suffering love not triumphant love when it enters history. God's revelation gives history new meaning, but does not bring it to fulfillment. Christ does not so much transform human existence as inject a new tension into it. Love now transcends law but remains bound by the limits of human nature. God's grace is empowering, infusing culture and personality with new potential, yet it is also negative, condemning the swelling satisfaction that men take in their own achievements. And it is ultimately forgiving, showing men mercy for their transgressions. Human history is so significant in the Christian view, that God himself takes flesh in it, but the Incarnation is paradoxical: God is present but absent. He remains hidden despite His intervention. Human history sits poised in the interim between First and Second Coming, between the revelation of meaning and the realization of it. In that charged atmosphere Christians attempt to embody Christ's love while also combating their own temptation to self-righteousness.[21]

Niebuhr is famous for the following aphorism: "Man's capacity for justice makes democracy possible, but his inclination to injustice makes democracy necessary."[22] He adds to that an understanding of the perpetuity of politics. Politics cannot be seen as merely a transitory means to a final resolution of history's dilemmas. "Democracy is a method of finding proximate solutions for insoluble problems." His work provides important resources to chastise human hubris and it has been a profound catalyst to generations of social critics.

E. J. Dionne has commented: "Niebuhr's recovery of the importance of original sin was a reaction against what he saw as a potentially dangerous naivete in the Social Gospel movement that arose in tandem with the Progressive era." Dionne goes on to add that

> the forms of engagement in public life that are rooted in doubt and humility are far more likely to be effective—and far more apt to be just—than approaches rooted in utter assurance and arrogance, in total identification of a human political agenda with the cause of God. Lincoln demonstrated as clearly as any statesman that it is possible to undertake great tasks in politics with firmness, commitment, principle, and courage and still not pretend to absolute certainty about one's course, one's intentions, and the purity of one's motives. It is a style of public religion that badly needs to be rediscovered and put into practice.[23]

With Dionne, I share the conviction that a more just and constructive politics depends on a renewed conversation between the social gospel tradition and the kinds of prophetic Christianity for which Niebuhr spoke so eloquently. But in my judgment the need for openness and humility extends beyond the range of policy and moral value to the question of the sources of those values. Dionne surely does not rule out conversations with atheists on moral values nor does he embrace the notion that one must be Christian or even theistic at all to be moral. And commendably, Dionne recognizes that his faith is not fully demonstrable nor are those who reject it necessarily ignorant or perverse.

If he is to be faulted, it is for a sin of omission. There are forms of philosophical discourse that while rejecting conventional theism or teleological views of nature also reject the conventional secular posture of a law-like world known and governed by man. Such perspectives, sometimes dismissively labeled postmodern and which I have termed deep pluralist, can contribute to the very humility Dionne endorses in two ways. They explicitly raise a vital question in today's pluralizing world—whether just and egalitarian order is better secured by debate and negotiation among differing foundational systems each of which acknowledges the unlikelihood of establishing itself fully by debate and argument. Or is belief in some ultimate singular ground of being, albeit one to be established only through democratic means, a necessary motive and adequate ground for a just and relatively egalitarian order? Recognition and consideration of these nontheistic alternatives also raise the question of whether recognition of a pluralistic universe could better—or at least as well—attune reformers to the limits of reform as did Niebuhrian prophetic Christianity. And finally, in an era where environmental issues are so prominent, nontheological alternatives to mechanistic understandings of nature could be especially important.

Broadening the discourse is strategically important as well. The prophetic vision of perpetual striving for an ideal that can never be fully realized could evoke in some a sense of despair. At the very least, the notion of history gaining meaning through God's willingness to intervene in it is a standard so abstract as to fail to communicate or motivate some.

Others like Keller, within the tradition of process theology, while indebted to Niebuhr in some ways, suggest that divine agape influences us not merely as example but as a larger spirit that infuses us and shapes and is shaped by an equally divine inspired Eros. These oscillations are not smooth or easily predictable and they create and grow out of defects in the larger social order needed to contain and express them. Anxiety and with it closure can result, especially when too much privilege or suffering or even habit become too dominant, but I read in Keller a stronger sense of a spiritual depth that can inspire or be tapped to inspire a continual openness to the becoming of the world. Through these means it also yields more resources with which to confront both natural and social tragedy.

Finally, for some others, the meaning of Crucifixion and Resurrection have been so thoroughly taken over by literalist or fundamentalist readings that it becomes hard to give Niebuhr's or even Keller's reading a fair hearing. In subsequent chapters, I will invoke other religions and philosophical visions that might enter into fruitful conversation with both. For now I will provide a tour of the major historical transformations of U.S. society, from the New Deal through the Montgomery bus boycott and the early stirrings of the civil right movement, a tour informed by Niebuhr's concerns about messianic imperialism and Keller's celebration of the inspirational impact and continuing challenges offered by agapic voices.

From FDR to Montgomery: The Limits of Reform

We think of the Roosevelt administration as the defender of unions, the author of Social Security, and welfare for the very poor. These perspectives are true, but misleading. In fact, Roosevelt's Social Gospel vision had considerable elements of noblesse oblige, the package of rights he endorsed were relatively narrow, even when seen by the standards of the time, and the citizenry who qualified for those rights even more limited.

Franklin Roosevelt is famous for support of the 1935 Wagner Labor Act, granting workers the right to petition the US government for supervised elections as to whether to unionize. Yet even this act, basic as it has been to modern labor, supplanted a different form of labor protection that had enjoyed modest success. Furthermore, the Wagner Act locked labor into working through complex federal bureaucracies. The Norris-Laguardia Anti-Injunction act of 1932 prohibited injunctions against union organizing campaigns as "conspiracies in restraint of trade," the tool that employers had long used to break strikes.

Of course, lifting an injunction did not guarantee success of an organizing campaign, even if a majority supported it, but the Wagner Act itself required workers seeking a union to petition the government for an election and then to go through a long and complex process closely monitored by the government. As long as government itself was generally favorable to unions, progress could be made. But once government support had waned or government had become completely pro-management, the complex process would become a virtual obstacle course. Workers were far more likely to succeed through direct grass root actions by employees outside of government channels. And one can also argue that the whole thrust of the Wagner Act, with its definitions of what were considered issues over which management had to or did not have to bargain, in effect contributed to the emergence of a labor movement focused primarily on wages rather than broader workplace control issues.

Social Security raised other issues. Often pointed to as a European-style universal program, the original Act excluded agricultural and domestic workers and it was not until the 1950s that they were brought into the program. Their exclusion was the result of a carefully crafted compromise by FDR to bring Southern Democrats into the fold. Southern Democrats worried that any form of pension support for African American farm workers would reduce the leverage they held over these workers. Defenders of Roosevelt argue that the compromise was politically necessary and that the success of the initial program paved the way for later inclusion of farm and domestic workers. There is something to this argument, but these compromises came with a price. Political theory and political activism would do well always to keep the price of such exclusions in mind, even as compromises are inevitably negotiated. The nearly two-decade exclusion from social security is just one more fact contributing to the cumulative inequality of African Americans. In addition, some of the original deficiencies of the system have never been repaired. As part of the compromise to assure

Southern support, the welfare and unemployment parts of the legislation were established with joint federal/state administration and responsibility. In practice this has meant, from the very inception of the program that significantly lower public assistance and unemployment support has been available in the South, where these programs are also thought to "interfere" with the incentives of African Americans to seek work. Some of the implications for our current economic crisis of the inadequacies and racial and gender exclusions of New Deal era policies will be discussed in the final chapter.

Rosa Parks's Legacy

Rosa Parks was of course one of the major figures in redressing the injustices left standing by the New Deal. For many commentators, her success, soon followed by voting rights and civil rights for African Americans, represented the culmination and termination of a great struggle. Yet the ugly and well-publicized events surrounding Katrina suggest that Parks's legacy might be better understood from a more prophetic perspective. Parks iconic status hides a vital question. What are we celebrating in her passing? The commemorations of Parks's life read as narratives that celebrate America as the quintessentially just society. Her brave acts forced this nation finally to embrace and implement the full meaning of its professed faith in the rights and equality of all citizens.

A closer look at Parks's struggle opens other interpretations of her significance. Perhaps the greatest gift Parks can bequeath is a willingness to ask further questions. Have we as a nation extended basic rights as broadly as we claim and are our currently sanctioned list of rights sufficiently broad?

It was the commonsense of Southern society, inscribed both in law and in social custom, that whites enjoyed preferential treatment on buses and other "public" transit. Rosa Parks challenged this commonsense, but she was not the first. The obituary of Parks in the *New York Times* tells an often forgotten part of her story:

> Her arrest was the answer to prayers... Blacks had been arrested, and even killed, for disobeying bus drivers. They had begun to build a case around a 15-year-old girl's arrest for refusing to give up her seat, and Mrs. Parks had been among those raising money for the girl's defense. But when they learned that the girl was pregnant, they decided that she was an unsuitable symbol for their cause. Mrs. Parks, on the other hand, was regarded as "one of the finest citizens of Montgomery—not one of the finest Negro citizens—but one of the finest citizens of Montgomery," Dr. King said.[24]

It is hard to question the tactical savvy in abandoning the cause of the pregnant teenager to choose the quiet, married department store clerk as the poster child for one's political cause. To challenge one set of social conventions, building on others is often a necessity.

Yet however tactically necessary, does that choice not also entail possible elements of current or future injustice? Aren't even pregnant teenage girls entitled to a seat on the bus? One can of course argue that choosing a meritorious woman like Rosa Parks will allow progressives to win the struggles that may eventually benefit everyone.

The operative word here is "may." Winning the struggle for rights to equal seating on buses on the grounds that segregated transit hurts such upstanding members of the community as quiet married store clerks can also entrench and further reinforce conceptions about unmarried pregnant teens and unemployed African American teenagers. Conceptions of the unemployed and pregnant teens as in need of pity at best and continuous supervision or discipline at worst historically worked into and became entrenched in employment practices and welfare policies. If they are seen as intrinsically lacking, how are they to get the education, job training, or jobs needed to lift them out of poverty?

The civil rights activists of Parks's era faced other unpleasant surprises. Extraordinary levels of violence were unleashed against activists. In addition, after their victory in the courts, Parks herself could no longer get a job. She and her husband were forced to move in search of employment. The right to a seat on a bus, even when fully established, does not imply or even necessarily advance the right to a job.

Late in her life, Parks openly wondered about the use of Martin Luther King in our mainstream media. She objected to portrayals of him as a dreamer rather than a social activist. For her the importance of King lay in taking on new injustices rather than in commemorating past accomplishments as proof of final rectitude. She recognized that even the most well-motivated struggles for justice can still leave ugly remainders in their wake.

Today, when even prominent blacks such as Bill Cosby suggest that the poverty of urban ghettoes is a consequence of the negligence and lasciviousness of young male fathers, they would do well to listen to other voices. Are young African American males likely to be desirable as mates if few have job prospects? And if family is important for children—and surely virtually all agree that it is—are we sure that the nuclear, heterosexual couple is the only way to raise thriving children? And if divorce is a major factor in the lives of troubled children, does divorce itself reflect personal moral sloth or overly rigid definitions of marriage as well as inadequate support for parents of young children?

During President Bush's first term, Colin Powell and Condoleezza Rice both acknowledged that affirmative action programs had contributed to the success of their careers. These remarks constituted an admission that lingering stereotypes had made equal employment opportunities elusive half a century after Montgomery even for middle-class African Americans. The Rosa Parks I honor would continue to ask unsettling questions and thus risk losing mainstream iconic status. Are schools, healthcare, housing, access to transit, and entry-level jobs equally available to the African American underclass Cosby condemns?

A generous welfare state will emerge only through a reconstitution of the Social Gospel tradition, but the best hope for reconstituting that tradition lies in awareness of its own past hubris and openness to its future limits. In the wake of Katrina and the social and environmental scars it revealed, we clearly need some fundamental political reconstruction. We need an environmental politics that places the conventional forms of economic growth, including consumerism, transit options, and suburban sprawl front and center. But we also need a perspective that attunes itself to questions of inclusion—who has been excluded in our traditional grants of rights. And are these rights not open to further change and elaboration. Placing such issues as the length of the standard workweek and labor's right to negotiate shorter hours strikes me as being just as pivotal today as it was in the late 1930s. But today the issue is not merely one of creating more jobs. It also creates opportunities for overworked Americans to experience different sides of a human personality that blessedly is too complex and protean to be confined by narrow standards and fixed identities. With more opportunities for their own self-expression, perhaps fewer of us will take our own frustrations out on those we too eagerly perceive as loafers and self-indulgent abusers of the public trust. We might be more willing to give both Rosa and that anonymous pregnant teen a seat on the bus.

There is also an international dimension to this struggle. I began chapter one by mentioning that my work on this project was bookended by hurricane Katrina and the Haitian earthquake. In a personal communication, Harriet Price, author of *Maine's Black History*, called my attention to the deep connections between Haiti and Louisiana. Both

were the most important sites of the racial revolution in the New World. Haiti's revolution of the late 1700s, which terrified white power, spilled over into Louisiana where whites and some mulattoes fled with their black slaves/servants. The terror to whites was that the black revolution was being exported to white soil. It permeated the East Coast, too, for a different reason—black seamen carried the message and black educated men (the greatest revolutionaries) led resettlement movements to Haiti. Louisiana and New Orleans played out differently, but the fear was the same, perhaps more repressed because of the racial mixture.

Today, as two centuries ago, fear of Haiti and domestic racial tensions and exclusions both intensify each other. Haitians suffer appalling conditions as aid for the earthquake fails to meet even its minimal promises. No longer under formal colonial rule, it suffers from crushing debt and denial of real political equality while New Orleans "restores" itself as an enclave for affluent whites. US policy remains disdainful of any reforms that might give Haiti true political democracy and economic justice Haitian poverty in turn is portrayed as proof of its backward status and justification of efforts to block reform or desperate acts of emigration from the island.

Hurricane Katrina and New Orleans are an American parable. Moralistic views of international politics and domestic strife build on each other and intensify class and race divisions. The fear of sudden and violent death has further intensified social divisions and fundamentalist moral currents. But there may be other options.

The New Orleans that I celebrate is a city that in its funerals moved beyond mourning death to celebrate the artistry of its most prominent lives. Cornel West puts it well:

> New Orleans has always been a city that lived on the edge. When you live so close to death, behind the levees, you live more intensely, sexually, gastronomically, psychologically. Louis Armstrong came out of that unbelievable cultural breakthrough unprecedented in the history of American civilization. The rural blues, the urban jazz. It is the tragi-comic lyricism that gives you the courage to get through the darkest storm. Charlie Parker would have killed somebody if he had not blown his horn. The history of black people in America is one of unbelievable resilience in the face of crushing white supremacist powers. This kind of dignity in your struggle cuts both ways, though, because it does not mobilize a collective uprising against the elites. That was the Black Panther movement. You probably need both. There would have been no Panthers without jazz.

West goes on to add:

> Bush talks about God, but he has forgotten the point of prophetic Christianity is compassion and justice for those who have least. Hip-hop has the anger that comes out of postindustrial, free-market America, but it lacks the progressiveness that produces organizations that will threaten the status quo. There has not been a giant since King, someone prepared to die and create an insurgency where many are prepared to die to upset the corporate elite. The Democrats are spineless.[25]

Thus the quest for an expansive multicultural politics may require for its inspiration more than collective or individual guilt about past injustices. It needs its prophetic panthers and jazz's spontaneous celebration of human pluripotentiality.

Katrina suggests one other lesson as well. We may need views of nature itself that challenge our prevailing sense that the material and animal worlds are domains to be conquered by men, the failure of which leads to despair and vindictive attacks on the most vulnerable.

CHAPTER THREE

FROM THE MODEL T TO THE HUMMER: THE ECONOMICS AND AESTHETICS OF THE AMERICAN AUTOMOBILE

About ten years ago a newspaper in Saskatchewan, which has a population roughly equal to my home state of Maine's 1.3 million, ran an eye-popping headline: "165 People Killed! 7,562 Injured! Over $100,000,000 in Property Damage! Provincial Government Helpless! Expects Same Carnage Next Year!"[1]

Were Saskatchewan residents worried about future Gulf Coast hurricanes veering off course? No, the headline refers to the cumulative annual damage from what the paper calls the province's "meat grinder transportation system." Monetizing the value of a human life merely in terms of lost lifetime income, the paper calculated that the cost to the Province at three-quarters of a billion dollars. And even these costs don't factor in fatal and nonfatal respiratory problems occasioned by the auto, the full costs of policing roads, and the military costs involved in keeping oil flowing freely.

An invading force that killed a tenth as many of our citizens would have been nuked into the Stone Age long ago. Though the editors of the Saskatchewan paper are probably not deep pluralist political theorists their headline might be taken as a critical commentary on the auto's privileged, almost iconic place in our identity. The auto is sustained by a visual aesthetics and a cultural commentary that connects it to other core features of American identity and to understandings of the natural world that have been at the center of our capitalist economy. Unthinking the auto requires critical reflection on its culture, a prophetic look at its history, and most importantly contemplation of alternative identities and understandings of nature.

Historically, views of nature as a great chain of being in which humans were embedded served to ground a less invasive orientation to technology and economic growth. Yet this view was both encouraged and sustained by an understanding of natural social hierarchy viewed as unjust even by most conservatives today. Alternatives to holistic and mechanistic views of nature have been developed within both Christianity and nontheistic philosophy as well.

Our attraction to and understanding of the auto is shaped by and in turn influences these debates, even if seldom on a fully conscious level. If we are to achieve a safe and noncoercive escape from the ecological and military consequences of the auto age, we must engage the entire political and philosophical economy of the auto.

Auto Dependence: Addiction or Choice?

Years ago when my wife asked a public health professional why far more attention is devoted to teenage smoking than to the auto, she was told that "we choose to smoke, but everyone has to drive."

Even President Bush, however, did at least hint at a slightly more challenging perspective on our "choice" when he commented after Katrina that we are "addicted to oil."[2] I regard driving as another addiction. The bad news is that "caraholism" is a public health crisis the magnitude of which is probably exceeded only by World War II or perhaps the flu pandemic of 1918. The good news is that it could be treated by methods far less painful and intrusive than those employed against many of our other public health crises.

Whether it be called a lifestyle choice or an addiction, many mainstream economists properly offer one constructive response to such problems. Since the full costs implicated in running a car are not factored into the cost of the purchase, the gas tax should be increased to reflect not only the cost of roads but the respiratory, military, and road-related fatalities associated with the auto. Yet an increase in the gas tax for virtually any other purpose than roads always seems to be a political nonstarter in this country.

If the popularity of the auto is an outgrowth of individual consumer choice and the magic of the market, shouldn't consumers and voters embrace a market-oriented approach to autos that would steer us toward cost-effective solutions to these problems? Efforts to fold the full environmental damage of the car and other carbon burning products into their cost have met with some ardent opposition. Senator Inhofe of Oklahoma once infamously suggested: "Why did the UN cook up the idea of global warming? To 'shut down the machine called America.'"[3] In fact, as we learned, global warming is a plot to destroy the US economy and to initiate one-world government—a goal not only of the UN but also of the American political left more broadly. Establishing his Christian credentials, Inhofe invoked Romans 1:25 (For they exchanged the truth of God for a lie, and worshiped and served the creature rather than the Creator, who is blessed forever) to suggest that taking steps to ameliorate global warming would constitute a form of idol worship.

Environmentalists have responded to arguments like those of Inhofe with dire warnings of the imminence of environmental collapse. Commenting on the slow progress of climate change legislation in major Western governments, Bill McKibben remarked:

> The trouble is, physics and chemistry aren't adjusting their schedule to fit our political and economic convenience. Each week brings new accounts of crashing ice sheets and spreading droughts. The scientific journal Nature said in its April 29 cover story that "a growing number of scientists agree that the CO2 challenge is even greater than had been previously thought."
>
> As politics gets slower, global warming speeds up. The problem isn't feckless officials. Obama has a dream team of climate specialists: Clinton administration EPA veteran Carol Browner as energy czar, Harvard physicist John Holdren as top science advisor, Nobel Prize-winning physicist Steven Chu as Energy secretary and Oakland activist Van Jones as White House green jobs coordinator.
>
> And the problem isn't that environmental groups aren't working hard enough. I've never seen them work more tirelessly, with lobbying efforts in capitals around the world.
>
> In fact, the problem is pretty simple: The environmental movement isn't big enough. It's one of the most selfless of advocacy efforts. But the movement has been sized to save whales and build national parks and force carmakers to stick catalytic converters on exhaust systems. It's nowhere near big enough to take on the fossil fuel industry, the biggest player in our global economy. It's like sending the Food and Drug Administration to fight the war in Afghanistan.[4]

I am more sympathetic to McKibben's apocalyptic message than to Inhofe's, but there are still dangers and inadequacies in the latter's view. Even the best of this science still has a range of unpredictability, especially when it comes to the effects on specific regions. And since local, short-term predictions are impossible, skeptical citizens can still engage in denial, especially if they remain enchanted by or caught up in current patterns of economic growth.

Many citizens need an alternative understanding of economic growth and development that is practically and morally compelling. In addition, pointing to the end of the world will not rally those who already embrace, for whatever reason, such scenarios as ultimately redemptive. If they are to be touched at all, it would only be through more direct and religiously inflected alternatives to doomsday scenarios. Finally, McKibben is surely correct in citing the powerful economic array opposed to environmental regulation, but such talk can mask the ways that inadequacies in the movement itself may have limited its political reach. A movement led by selfless natural scientists can still have its economic and cultural blind spots. In this chapter I will discuss the cultural and economic imperatives that have driven our reliance on the auto and our prevailing pattern of economic growth. Then I will present religious and philosophical alternatives to the conventional views driving our growth-oriented society. Christianity itself is no monolith on this topic, and various strands in process theology and the social justice tradition can play a very constructive role. And deep pluralists have important contributions to make and gains to be achieved from dialogue on this topic.

Fortunately climate change denial is now less common among leading business lobbies, but they take a tack still indebted to the logic that concern for the issue would carry extreme consequences. They claim that any serious attempt to slow the pace of global warming will do serious damage to the national economy. They can reach this conclusion because they equate their short-term bottom line with "the economy," and surprisingly many in the media follow them in this judgment. A successful environmental movement must start by emphasizing how limited and self-interested the industry's conception of the economy is and how that conception violates even conventional market-oriented norms.

Oil industry defenders portray leading climate scientists as hell bent on placing draconian curbs on the US economy. Yet prominent climate scientists are, if anything, too restrained—and conventional—in their political and economic pronouncements. Even the most conservative introductory economics texts, such as that by former Bush administration CEA chair Gregory Mankiw, recognize that markets have imperfections.[5] When the purchase and use of a commodity harms third parties, the government has an appropriate role in taxing and thus discouraging consumption of that commodity. In the world of economic textbooks, a neutral and informed government calculates the extent of the damage and enacts an appropriate tax.

Yet in our contemporary corporate economy, oil, auto, and private utility interests have enormous market power, which they eagerly translate into political power. They already enjoy vast favors in the forms of subsidized leases, government-supported highways and emergency services, and lower tax rates. A tax on gas that reflected not only carbon content but also much of our military cost as well as air pollution, congestion, and highway accidents would substantially impact several key corporations. Nonetheless, is their welfare synonymous with "the economy"?

Tax and regulatory policy in the late 1980s and 1990s led to major gains in energy efficiency and if anything were very beneficial to overall economic development. James Hansen, one of the mad scientists most reviled by leading oil companies, has put this case in language that reads as though it came straight out of market economics 101:

> The US is still only half as efficient in its use of energy as Western Europe, i.e., the US emits twice as much CO_2 to produce a unit of GNP, partly because Europe encourages efficiency by fossil fuel taxes. Available technologies would allow great improvement of energy efficiency, even in Europe. Economists agree that the potential could be achieved most effectively by a tax on carbon emissions...The tax could be revenue-neutral...leaving government revenue unchanged; and it should be introduced gradually. The consumer who makes a special effort to save energy could gain, benefiting from the tax credit or decrease while buying less fuel; the well-to-do consumer who insisted on having three Hummers would pay for his own excesses.[6]

Such a course of action represents a market friendly way to leverage less reliance on militarily costly foreign oil markets, less-polluting and more efficient transportation system, and whole new markets in energy-saving technologies.

More broadly, those who equate the economy with business as usual would do well to consider the ice storm that rocked my home state of Maine nearly a decade ago. Much of the state lost power for more than a week; the cleanup costs were immense, and it took even longer to get back to business as usual. Recently the *Toronto Star* reported on a Canadian study of the storm, which also struck much of Southern Ontario. The ice storm gave the biggest single boost to Ontario's economy in history, a 1.6 billion dollar gain attributed to necessary repairs to houses, roads, and bridges. Some of the repairs are still not complete, but the Gross Domestic Product (GDP) got a huge boost. If the greenhouse effect is associated with more extreme weather events, then economic growth will really take off.

Is this the kind of growth we want? The GDP also rises if more citizens go to hospital emergency rooms for asthma or auto crashes or hire more babysitters to cover for time lost in traffic jams. The economic growth most celebrated by the dominant players in our global economy isn't helping most of our citizens. Too many of our corporate giants feel entitled to the kind of "growth" that suits their needs. Oil and auto industry apologists argue that scientists are using greenhouse analysis to trump consumer freedoms. Yet it is they who have used their political and economic power to narrow our options, to the detriment not only of today's consumers but also of future generations.

I am more sympathetic to Hansen and the Intergovernmental Panel on Climate Change (IPPC), but his rejoinder to Senator Inhofe is not adequate. A capitalism more attentive to environmental costs can grow faster and perhaps that growth could even be sustainable. We need efficient growth to meet pressing needs for housing, food, and transportation of some form here and in developing nations. But is more material consumption either a desirable or psychologically sustainable goal? Should or could future capitalist growth take other forms besides expansion of goods and services? And what would it make if we could come to look at nature as more than a resource for future commodities or as a vengeful force to punish our excesses, something neither capitalism nor socialism has ever achieved. Would seeing nature in other ways and the related task of finding other ways of growth not provide a better and more compelling motive to change our course than scenarios of ecological doom?

Economists need to think more about the political and cultural contexts in which such debates play out and about the model of the informed and autonomous consumer on which some economists premise their policy recommendations. Perhaps we need to question our ordinary, commonsense understanding of how and why consumers behave as they do.

Toward this end, I would like to turn to an alternative narrative about the auto. I believe that this narrative also has some flaws. When deep pluralists or prophetic Christians scrutinize it, they may perceive important gaps and persistent problems, especially in its rather Manichean portrayal of corporate greed versus passive consumers. Nonetheless, this narrative opens up another line of debate on this problem. Call it the "Roger and Me" school of political economy.

I am referring of course to Michael Moore's *Roger and Me*, a film that two decades ago attributed the decline of working-class communities such as Flint, Michigan, to the singular greed of Roger Smith, the CEO of General Motors, and his corporate cronies. Though the film did not directly address transit, it might well have added to its litany of complaints the findings of an earlier Senate Anti-Trust subcommittee investigation regarding GM's role in the decline of mass transit in this nation. A joint subsidiary of GM, Standard Oil, and Firestone Tire company bought up many urban mass transit systems in the 1930s, mostly electrified rail, converted the systems to diesel buses, the popularity of which declined, in the process leading to the decimation of mass transit and the triumph of the automobile.

There is no doubt in my mind that this scenario unfolded pretty much as the Senate committee would have us believe, that it was a conscious business strategy, and that it was an effort to shape and distort a market through monopoly power rather than merely respond to consumer desires.

But as a broad-gauge historical theory, it has some major inadequacies. Even by the late 1920s, the automobile industry had changed in remarkable ways certain to impel it toward ever-greater market penetration.

The auto had become at the time the premier positional good in an economy that had become both increasingly inegalitarian and ever more prone to the problem of overproduction and underconsumption. By a positional good, a concept drawn from Fred Hirsch's *The Social Limits to Economic Growth* and revised and expanded in the work of Michael Best and William Connolly,[7] I mean a good that conveys great value and reward to those who get there first, but as the good expands to wider markets, its utility to all who purchase it begins to diminish. Nonetheless, with wider penetration, it also becomes more of a necessity for all consumers. The auto is a premier example. Once the rich have them and redesign their employment, living, and shopping arrangements around them, middle-class citizens need them as well. But as everyone gets a car, the utility to each consumer diminishes, unlike the case of public transit, a social or collective good, which increases in value as more routes and vehicles are added to a system and the cost of which diminishes as more people use it.

In addition, the auto became positional earlier in another related sense. Under the leadership of Alfred Sloan in the 1920s General Motors was a leader in establishing three practices that became staples of our consumer culture—the annual model change, a segmented product (different divisions and autos targeted to different levels of the society), and consumer credit. All of these were strategies designed not only to promote a particular product but also to cement work, growth in material consumption, and status anxiety as natural and permanent aspects of society.

Today hard work is supposed to be as American as apple pie, but American capitalism was once celebrated for its capacity to deliver us from work. In the mid-1950s, futuristic books celebrated a world where machines—including robots—would help us work less. Machines kept their part of the bargain, but many business and political leaders viewed the prospect with alarm. Fred Kaplan, writing for *Orion*, points out that as long ago as 1927 it was seen that 14 percent of American shoe factories could produce a year's supply of footwear. One writer speculated: "the world's needs ultimately will be produced by three days' work a week."[8]

Kaplan comments that surprisingly business leaders were "less than enthusiastic about the prospect of a society no longer centered on the production of goods." A society no longer premised on the centrality of work was not merely a concern in terms of profits but a threat to their political beliefs and even core personal identity. John E. Edgerton, president of the National Association of Manufacturers during the Roaring Twenties, declared: "I am for everything that will make work happier but against everything that will further subordinate its importance. The empha-sis should be put on work-more work and better work." "Nothing," he claimed, "breeds radicalism more than...leisure."

American business leaders found a way out of this dilemma. As Kaplan argues, "people could be convinced that however much they have, it isn't enough." President Herbert Hoover's 1929 Committee on Recent Economic Changes celebrated the results: "By advertising and other pro-motional devices...a measurable pull on production has been created which releases capital otherwise tied up."

Today, many Americans are convinced that it is "human nature" to want, even to crave new toys. They work long hours to fulfill their personal desires. Yet the story is much more complicated. Most advertising hardly educates consumers. It sows anxieties, often by subtle cinematic and psy-chological techniques concealed from the consumer.

Political—not market—forces have given advertising a place it enjoys in no other capitalist country. Advertising is tax deductible. Commercial broadcasters are awarded precious space on the airwaves. These practices assure that the virtues of consumption constitute a steady drumbeat from childhood on. More than any other contemporary political economist, Juliet Schor has analyzed and critiqued the twinned imperatives of work and consumption in modern US society.[9]

Today's parents work longer hours than ever before. Some families have more discretionary income but also less time to spend with their children. Children have always played some role in decisions about family purchases, but now the children have more money, both because parents earn more and because some parents—the "guilt factor"—seek to compensate for the lack of time by giving their children more money.[10]

Corporate marketers—knowing that brand loyalty is established early— have moved into this newly emerging territory. Every corner of children's lives is now viewed as potentially exploitable. Children have niche media networks of their own, video games, and DVDs, all with their own product tie-ins and advertisements. Many schools have established marketing relationships with suppliers of soft drinks and other junk foods. Channel One, the corporate-sponsored news program for high-school students, is a mandatory part of the school day in many US public schools. The volume of ads designed specifically for children has escalated. Most importantly, so has the content of those ads. Whereas in the 1920s advertisers had to convince mothers that the product was good for the child, today's ads are based on the "nag factor," encouraging the child to nag the parents into the purchase. Advertisers portray themselves in league with the child to promote children's autonomy.

There is much to be said for giving children more voice in their own consumer and lifestyle choices. Schor recognizes and values changes in contemporary understandings of childhood. She has no sympathy for an era when children could be seen but not heard. Nonetheless, she reminds us that it is a strange notion of autonomy that is so clearly dominated and inspired by one set of corporate-defined options. Children have little real autonomy when their days are dominated by ad campaigns that routinely suggest their academic or social inadequacies absent the latest car, video game, and makeup.

Children neither enjoy nor benefit from this latest dose of corporate-sponsored autonomy. In a recent poll among children aged nine–fourteen, more than 60 percent expressed concerns about ads continually trying to persuade them to buy things and nearly three-quarters lamented a world where "you have to buy certain things to be cool." Schor's own work shows a clear causal connection between heavy levels of exposure to such commercial imagery and a range of behavioral problems.

Despite much talk about the conservatism of this era, citizens all across the political spectrum have been concerned about the corporate consolidation of the mass media, which remain less popular than most politicians. A political push to eliminate commercial advertising from children's media and schools could gain traction. Short of that, Schor points out that some school districts have now given middle-school children the facilities and training to prepare news programming on their own—a child-inspired answer to Channel One. More broadly, the salience of such issues as childhood obesity suggest both the need and the possibility that parents and children can put larger issues about the control of time and culture on the political agenda.

Schools' homework policies and workplace employment rules are structured to minimize the knowledge and allure of alternatives. For many workers, refusing overtime can lead to firing. Many others who "choose" overtime do so because they fear future job loss. Those fears are well grounded in an economy where federal policy promotes enough unemployment to keep workers in their place.

Beyond the normal business strategies, consolidation, advertising, and market creation, it is important also to take a look at adult consumers and their day-to-day lives in neighborhoods and workplaces over the last half century if we are going to understand the culture of the auto. I do not accept the contention that it is natural to want a sports utility, but nor do I believe that a narrow and single-minded corporate elite imposed these on the rest of us suckers.

A provocative piece some years ago in the *New York Times* provides some insights into the popularity of this vehicle. That these vehicles are purchased primarily for utilitarian reasons is on the face of it a hard argument to sustain. Industry research shows that only a quarter of the purchasers of these vehicles use them for off road adventure or towing heavy loads. There is something more subtle going on for most purchasers. Jerry Hirschberg, Nissan's president of North American design, is quoted as saying: 'There's a feeling, when I am in my car, I am in command of my future. Home and work have not been symbols of stability" (March 23, 1997).[11]

Hirschberg is implying an understanding of consumer behavior here that is subtler than either the neoclassical view or the simplistic left notion of corporate consolidation and brainwashing. In this regard, I think that once again Schor's earlier work, *The Overspent American* (1998), provides a more fertile way into our understanding of this phenomenon.

Schor's fundamental premise is that we are social beings. We are lost without some set of socially constructed norms to guide us. In a society where some version of the Protestant work ethic has always valorized work and material success as its just rewards, getting and spending have added meaning to life. Consumer goods, especially the ones that are visible, are statements about ourselves.

But if social and personal identity is necessary simply to be, must that identity be regarded as forever unalterable, subject neither to contestation nor to limits? Does that identity express all we can become? And in fact do none of us harbor inner doubts about this consumer life or moments of rebellion, even if we don't or can't act on these? By implication, Schor argues that an identity of getting and spending has taken a social toll at least as severe as its environmental toll, and that challenges and limits to this identity are possible.

Keeping up with the Joneses is more American than apple pie. In the 1950s and 1960s, it may have occasioned the kind of bland and occasionally oppressive conformity symbolized by Levittown, but the standards were often set as much by neighbors as by distant authority. And in neighborhoods where income ranges were relatively small, the standards could be met by many.

Today's consumerism is qualitatively far more problematic, and it is this form of consumerism that lies at the heart of the sport utility vehicle (SUV) phenomenon. The role of the neighborhood in our lives is much less substantial. Even in two-parent families, mom is ever less likely to be at home. Mom and dad are both working and the Joneses with whom they strive to keep pace are coworkers and supervisors. And for almost everyone, television with its ads and opulent lifestyles is the new neighborhood.

In the modern workplace, the power and income spread has reached unprecedented levels. Keeping up appearances is thus a daunting task. Schor demonstrates, through studies of purchasing patterns for such highly visible consumer goods as cosmetics and branded clothing, and through consumer surveys that much consumer spending is designed for positioning ourselves in this increasingly stratified and competitive universe. Similarly, purchase of an SUV makes a very conspicuous statement. And it isn't merely the fact that the vehicle is large and expensive. It suggests a certain kind of life—access to the country, to the leisure and camping activities that the most affluent and successful professionals and families of wealth have always enjoyed.

The obsession to spend more on consumer goods denudes the public sector. In language reminiscent of Rousseau, Schor portrays a world where extreme individualism and massive inequalities eviscerate political life. As taxes are cut and individuals pour ever more resources into private solutions to their problems, public functions are performed ever less well. In this context as well, even the utilitarian aspects of the SUV take on new significance. One reason for their attraction is the decline of the public sphere. In this sense, Moore is right, but this decline is attributable to far more than a GM conspiracy.

The decline of the public sphere takes on great significance in terms of the kind of private good we buy. There has been a long-term decline in public spending for such items as roads and bridges. Potholes have proliferated. In addition, ever more crowded and trafficked urban areas do cause many traffic accidents. These vehicles are safer. The utilitarian defense of these vehicles makes some sense, but sits within a larger context of social policy and social evolution.

Nonetheless, far from breeding a sense of satisfaction, this new consumerism seems increasingly to disappoint. Much of what we buy we hardly use and often discard; and not surprisingly so. Keeping up with the higher ups at work requires endless new consumption. American consumers are often characterized as materialistic, but in an interesting twist our consumer patterns demonstrate no intrinsic interest in the material good. Goods are continually discarded as their social value is spent. And even as some of us gradually gain the material level to which we aspire, many others have also and the bar is then raised.

The SUV is a perfect illustration of this phenomenon as well. The first few purchasers do enjoy some safety advantage and the bragging rights. But as the *Times* pointed out, even by 1997 14 percent of all vehicles sold were SUVs and not only does status suffer but safety does as well. As one Sierra Club official remarked, "You can't see over the traffic any more, you just see the SUV in front of you."

Not to be outdone, some corporations are now making even larger versions. An obsession to spend ever more often sets in even while many despair of where their lives are going. More than a quarter of those earning over one hundred thousand report that they would need very large increases in income just to meet their "needs." And meeting those "needs" often fails to satisfy. Thomas Dumm points out in *A Politics of the Ordinary* (1999) that our ordinary, obsessive pursuit of more goods shields us from other ordinary aspects of life, the hidden places and sources of satisfaction that can well up amid other daily activities:

> As many of us would tacitly acknowledge—though this acknowledgement fails to influence most of our practical reasoning—the crush of goods is never so good as to save us from the need to pursue more of them. In fact, perhaps, the most commonly recurring theme in the pursuit of happiness in the United States is the general failure by Americans to achieve the happiness we pursue. Entire genres of literature and film present us instead with the serendipitous discovery of happiness where it has been overlooked.[12]

The auto as fortress and status symbol, the centrality of work, the always elusive quest for position come in focus even more clearly if we examine another recent phenomenon, the cell phone.

I hate cell phones. They are unattractive. Cutesy "ring tones" interrupt meetings, concerts, and lectures where concentration is required. On the few occasions when I have felt compelled or was persuaded to borrow one, I could hardly figure out where to talk and where to listen. Dialing remains a mystery to me. I can't even stand being on the other side of cell phone calls. At least half break up, necessitating repeat calls, thereby further disrupting my work. I wish they had never been invented.

I know, I can hear what some of you are saying or thinking: "He is some sort of anti-technology nut, a modern day Luddite who wants to smash the machines that lift the burdens off our backs. If he doesn't like cell phones, there is a simple answer. Don't buy one."

For the record, I am not a Luddite. I was one of the first to buy a VCR. It allowed me to follow my beloved sports teams on their periodic West Coast swings without having to stay up all hours of the night.

I wish decisions about cell phones were as simple. VCR purchases by neighbors had little effect on my life and were no factor in my purchase. For cell phones, however, the case is murkier. For over a decade I played tennis periodically during the winter at a Holiday Inn in Ellsworth, Maine, half an hour from my home. If I was running late or needed to get in touch with family members at home, a pay phone was available in the hallway outside the courts. That phone is now gone, a casualty of an era where the purchase of cell phones by most affluent and even many working-class consumers has led phone companies to discontinue public pay phones as insufficiently profitable.

My travel is also more difficult. I was recently invited to Denver to give a talk. The airport is a cavernous labyrinth and I had trouble finding my host. I figured I'd locate a pay phone to establish a new rendezvous point. I asked an airport security person where the nearest pay phone was, only to be told that most public phones had been eliminated but there might be one in a concourse about three football fields from where we were standing. (Fortunately for me, he was right.)

Many professionals in various fields also face dilemmas. Lawyers, accountants, and contractors risk losing clients if they aren't readily accessible by cell phone, but there is a little noted paradox here. The first few purchasers of cell phones reap a decided advantage, but as soon as most lawyers, accountants, and contractors have their own, no one has an advantage. Everyone in fact is paying several hundred dollars a year more just to stay at square one.

Autos and SUVs go together in a self-reinforcing pattern of consumer addiction. Cell phones make us more accident prone, all the more reason to "need" an SUV. Endless hours of time in traffic? No problem, you can work as much as you need to via your cell phone.

Markets, technological innovation, and consumer freedom are great achievements of modern capitalist societies. I love my VCR. Nonetheless, technology and the free market are not as simple and unalloyed gifts as they are often portrayed. In a world of increasing interdependence the spillover effects of products and technologies go beyond such issues as the discharge of pollutants into the air and water. If consumer freedom is not to lead to ever more self-defeating traps and bottlenecks for most consumers, that freedom will require regulation and periodic readjustment. Today it would hardly be unreasonable to tax cell phones to pay for a minimum level of public phones and to impose much stricter limits on their use in cars. Even more importantly, the auto industry today would be more stable and the average driver far less burdened if politicians and regulators had insisted on applying safety and fuel economy standards across the board.

Making these policy changes is of course far from simply a matter of dollars and cents debate within a policy arena. Nor is resistance to a cell phone tax merely a factor of individuals' already having invested in these and not wishing to make any further sacrifice. More than our economic security or social status is tied up in our possessions.

Autos and public transit are not simply interchangeable commodities. They also represent and express different understandings of human freedom and the good life. Despite its deficiencies and inconveniences, the private auto still represents a sense of the individual's autonomy, his or her ability to travel where and when they wish, and a sense of one's place in the world, as symbolized by the relative luxury of the auto. And particular autos are also, as Schor's analysis suggests, connected to our identity and our sense of ourselves as worthy human beings.

A Theology of the Auto

Religion in its many forms plays a major role. The devotion to certain commodities expresses and in some ways is undergirded by religious or philosophical convictions. To be human is to have some not always fully articulated or fully provable sense of the way things just are. We need this sense to lend some degree of order and coherence to our lives and keep our minds from being overloaded. I term the conscious aspect of how things are our "commonsense ontologies," or perspectives on the nature of reality itself. I will focus on one mainstream view, which, though not embraced in all its dimensions, colors the view of many Americans.

The mainstream view suggests that an omnipotent God created the world ex nihilo, with man (and I do mean man) being directly created by God. Man is given both freedom and dominion over the earth and with these gifts the responsibility to obey God's simple laws. The world created by God is like a well-oiled machine and human beings can achieve increasing control of nature and greater wealth. In some versions, wealth and technological wizardry are one proof of our healthy relationship with God. Maintenance of any commonsense ontology is both necessary and yet difficult. In today's world, where the pace of cultural encounter is rapid, human beings inevitably experience both individuals and cultures that hold other views. They also confront events that can challenge or provoke their commonsense ontologies and evoke deeper fears and feelings of disgust that we often cannot fully articulate or understand. Earthquakes and tsunamis may happen thousands of miles away, but we often have home videos of the events within days or hours. Many white southerners in the 1960s were angered and disgusted by both reports and pictures of mixed marriages. Today, images of same sex marriages can be flashed across screens 24/7, and populations with diverse values and lifestyles are but a plane ride or an eighteen-wheeler away. Whether in response to an intrinsic anxiety about our finitude or because our religious narratives exacerbate fears of death and tend toward exclusivity and dogmatism, we often vilify those whose actual or apparent lifestyles seem to question prevailing social norms, especially the quest to control nature, become wealthy, and display that wealth. To borrow from President Bush, we hate them for what they are, not for what they do.

Americans spend increasing numbers of hours in traffic jams. Nonetheless, the vision of the auto is captured in endless series of advertising copy shot in remote and often arcadian locations and coded with subtexts of power over nature and social success. More recently auto ads have resorted to a stunning array of visual techniques. Backdrops and camera angles change rapidly, suggesting the auto both transcends and escapes current constraints, and the rapidity of the change and the infinitely receding backdrop associate the car with power and mystery. I believe much of this imagery subconsciously evokes, if you will pardon the phrase, shock and awe. In addition, such ads can have a hold on most of us even well before we are old enough to own our own cars

The industry skillfully draws on these ideals and insecurities. The International Hummer Owners Group (IHOG) claims:

> The H2 is an American icon. It's a symbol of what we all hold so dearly above all else, the fact we have the freedom of choice, the freedom of happiness, the freedom of adventure and discovery, and the ultimate freedom of expression. Those who deface a Hummer in words or deeds...deface the American flag and what it stands for.

While writing the first draft of this chapter (June 2006), I saw a TV ad in which a mother is upset with another mother who let a child jump in front of hers to ride the playground slide. The next scene shows her at a Hummer dealer, soon driving off with a look of smug entitlement in a Hummer with a mile-high bumper. A friend has told me that a corollary ad aimed at men ends with the statement, "Take back your manhood." Hummer sells aggression and revenge. Some men and women buy the product.[13]

Public transit, on the other hand, has long been coded in different social and natural terms. It is viewed as both limited in capacity and as a necessity for life's losers. Many public high-school students regard the bus to school as not merely inconvenient but as a sign that they are not full, respected, powerful, and autonomous members of the adult community. When older citizens reach a point where driving becomes problematic, they often resent and resist losing the right to drive. There are obvious practical reasons for this anger, but I think there are psychic ones as well. The car is part of their psychic economy as fully respected beings in control of their world.

The very public form of any community transit entails different social relations—a need to interact with others across an ethnic and economic spectrum. (Even in a traffic jam, one has a degree of privacy in a car not experienced on a bus.) Public transit seems objectionable for the very reason that it is public. It is provided to everyone regardless of economic success and it even extends support to those who are widely deemed morally deficient. Baseball fans may remember Atlanta Braves pitcher John

Rocker's rant about the ethnic, racial, and lifestyle minorities encountered on and supported by New York City subways.

An effective response to the increasing crisis of our auto-and-oil dependent society requires us to do more than focus only on the register of "rational" cost-benefit analysis of various transit modes. Our orientation toward transit policy also forms along four other distinct additional registers: religious attitudes toward domination of nature; the ways in which we view others who are different from ourselves; the way we relate to others and to our commodities; and even our gut feelings and aesthetic sensibilities. Therefore, we need to address five registers in all. A self-consciously five-pronged approach may not be possible or even necessary for everyone, but the whole package is involved—and in such a way that the sum is greater than the parts.

We need an understanding of the human mind and its relation to nature that acknowledges the power of modern science without deluding ourselves that we can have full control or understanding of our social and natural world.

A Catholic Alternative

Historically Catholic theology's social gospel offered a broadly inclusive commitment to the well-being of the working class and the poor while not relying solely on the false promises of economic growth to right all social injustices. This theology, which continues to have a presence among liberal Catholics, is an important place to begin fruitful dialogues about how and in what terms to contest the current priorities as expressed in our auto celebratory culture.

Father John A. Ryan, an influential Catholic theologian of the 1930s, was also well-versed in economic thought and attuned to the problems of overproduction that resulted from the gaping inequalities of the capitalism of the 1920s.[14] Ryan recognized the role that socioeconomic inequality had played in the economic crisis of the 1930s. The wealthy had more than they could or wanted to spend and the poor did not have enough even to meet minimal needs. Demand for goods and services lagged behind the growing capacity to produce such goods.

Mainstream political economists and business leaders followed the lead of the Hoover commission in advocating the stimulation of needs through advertizing and hoped that new technologies and products would inspire more consumption by the affluent.

Ryan regarded faith in such remedies as both overly optimistic and misguided. The economic crisis flowed from society's violation of natural law. Society has a firm moral obligation to assure workers the right to a decent material standard of living before indulging in the luxuries of the wealthy. Economic growth rather than being independent of or a sign of ethical progress had to be subject to larger ethical tests. The material world is an instrument of and subordinate to higher ends, including preservation of the family and ultimately contemplation of God.

On the policy front, Ryan advocated stronger minimum wage laws and redistributive taxation both to advance a more egalitarian notion of community and to forestall economic stagnation. In addition, he argued for gradual reduction in working hours as productivity increased. He viewed the latter as crucial not merely to keep demand for labor high and thereby buttress the position of the poor and the working class but also to advance moral ends. As productivity increased, its dividends could be taken in the form of time for family and for communion with God.

Ryan's work had an enduring influence on labor, social justice, and environmental movements, but it is not without its problems and challenges. The notion of the relatively egalitarian community as the natural outcome and foundation of democratic politics does and has inspired many reformers. These reformers see such a belief as both well grounded and as pragmatically and existentially necessary to inspire the kind of cooperation reform movements require. This perspective surely has a role to play in the dialogue and debate enabling ecological and economic reform. Others, however, detect possible dangers in the celebration of the harmonious community toward which nature and God are pointing us. Society requires law and minimal order, but must or can these be founded only on shared, fundamental beliefs? Can society be better sustained by willingness to engage and debate multiple foundations for the rights and obligations we share and by a willingness to contemplate the expansion of the catalogue of rights and those who are entitled to them?

Not only does Ryan's social ontology perhaps blind us to exclusions, the Catholic natural law tradition, by positing an ultimate harmony of humans and nature, can be seen as one more narcissistic concept of nature as fully amenable to our purposes. Though such conceptions have managed to curb acquisitive instincts in some, for many moderns notions of natural hierarchies and harmonies are not plausible.

Prophetic Christianity is suspicious of natural law and hard teleology as a way of absolutizing finite moral perspectives or current procedures regarded as the tools to move society toward higher truths. Celebrating the community as the buffer or container of economic life has much merit, but even relatively economically egalitarian and democratic communities may be worthy only as long as we are attuned to other forms of injustice that may be embodied in our understandings of community. The Catholic Church's long-term stance regarding the role of women in the Church, the workplace, and the family has rightly become a major issue since Ryan's time, but notions of history as moving toward a fixed teleology can be seen as factors that blunted much earlier receptivity to emerging or diffuse concerns about such issues. These teleologies, even when they embrace an affirmation of democracy and participation, tend to treat politics as an eventually dispensable outpost on a road to final consensus. If they inspire efforts to build cross-class, cross-cultural reform movements for some, they may deter others who would be more inspired by visions of an evolving, multicentered coalition and the tensions and vitalities it would represent and evoke.

Along these lines, Ryan's aspiration for leisure time for contemplation of God is admirable—as long as it is tethered to pluralistic understandings both of God and the process of contemplation itself. For Ryan, static or unitary understandings of God may suffice both to provide comfort and to energize reform, but for others such a God fails both tests. Understandings of God as fallible or limited can not only inspire others but also provide a powerful counter giving more conventional theists a deeper understanding of their own commitments.

"Contemplation of God" may also evoke too intellectualistic an image even for conventional religious practice, which is replete with ritual, artistic visualization, music, and postural practices and disciplines. Just as Catholics' communion with their God involves bodily disposition and activity, those committed to a limited or fallible God will engage that God along several different registers.

Other Voices: Process Theology, Complexity Theory, Immanent Naturalism

With regard to the bodily dimensions of spiritual experience, one might also engage Ryan's discussion of the material world itself. His understanding that material progress is a means and not an end has been one impetus to blunt environmentally destructive and unsustainable forms of resource exploitation. But need we ground sustainable development solely around a view of natural limits or nature as a home or a celebration of man's intellectual pursuits? An interesting counter or addition to the perspectives of the Ryan and the Catholic Social Gospel can be found in Christianity's process theology.

One place to start is with Genesis itself. Genesis is the prime text not only for the cultural right's Creationism but also for industrial capitalism's celebration of a hard predictive natural science and material progress. It is perhaps a cosmic irony that Creationists debunk contemporary science even as the cultural and religious right provides troops and support for the modern crony/disaster capitalism I describe in chapter four. That capitalism fosters and builds upon the very faith in linear science Creationists abhor. We may start to break the grip of both Creationism and the hubristic forms of linear and reductionist science through Catherine Keller's provocative rereading of Genesis.

Theology generally interprets Genesis as proof of God's creation of the world from absolutely nothing. Both Testaments do picture a creation through divine speech, a dramatic beginning of the world different from a static or cyclical creations. It is not a purposeless universe.

Conventional theology, however, is wrong to presume that creation ex nihilo is the only alternative to nihilism. The Bible narrates various versions of a more mysterious process, "creation from the deep, known as the watery chaos." This constitutes an alternative to God's top-down, once-and-for-all creation or to mechanistic understandings of the world.

Keller asks us to bracket all we have been taught about Genesis and reread the first few verses. She asks us to notice: "there is no nothingness, but a whole lot of not quite somethingness." Earth exists as a potential planet, its condition best translated as "waste and wild," a phrase chosen for its onomatopoetic rhyme and rhythm. She goes on to add:

> The playful poetic repetition of the Hebrew may be the essence of its meaning: for matter, as we are learning from the new physics, is at base rhythm. Indeed, superstring theory "suggests that the microscopic landscape is suffused with tiny strings whose vibrational patterns orchestrate the evolution of the cosmos." The earth's [waste and wild] suggests a rhyme that has not yet found its reason...The breath of God pulses over a watery chaos, but flow in nature is not of a smooth, continuous motion but of pulsation...as in the ebb and flow of waves keeping the ocean moving...These waters express the widespread myth of a primal chaos, an infinity of unformed and unfathomable potentiality.[15]

God does not micromanage this process. Indeed from the very beginning not only humans but also the rest of matter is involved as collaborators in the process of creativity. God sees, not says that it is good. The element of surprise has been noted too little.

Keller goes on to note that for some scientists, God creates through self-organizing systems. She follows Whitehead in regarding God as "the ground of order and novelty, offering an initial aim or lure to each emerging occasion. Rather than Intelligent Design, we might speak of Creative Wisdom. The wisdom does not impose order but calls forth self-organizing complexity." Emerging from the primordial depths, creatures become increasingly other from the mother, capable of relationships but never altogether separate. Genesis involves generations of forthcoming, multi-plying creatures. The gathering cooperation unfolds as a rhythm, a cosmic liturgy: divine lure, creaturely improvisation, and divine reception—ooh, good!"

In language that I find eerily apt when one considers our current eco-nomic distress that in turn is illuminated by that distress, Keller goes on to add:

> When the level of order, of what biologists call "self-organizing complex-ity," reaches a new level, so does the risk of chaos. But since complexity theory teaches that creativity in the universe—the evolutionary leaps in organic versatility—emerges "at the edge of chaos," this risk also expresses the creative wisdom. The creation called forth in Genesis is a kosmos, in the Greek sense of a decorative order. But unlike classical, symmetrical aes-thetic, this cosmos unfolds an art of flows, waves, disruptions, and sur-prises. A disciplined improvisation is called forth in creatures at great risk. Genesis names not a static and settled cosmos but something more like what James Joyce playfully dubbed chaosmos. In the interplay of formless-ness and form, chaos and order, emergence and collapse, the possibilities in what process theology calls "the divine lure" finds actualizastion. The genesis collective thus continues, moment by moment, amidst all its losses, to emerge.[16]

Human beings are thus not unique, but a distinctive aspect of Creation. Humans "are able to participate in the self-organizational capacity of the genesis collective with a self-conscious creativity." Keller goes on to add, in a theme reminiscent of Niebuhr, that

> that self-consciousness is both our gift and our curse. It can fill us with ourselves—me-me-me—and therefore cancel out the imago dei: the con-sciousness of the multiplicity of creation that we share with the creator. So here begin all the painful self-contradictions of human history: self-organizing complexity tangling us up in ourselves.[17]

Will we as individual human beings or whole societies follow the cre-ative lure, strive to keep ourselves open to new possibilities amid the con-tinual need for order? Could narratives like Keller's lead Creationists to reconsider their views or give pause to those who see creation ex nihilo as sanctioning a rapacious orientation to nature? I don't know, but my own speculation is that the level of commitment to these doctrines among some social conservatives is less than absolute. They might well respond to a narrative that so carefully retells the Genesis narrative in a way they would not necessarily respond to nontheistic versions of chaos theory or to deep pluralist interrogations of linear causality. In any case, it is incumbent on those of us who are appalled by the consequences of conventional readings of nature to present alternatives and engage in discussion of these when the opportunity presents itself. We cannot anticipate results in advance. Neither history nor God makes that determination. From Keller's perspective, however, that uncertainty at the highest level is a necessary aspect of the goodness of the world God has created.

Genesis and Keller's reading of it are not science. Nonetheless, they open us up to an intriguing set of developments in both science and modern philosophy. Analogous perspectives have been developed by some chemists and physicists. A growing minority within the scientific community now doubts that science itself can yield fully predictive models of the natural world. The view that nature is wholly predictable may be the ultimate narcissistic fallacy, as though it were designed to serve our purposes. These scientists take as paradigmatic a range of chemical reactions at far from equilibrium conditions. When these reactions are subject to changes in such parameters as temperature or pressure they can yield several distinctive outcomes.

More broadly, Stuart Kauffman has addressed these issues with respect to all of nature. The belief in law like models or even the notions that every phenomenon can be reduced to the unfolding of simple and replicable components has been questioned even at the levels of physics, biochemistry, and evolutionary biology. Consider the work that Kauffman has done in explicating Darwin and what is now known as preadaptations. As an example, paleontologists have traced the evolution of swim bladders in fish from early fish with lungs. Some lived in oxygen poor water. Lungs grew as outpouchings from the gut so that air could be absorbed, making it easier for the fish to survive. But now water and air were in a single lung and the lung was preadapted to serve a new function, a swim bladder that adjusted neutral buoyancy in a water column. If ocean and river conditions changed, requiring fish to adjust their buoyancy in the water column, they were prepared.

Kauffman then asks if a scientist could predict all future preadaptations. His answer is no. Part of the problem is that we would have to prestate all possible selective environments. Kauffman points out that we cannot possibly have an idea as to what all possible selective environments can be. Furthermore, each successful preadaptation alters the environment in which future selective changes occur. This requirement creates major difficulties for models of science based on the conviction that all phenomena are at least in principle describable eventually as law-like regularities.[18]

After the fact we can explain why certain modifications managed to increase the survival prospects of those members of the species that experienced these changes. Swim bladders violate no laws of physics, they are not magic, but eons ago we could not have extrapolated from these simple laws to predict their occurrence.

Kauffman makes clear that he is not denying all orderliness or predictability in the universe. With relatively closed systems or those that are in equilibrium, order, causal laws, and relative predictability are possible. Indeed, we depend on such predictability all the time. But the very existence of such stability often fosters changes that either disrupt equilibria or bring formerly closed systems into proximity and interdependence with others.

This science does not speak of literal chaos. Probabilities can be established. At equilibrium conditions predictable order is maintained. Nonetheless, even in principle it is impossible to establish certainties when systems diverge far from equilibrium. Order and predictability thus may pertain for a time, but time itself must be viewed as punctuated. New circumstances, often intervening variables originating from other open systems operating on different time scales, can generate conditions that disrupt order, leading to a finite range of outcomes, no one of which can be predicted.

Life and the emergence of human creativity are then understood as grandly fortuitous events amid the partially indeterminate flux of nature. Several open systems operating on different time scales lead to unpredictable results, both joyous and terrifying.

New readings of both organic and inorganic nature add important insights. Jane Bennett has called to our attention Charles Darwin's work on worms. She provides another powerful take on Darwinian preadaptations.

Darwin maintained that worms play a significant role in human history, and that role cannot be explained by or simply reduced to an unvarying inherited impulse. Worms turn vegetative material into topsoil and they do so by adjusting their technique to the materials at hand, in much the way a person would. Furthermore, worms, like humans, can be so absorbed in a task as to override their normal instinctual tendency to flee to a burrow to avoid bright light.[19]

Ontological understandings of the vagaries of organic and even inorganic nature can have broader ethical and social consequences as well. Finding joy in the surprises offered by vibrant matter can blunt the self-defeating urge to accumulate and soon discard more and more stuff. Bennett's recasting of the Nicene Creed cleverly suggests this possibility:

> I believe in one matter-energy, the maker of things seen and unseen. I believe that this pluriverse is traversed by heterogeneities that are continually doing things. I believe that it is wrong to deny vitality to nonhuman

bodies, forces, and forms and that a careful course of anthropomorphization can help reveal that vitality, even though it resists full translation and exceeds my comprehensive grasp. I believe that encounters with lively matter can chasten my fantasies of human mastery, highlight the common materiality of all that is, expose a wider distribution of agency, and reshape the self and its interests.[20]

For me, several philosophical/theological currents resonate with while challenging each other in fruitful ways. Reinhold Niebuhr, whose work I discussed more fully in chapter one, explicitly denies that death is God's punishment for sin. Rather sin itself arises from the propensity to still the anxiety of finitude. That anxiety issues in comprehensive social ideologies sealed against challenge. Sin, he says, is to be redressed by the example of agape. The Coming of Jesus as the Christ and the power of the example of his life symbolizes the worth and meaning of history and the efficacy of love. The Crucifixion is a symbolic statement of the inability to fully apply standards of complete love to our world. History always points to something beyond itself. Nonetheless, the Resurrection symbolizes the continual relevance of that standard as a challenge that continually inflects worldly concerns. Neibuhr's concept calls our attention to our perpetual human urge to respond to the temptation of final knowledge. He reminds us to attend to the continuing possibilities of injustice evoked by even our most broadly consensual laws and reforms. At the very least we must not forget the real harm we do even as we (necessarily) imprison the violent among us.

Yet the tragic vision—that of a justice that can never be reached and that always judges us—can itself be overwhelming and a source of despair. It may be a necessary antidote for those who have lived privileged lives and may open them to other possible moral visions and worldviews. But for others the tragic sense can become overwhelming and self-defeating.

For Bennett, care for diverse and pluralizing currents within ourselves, our fellow humans, and nature itself need not depend on any theistic tradition. It springs from the recognition of the inexhaustible dynamism of the human and nonhuman worlds. Bennett's discussions of simple "thing power" and more complex agencies of assemblage, to be discussed later, not only add to our understanding of the dimensions of pluripotentiality but also convincingly address its ethical potential.

The capacity to recognize and appreciate this multifaceted creativity can be cultivated in most of us. Bennett recommends that rather than deriving our ethical sensibility from acknowledging that life will always exceed our knowledge and control,

> the starting point of ethics [may be] less the acceptance of this impossibility and more the recognition of human participation in a shared, vital

materiality. We are vital materiality and we are surrounded by it, though we don't always see it that way. The ethical task at hand here is to cultivate the ability to discern nonhuman vitality, to become perpetually open to it.[21]

Personal and social tragedy is a part of the human condition. It is terrible in its own right and it can often blunt our capacity to embrace natural potential. Nonetheless, tragedy need not lead to irredeemable or unrelenting despair as if we can remain attuned to nature as a source of mystery and surprise, the mystery that brought us life itself. Writing on the basis of her reading of Genesis, Keller responds to the reality of the unpredictable by suggesting that we can lessen the burden of that suffering when we no longer attribute it to the direct intervention of God. God, the God who affirmed a world of primal and unfathomable surprises, does not will our specific suffering. A world micromanaged by God would be a lesser, more boring world.

> God does will a living, whirling, open system of a world. That world happens to be this creation, this real world of finite creatures who live, feed, exult, risk, and die, a world of change and interdependence in which suffering is inevitable. Yet this genesis collective is so intensely alive, even or precisely in its chaos, that new life is also always happening. Therefore, even for one as tragically hurt as Job, new life can take place. This may only be possible because he has refused to suppress piously the turbulent truth of his own experience but has grieved and raged and confronted the meaning of life. Ex profundis.[22]

If there is no grand design to nature and if nature is too unpredictable to be completely mastered, death—even death at an early age—is not automatic proof of a human failing. At best, death will be regarded as serene oblivion. Or, following Epicurus, we should

> get used to believing that death is nothing to us. For all good and evil lies in sensation and death is the end of all sensation. Therefore a right understanding that death is nothing to us makes the mortality of life enjoyable, not by adding to limitless duration, but by taking away the yearning for immortality... But the wise man neither looks for the escape from life nor for its cessation... And just as men do not seek simply and only the largest portion of good but the pleasantest, so the wise seek to enjoy the time which is most pleasant and not merely that which is the longest.[23]

At the very least, such a perspective can help blunt the cultural urge instilled within many toward self-flagellation for the putative failure to live up to some established standard or lifetime requirements, requirements that are themselves infinitely expanding. It becomes instead merely a lamentable closing of a window upon future personal, social, and natural surprises. From this perspective, even the orthodox Christian heaven, with its perpetual bliss, amounts to pervasive boredom and is a hollow offer.

Both Keller and Bennett recognize and acknowledge that they speak from faith, albeit differently grounded. Bennett's explication of vibrant matter commendably admits its own elements of speculation and her role in understanding matter in this light. She makes, however, a strong brief on behalf of her views. Bennett's assemblages give life and plausibility to Kauffman's more abstract discussion of the limits of reductionism and determinism. She evokes sensitivity to her theme even as she addresses standard philosophical concerns. Her playful style, her engagement with vibrant nature in daily life, and her trenchant treatment of such perplexing political issues as stem cells and electrical blackouts highlight the ways some notion of "vibrant matter" has found its way into ordinary discourse.

Bennett sees worms in an ecosystem and even electrical currents in a complex wire and institutional grid as having some modicum of self-organizational capacity—at least in situations far from equilibrium. This capacity can disrupt or enliven and enrich the cultural and natural landscape. Some critics might choose to write this ontological perspective off as just the projection of an overly imaginative human mind. In my eyes, Bennett can reply effectively that the very capacity of the human mind to build such "fantasies" depends on the complex concatenation of active waves and particles we call the brain.[24]

If matter is not merely on occasion resistant to our designs but an active participant in complex assemblages, holding humans solely responsible for deleterious outcomes is not merely unjust, it also reinforces a technological hubris that contributes to our problems.

As with the discussion of God and love in chapter one, Bennett's posture also does not issue in passivity. None of this means that we must completely forego specific attributions of responsibility. The emergent human capacity through consciousness, language, and technology, though itself grounded in the material world, has an extraordinary capacity to shape the context in which cultural and natural change occur and to avail itself of regularities that do pertain. Notions of responsibility both individual and collective help instill in us and remind us of that capacity. But responsibility itself needs to be recast and amended in the light of our recognition of the complex web in which actions emerge. The relative roles of context, law, cultural understandings, organic and inorganic actants, and economic institutions must be periodically reevaluated with an eye both to revise law and adjust the severity of punishment. More broadly, responsibility now requires greater attunement to its own limits and to the injustices that may flow from revenge against the inevitability of mortality and a world humans cannot fully understand and control. Finally, recognition of the ways the world is so vibrant and can bring us to the brink of catastrophe should lead us to construct economic systems and technologies premised on the possibility of unpredictability.

I suspect that even some of those whose primary theological commitment is to some version of the historical Jesus and or prophetic Christianity can take comfort in this view of nature and find in it inspiration to continue their quest for justice and their care not to judge.

Those who embrace various subsets of these visions are not "relativists" or anarchists as sometimes charged. They know that rules and standards are necessary even to sustain a care for life and the earth. How these boundaries are policed, however, makes a big difference. Devotees of these views demand sensitivity to the tragic dimension of law enforcement and to the ways that law can become insensitive to the emerging currents its very stabilities enable.

More openness to others, to nature and its delights and vagaries, and to the limits of our resources and capacities could encourage policies that both addressed environmental concerns and at the same time relieved some of the insecurities that encourage the most strident fundamentalisms in our culture. Let's get back to the World War II analogy. Detroit, my hometown, became the arsenal of democracy. Today, a sagging auto industry could be put on a new wartime footing to produce large numbers of vans, buses, and alternative fueled vehicles, and most especially whole new generations of comfortable mid-range vans for rural and suburban park and ride alternatives. This program would reduce local and regional unemployment, attack growing economic inequality, and make industry more efficient and competitive.

Taxing the externalities associated with the auto is vital, but that tax needs to be offset by other more progressive tax measures to end the regressivity of such a step and more importantly, it needs to be paired and associated with positive programs and visions.

Progressive environmentalists should learn some lessons from Madison Avenue. We need an aesthetics and a popular culture that valorizes public transit and more broadly alternatives to the energy intense work and spend culture so prevalent. Public transit needs to be connected symbolically to images of leisure, release from daily challenges, and new and expanded visual possibilities that the picture windows of trains and the freedom from intense driving concentration can frame and enable. In addition we need imaginative portrayals of positive cultural encounter in such settings. Today, we have few ads for transit alternatives and most of these stress its utilitarian aspects—BART tells citizens that they save money by taking the transit system to work. Much of the environmental community, highlighting the danger and risk of cars or other forms of consumerism, have failed in this larger positive task of valorizing leisure and free time and alternatives to mass consumption. This failure may reflect or be intensified by some forms of demonization in which progressives themselves have engaged.

Viewers of Fahrenheit 911 may remember the scene where Michael Moore portrays President Bush's decision to vacation in response to professional crises as a sign of moral deficiency. Bush's most endearing trait, however, may have been that he was not a workaholic. It is a strange sort of left politics that implicitly celebrates long working hours rather than validate the contribution leisure makes to human development. Moore's sarcasm suggests inadvertently the ways even left culture has been captured by mainstream norms and may reflect some submerged anger regarding the toll that work life has taken.

Leisure is both a subject of conscious or latent desire as well as a condition for the emergence of more inclusive states of consciousness. Various protests centered on leisure time, whether from students vis-à-vis homework, French and German workers striking to preserve the thirty-five-hour week, or women demanding relief from the second shift, seem to converge in interesting ways. The good news is that time pressure on working-class families is emerging as a significant issue. When workers have more free time, they can experience more sides of their own diverse personalities and at least potentially revisit assumptions they have brought to their judgments on other ways of life and cultures. And finally, more free time is time also, at least on occasion, for politics, for the mobilization of the very constituencies needed if issues of alternative transit and social justice are to be pursued and periodically renegotiated.

In this context, just as progressives need to avoid their own forms of demonization and be attuned to the emergence of new and plausible rights claims, they must be as inclusive as possible in the philosophical underpinning invited to this conversation. The movement to enact more sensible transit options might include fundamentalist greens, who see in nature itself a set of steady harmonies and values, as well as older, Christian groups inspired by John Ryan's Social Gospel tradition and eager to give a leg up to the poor. Finally, even within the evangelical community itself splits are appearing, including the emergence of groups concerned about the greenhouse who are effect committed to stewardship of the earth as a priority.

Does driving as much and as fast as we do have to be our birthright? Let's go back to World War II for a moment. America was a less auto-dependent society but a majority of adult workers still owned cars and routinely used them for business and pleasure. Gas rationing dramatically changed commuting and recreational patterns. More interestingly, rationing—unlike Prohibition—provoked relatively few attempts by well-placed individuals to undermine the system or defeat it at the polls.

In the 1940s policy and lifestyle changes were successful. They were, however, impelled not merely by fear of a common enemy but also by strong nationalistic and civic commitments. These commitments also, however, carry obvious risks. The willingness to accept rationing was eased by the commonly shared conviction that the United States was the greatest nation in the world and that sacrifice today would spur the return to even greater glory of the US consumer production machine. An older neighbor of ours pointed out to me that as soon as rationing was lifted, many of his neighbors immediately went on long car rides. So the question for me becomes not whether driving as much as we do is inevitable, but how can we put more humane and environmentally sound alternatives on a psychologically sustainable foundation, one that will make us more law abiding, less bellicose in our community, and more willing to adapt to the unpredictable fortunes of nature and culture.

Let me return to Maine and perform an intellectual experiment. Imagine the cost of gas suddenly went to twenty dollars a gallon. It would surely change habits rapidly and more optimistically it might catalyze different policies and ways of life, especially if we prepare ourselves intellectually and emotionally. Adults and teens would dramatically change their habits. Car pooling, not merely to work but to grocery stores and other retail establishments, would become commonplace. Business and working schedules would adjust to accommodate car pools. Here on MDI, every Island Explorer (a fleet of minibuses used to convey tourists in summer and early fall) would be pressed into year-round use and more such busing systems would be demanded. Buses to school would be something more than second-class transit. Extracurricular schedules would be adapted to public transit options, freeing time for parents of younger children. In the right intellectual and political climate a tipping point would be reached that would catalyze and congeal two new rights, the right to free time and the right to live without a car, a collection of rights that may come to seem more necessary and possible as the population ages. Working at home with expanded use of Internet and other communication technologies, the full potential of which has scarcely been tapped, would be dramatically expanded. Properly addressed, and with tax compensation for poor and working-class citizens most hurt by gas price increases, a dramatic escalation in price could give us more time at home, more opportunity to interact with a community that grows in its interests and diversity by the day, and more time to experience the beauties of a rugged and changing nature that so many pay so much to drive to and experience.

The nature that more free time might make available need not be found only on rock-lined coasts. While reading Bennett's work, I had an experience that both confirmed for me a sense of the animal world as actants in our lives and of the joys that can emerge from attunement to that possibility. As I sat in the kitchen one evening, a stray ping-pong ball fell off the counter and into a corner in our tiled kitchen. Ginger, a large black cat with white chest and white paws, leaped from the seat beside me onto the floor. Like a worm taking the new possibilities offered her she started whacking the ball off the wall and chasing its random rebounds. And like those worms she was not to be deterred from her task, which seemed to be to develop her own game. Eventually she began striking the ball at such an angle that it consistently came back to her. I tried to retrieve both ball and cat, only to be rebuffed with a disapproving meow. I was awestruck by her skill and tenacity, like a tennis pro sharpening volleys against a gymnasium wall. I am tempted to say that she displayed cat-like reflexes.

Several chance events had to come together that night for Ginger to play her ping-pong game and for me to become transfixed by it. The ball had to be in the room and be swept by an air current to the floor within a few feet of her. I had to be attuned through my own recent recollections to Ginger's purposive play and to resist the temptation to stop her. Ginger, like Bennett's worms, had to turn aside all distractions and concentrate on the ball. A particular and unexpected concatenation of events came together and gripped me. I cannot prove the view of evolution that underlay my experience, but nor can exponents of law-like models prove theirs, as we shall see in chapter four. I can say my attentiveness to organic and inorganic actants in the world has changed me.

CHAPTER FOUR

THE IMMIGRANTS ARE COMING!
THE IMMIGRANTS ARE COMING!

Four years ago, in an op ed column for my local paper, I wrote on threats to water resources posed by privatization and commercial bottled water. I expected e-mails defending private water rights or bottled water. Instead, one respondent commented: "As with almost all stories about wages falling, overpopulation, increases and diminishing resources we never see the actual cause identified-immigration... King George realizes that by increasing the labor supply wages go down while unemployment skyrockets." Other op eds in which I have commented on labor law reform have brought on angry e-mails asking me to address our real economic problem, "illegal immigrants." What part of illegal am I failing to understand, some of my readers angrily ask.

More recently, during the early days of the massive financial crisis that gripped Wall Street and the nation, the *National Review* website carried a story attributing the banking collapse to loans to "illegal immigrants." Although the *Wall Street Journal* soon countered this analysis, it gained considerable attention.[1]

Immigrants have become one of the hot button issues of our time, even in Maine. There are, however, grave dangers in what I take to be scapegoating of immigrants. These dangers go beyond the obvious injustices to the immigrants themselves. This heated rhetoric may distract us from considering the contribution that mainstream values and practices make to our most pressing problems, even to the high rate of immigration itself. And a reflexive hostility to immigrants may accompany and intensify a rigid rejection of all that is new, and thereby impoverish our own lives.

Seen from the perspective of the deep pluralist theory discussed in chapter one, much contemporary immigration politics is a further effort to resolve the paradox of politics and cement a secure identity. Immigrants have not always been seen as threats to our way of life, but they are regularly constructed in ways that serve to secure a prevailing identity. Recall that Rousseau blunts the full thrust of the paradox of politics by displacing it to the foundation of the Republic and assigning its resolution to a disinterested, heroic founder. But as Bonnie Honig reminds us, foundational problems recur on a daily basis. Every day new citizens arrive in established democracies both through birth and immigration.

Rousseau argues that the potentially alien force of the law can be blunted when citizens participate in willing a pure general will or common good. Yet apart from the very narrow conditions on which such a process depends (such as relative economic equality, shared culture, small population, and geographic area), the process also entails more than periodic voting. As Honig puts it:

> Recall that for Rousseau, a legitimate regime is one in which the law, which is always alien, can be made our own by willing it. Rousseau understood that merely periodic practices such as voting do not position citizens to experience the law as their own. Hence, he argued, the law must be willed frequently, and this was possible under certain elusive circumstances... Those circumstances do not exist in the mass, heterogeneous democracy of the United States. While some liberals have argued that American democracy legitimates itself through tacit consent, there is also another mechanism of legitimation at work here, one that operates through the agency of foreignness. The regime's legitimacy is shored up by way of the explicit consent of those celebrated foreigners—immigrants—who, almost daily, are sworn into citizenship in the nation's naturalization ceremonies.[2]

This myth, we might say, encourages full acceptance or at least tolerance of immigrants. It is not, however, so simple, as Honig clearly articulates:

> But the dream of a national home, helped along by the symbolic foreigner, in turn animates a suspicion of immigrant foreigners at the same time. "Their" admirable hard work and boundless acquisition puts "us" out of jobs... "Their" traditional family values threaten to overturn our still new and fragile gains in gender equity... The foreigner who shores up and reinvigorates the regime also unsettles it at the same time. Since the presumed test of both a good and a bad foreigner is the measure of her contribution to the restoration of the nation than, say, to the nation's transformation or attenuation, nationalist xenophilia tends to feed and (re)produce nationalist xenophobia as its partner.[3]

Deep pluralist perspectives like Honig's suggest the role of immigration and immigration rhetoric in securing a core national identity against doubt or challenge. But they are not alone in this. Even more deeply entrenched strands of prophetic Christianity have played a vital role in attuning many Americans to the injustices in both racial and immigration politics. In conversation, both could play a large role in better encouraging just postnational alternatives to the "melting pot" on the one hand or to deportation on the other.

Immigrants and Lawlessness

Let's consider how the current anti-immigrant thrust results from and is tied in with an affirmation of core national and capitalist values. The focus on "illegal" immigrants is curious. In English, the adjective comes before the noun, almost suggesting that the essential core identity of these human beings is that they are violating the law. We, on the other hand, are a uniquely law-abiding people.

Those who attack immigrants because of their legal status conveniently neglect at least two other considerations. Americans, especially when it comes to economic laws, are not especially law-abiding. About 75 percent of undocumented immigrants work in the formal economy. They pay taxes, including Social Security, from which they will likely receive no benefits. Those who work off the books are generally the least well paid. Their cost in lost taxes is about three billion a year. The IRS estimates on the other hand that twenty-five million US citizens work off the books and cost the Treasury nearly two hundred billion a year.[4]

Many Americans have good reasons to disobey the law. I recently interviewed a young single mother who, not surprisingly, could not support herself and her two children on the $400 a month Temporary Assistance for Need Families and the $200 in food stamps she received. If she reported any significant income, she would lose her welfare and food stamps. She earns several thousand dollars a year "under the table." She feels guilty about her lawlessness, but "I am not going to let my family starve." Though I know of no polls on this, it would be interesting to know how many Americans who partake of the underground economy also resent Latin American immigrants for their breaking of immigration law.

Millions of Mexicans are in similar situations, and not because they are profligate with their resources. In nations throughout this hemisphere, the gap between the poor and working class on the one hand and wealthy elites on the other hand is growing. Sociologist James Petras points out that the rise of Latin American billionaires has been occasioned by policy agendas forced on these nations by the US-dominated World Bank and International Monetary Funds as well as by governments aided and supported by the United States. Mexican billionaires have benefited from the forced privatization of state assets and sale of these assets at bargain basement prices to well-placed elites, reductions in minimum wages, cuts in public expenditures on social services, regressive taxation, lax labor legislation, and a rise in state repression. The result "has been downward mobility for public employees and workers, the displacement of urban labor into the informal sector, the massive bankruptcy of small farmers, peasants and rural labor and the out-migration from the countryside to the urban slums and emigration abroad."[5]

Although in my journalism I can speak of this only anecdotally, it is my experience that at least some of the craft and unskilled workers with whom I have discussed the "lawlessness" of immigrants and the issue of the underground economy are willing to consider the parallels, especially in a contest where an effort is made to acknowledge fully the injustices they face.

The sense of the validity of a core national identity is sustained in another way as well. Part of the worry that we are being swamped by illegal immigrants is the confidence that everyone wants to live here. The most rapid increases in immigration, however, have occurred only within the last few years. There were just 2.5 million undocumented immigrants in the United States in 1995; 8 million have arrived since. NAFTA plays a major role in this exodus. The Mexican government had long sustained subsistence agriculture through price supports on corn and beans. NAFTA eliminated these subsidies and hypocritically insisted on opening Mexican agriculture to competition with subsidized US agribusiness. It is estimated that 2 million Mexican farmers were driven to the growing urban centers. Mexican wages fell precipitously.[6]

What role did Mexican peasants and factory workers have in these changes? Throughout much of the twentieth century, Mexico was ruled by a corrupt one-party system, often with the connivance and assistance of the United States. Had NAFTA been subject to a free and fair referendum in Mexico, it would surely have lost.

Immigration and Working-class Wages

Whatever the reason for Mexican immigration, has it been the cause of major working-class wage stagnation in this country? Lou Dobbs certainly thinks so, and his long-standing campaign on the subject has had a major impact on US political dialogue. His work deserves careful scrutiny. An April 2007 edition of then CNN media star Lou Dobbs's ongoing series on "Broken Borders" was a live broadcast of a town meeting from Hazelton, Pennsylvania. A guest at Dobbs's forum made an impassioned comment that his two sons had been unable to find work in New Jersey because they had lost their jobs to illegal immigrants. These immigrants had undercut their wages. Dobbs then suggested that jobs for American citizens were disappearing and working-class wages had been stagnant for four years because illegal immigrants were taking jobs and undercutting wages.

Dobbs insisted that any discussion of this topic must confront the hard facts. All facts, however, emerge from some set of basic understandings and concerns. Dobbs places severe limits on the questions and perspectives he brings to his broadcasts.

One of Dobbs's guests, a representative of the Chamber of Commerce, argued that with an unemployment rate of 4 percent, everyone who wanted a job could get one and that illegal immigrants were simply taking jobs Americans would not take. Dobbs replied by suggesting that four years of stagnation in working-class wages prove that an oversupply of illegal immigrant labor must be undermining working-class wages.

Have oscillations in illegal immigrant movement caused the rise and fall of jobs and wages? There are more compelling explanations, and in fact movements of immigrants may be a lagging rather than a leading indicator of economic growth or stagnation. Immigrants enter booming economies and flee stagnant ones. In 2001, the tech/stock market bubble burst, leading to substantial declines in corporate investment and a dramatic increase in unemployment. Federal Reserve intervention combined with Bush administration tax cuts for the wealthy subsequently counteracted the collapse of the tech bubble. Nonetheless, looked at over its whole course, the Bush administration's good years, between the collapse of the tech bubble and the collapse of the housing bubble—saw only tepid growth. Fed interest rate cuts following the burst of the tech bubble had only a modest impact on corporate investment. The wealthy beneficiaries of tax cuts save more of their extra dollars than poor and working-class citizens.

More generally, unemployment is affected by what some economists rather colorfully label the animal spirits of American capitalism. The largely unpredictable willingness of corporations to commit themselves to massive investments in new products and technologies is vastly more consequential than any wave of incoming immigrants, whether legal or illegal. Almost as important are the decisions of the Federal Reserve and the bond markets. In 2007 both worried more that real full employment would increase inflationary pressure and erode corporate or bondholder profits. They had little to fear from inflation, but those ill-grounded fears had grave consequences for employment levels.

Workers and new plants and technologies are both assets. When new workers arrive, they bring skills, interests, and new ideas. When workers arrive in an expanding economy or in one that is prepared to adopt the social policies needed to foster full employment and to incorporate them into the workforce, communities gain in the long run.

Between 1980 and today, the US economy has undergone a sea change, and that change is not primarily immigration. It might best be characterized as leaving the fate of the poor and the working class—if not the corporate elite—to the tender mercies of the market. Even Bill Clinton celebrated the end of the "era of big government." Government has shredded the safety net for the poor and reduced job-creating expenditures on infrastructure even as it has extended new privileges to its corporate clientele. In turn, many pampered corporations have carried out a systematic attack on unions and cavalierly violated even our current meager wage and hour standards.

During his diatribe against illegal immigrants, Dobbs mentioned a statistic that undercuts much of his analysis. He pointed out that US working-class wages have stagnated over the last quarter century. But immigration did not begin its dramatic increase until the last decade. The plight of working-class citizens owes far more to a quarter century of corporate lawlessness in its dealings with native US workers than it does to violations of law by incoming immigrants.

The last quarter century has seen a sustained assault on unions, a precipitous decline in the inflation-adjusted Federal minimum wage, so-called welfare reform that stripped protection from many poor families, and weaker unemployment compensation. The recent history of the meatpacking industry, which has been the subject of several Federal immigration raids, illustrates these themes. Meatpacking as an industry has not been amenable to major technological advances. In order to increase profitability, companies have closed many unionized plants in urban areas and relocated to rural venues where unions had no toehold. The work in these plants then became lower paying and more accident-prone. Contrary to the whining of the industry, this is not work that Americans are unwilling to do. Only as the work became ever more poorly compensated and more dangerous did it become harder to find native-born Americans to staff these plants.

The most plausible interpretations is that the presence of more undocumented workers makes it easier for employers to carry out an attack on unions and wage and labor standards that was well under way before the influx of immigrants. An undocumented worker is even less able to complain about union busting or violation of wage and labor standards. Immigration and Custom Enforcement raids on Midwestern meatpacking plants featured raids on six plants, five of which were union plants.[7]

Economic trauma, dislocation for working and middle classes, and the use of immigrants as strike breakers provide fertile soil for stoking racist and xenophobic fears that have long resided just below the surface. But protectionism or literally walling off Mexico will not really redress the right-wing assault on the working class and the safety net. Many production processes are now globalized, and labor in the developing world also deserves justice. In addition, driving undocumented workers back to

Mexico would both further destabilize the Mexican economy, lower wages there, and perhaps make Mexico even more attractive to big business flight from the United States. Protecting wage and organizing rights both in the United States and in trading partners is the best answer to the corporate globalization that impels rapid population shifts. Organizing across ethnicity and nationality for labor rights here is crucial and could in turn build support for reform of the current international trade system.

What stands in the way of such an agenda? Just as economic insecurity and inequality encourage the worst forms of racism and xenophobia, so also do these exclusive identities make it difficult to build a progressive alliance. Even liberal *NY Times* columnist Paul Krugman, though celebrating the contribution that immigration has made to our nation, has suggested that unless immigration is limited, ethnic tensions will further undermine the commitment of Americans to even a minimal safety net.[8] He makes his claim through historical and cross-cultural correlations of demographic trends and the generosity of social safety nets. But merely because a correlation works during one era is no proof that it holds now or that ways cannot be found around it. Relations between immigrants and citizens are different today than earlier in this century and the media play a different role.

I would suggest we consider the inverse of Krugman's argument. If immigrants are demonized, this demonization may repel many legal residents with strong emotional connections to the undocumented. And the very focus on "illegals" as the origin of our problems can blunt attention to economic structures and policies in need of reform. In the process there will be bad consequences even for most native working-class citizens. It seems highly unlikely that under any scenario all will be expelled. Driven further underground, they will give unscrupulous bosses even more leverage. And with a fragmented poor and working class, how will progressive forces gain the political might to crack down on bosses? Even during periods of relative prosperity and more liberal political agendas, racial, national, and ethnic antagonisms have been a big part of our politics and have limited the inclusivity of our political agenda.

It may be impossible to demonstrate statistically that immigration does not depress wages for the most vulnerable US citizens. Nonetheless, opposition to immigrants seems to cut across wide sectors of the population. That even in the face of the grave malfeasance of our financial institutions, the collapse of an eight trillion dollar housing bubble, and the huge attendant decline in jobs, so much focus would attach to immigration suggests the sustained role of identity formation in this struggle. How deep pluralists might confront and redress contemporary xenophobia is my next subject.

Civilizational Rhetoric and Multidimensional Alternatives

Samuel Huntington, famous for the "Clash of Civilizations" rhetoric, is an example of perspectives that must be contested if a different politics is to emerge. Huntington says America is defined neither by race nor ethnicity but by a common culture. Rather than a nation of immigrants, we are a nation of settlers. He articulates a law of first settlement, which states that the most enduring impact comes from whoever got here first. Those who arrived here first wanted to build a new culture rather than simply carry theirs over here. The culture they endorsed was Anglo-Protestant. It emphasized the rule of law, private property, and the work ethic. Subsequent immigrants, even those who were not explicitly Protestant, essentially shared that vision. But the modern-day Hispanic immigrants are different.[9]

This is because Mexican immigration is different from any other: it is more persistent, more regionally concentrated, less committed to education, and more attached to its native culture and values. The net effect of these factors is disturbing: "In the late twentieth century, developments occurred that, if continued, could transform 'America into a culturally bifurcated Anglo-Hispanic society with two national languages.'" In the popular media, analogous charges have included the contention that illegal Mexican immigrants are a drain on the public treasury.

Huntington's litany of charges against Mexican immigrants as well as popular attacks on immigrants' fiscal drag and lawlessness presents many problems. That previous immigrants fully shared or were viewed as fully sharing the Protestant work culture is open to question. As I pointed out in chapter two, the Italian immigrants who raised the concerns cited by early twentieth-century immigration opponents were certainly not viewed as sharing the Protestant work ethic.

That illegal immigrants loot the public till is repeated frequently but with none of the kind of evidence reporters and commentators would demand if similar charges were leveled against middle-class white citizens. A frequent contention is that Hispanic immigrants loot the public treasury through welfare assistance. Yet such a contention becomes hard to take seriously when one examines changes in welfare law since Clinton. Clinton's evisceration of welfare drastically reduced assistance even for legal permanent residents who entered the country after 1996. No assistance at all was available until they had been here five years.

Crime presents an even clearer story. During the run-up to Arizona's draconian laws, its defenders kept talking of a crime wave hitting the city despite the fact that rates of violent crime, as measured through the ways citizens usually assess crime, had actually declined in recent years.

Numerous studies drawing on the usually accepted reporting methods have confirmed that young people born abroad are less likely to commit crime. Unfortunately, however, mainstream media often disproportionately present Hispanics in the role of criminal suspects.[10]

Huntington accuses Mexican immigrants of being unwilling to learn English, but demand for courses in English as a second language in the Southwest far exceeds the supply. He faults Mexicans for repatriating much of what they earn, but he says nothing about the role that US multinational corporations play in repatriating their capital to those same foreign nations. Why can GM build a factory in Monterrey, but it is awful when Mexican peasants send a few dollars home? And these Mexican immigrants are hardly going to take us over if they are busy getting ready to move back to Mexico. One paradox of harsh border policies is that many end up spending longer in this country than they had planned.

Perhaps the real problem with these Mexican immigrants is that they want to have some connection to our culture and still retain ties to their own. Rather than a threat, this is also an opportunity for us to become a broader and more inclusive culture.

A Theology of Clear Borders

Unfortunately, the willingness to explore difference as at least potentially a source of opportunity can be stymied by certain forms of religious discourse. Notions of strengthening our borders often go hand in hand at the rhetorical level with our understandings of the boundaries between good and evil. Many e-mails from readers to me stressed that those who cross our borders have also crossed a moral border. Morality itself is seen as a clear line in the sand.

Cal Thomas, like George Bush, argues that evil springs from the unwillingness of this culture to accept the notion that there is a clear LINE between good and evil and to adhere to that line. Thomas quotes with approval a Senate chaplin who maintains:

> Abandoning an absolute ethical (and) moral standard leads irresistibly to the absence of ethics and morality. Each person determines his own ethical/moral code. That's anarchy. Humans become their own gods and decide, each in his own way, what is good and what is evil. Evil becomes good—good becomes evil. Upside down morality! Good is ridiculed! Evil is dignified!

The chaplain's words might be set against some of the great atrocities of the last few centuries, including the massacre of Native Americans, slavery, and the Holocaust. Each was perpetrated by a "civilization" firmly convinced that it abided by a clear and unitary moral code, a code that was not merely theirs but was divinely inspired. Even today, there is nothing in Thomas's remarks that Osama Bin Laden would have rejected. The clear lines and the sharp punishments that advocates of this theology and moral orientation advocate might also be viewed as institutionalized forms of revenge, revenge against the human condition and against those who even question their theological views.

Reinhold Niebuhr, whose work I cited in chapter one, once suggested that conventional moralists exaggerate the degree of sin in specific violations of moral codes even as they understate the sin in the denial and disregard of the damage that standards established by the state or the culture can do. I read immigration rhetoric as a dangerous example.

Cal Thomas threatens us with a familiar blackmail. Is the only alternative to a squishy relativism an ethic of fixed standards anchored in the word of an all powerful God? A God who will or might punish us?

Other Christians need to enter the fray. Simple injunctions by some secularists to leave religion out of politics are neither effective nor fair. Many liberal secularists properly oppose direct religious tests for government programs but fail to acknowledge and address the ways in which any political action and policy bears some underlying philosophical and even religious principle. The social right, not confronted by contrary narratives and emotionally resonant symbolism in defense of a pluralizing world, fill the void with exclusionary, judgmental theologies and practices that constitute a war on difference. These contribute to or resonate with the worst forms of xenophobic politics among some segments of a working class that has seen its fortunes and security plummet in recent years.

Other Christian Voices

John Howard Yoder's Mennonite Christianity provides a powerful counterpoint, and one with clear implications for debates growing out of ethnic migration and conflict. Political theorist Romand Coles has recently provided an insightful analysis of the contributions Yoder's provocative reading of the biblical narrative and the Christian tradition can make to a more inclusive and just politics. Coles's commentary on and interrogation of Yoder aid my own efforts to respond to fundamentalist agendas like those of Cal Thomas.

Fundamentalist readings of Christianity claim to possess sovereignty by securing a continuous relation to an authorizing origin. Yoder counters that "Jesus is Lord" has a different message from what Thomas has in mind. It calls us to a "perennially unfinished process of critiquing the developed tradition from the perspective of our own roots." The message of Jesus works to "deny absolute authority to any later epoch, especially to the present."[11]

For Yoder to reach back to scripture is not to find a final resting place that can answer all current moral dilemmas. The truth is always a finite historical incarnation. Scripture is important, but as a narrative of a process and an ethos that opens us to the unfolding mystery of God. Scripture celebrates the early church's coming to grips with the message of Jesus in the context of its own situation.[12]

The soundness of the church lies in its dialogic practices, not in a truth that is seen as some final resting place. Church unity is a commitment to dialogical processes of reconciliation figured by the efforts of the early church to grasp the meaning around Jesus's wisdom of the Cross. The vision of the early church community striving to find the meaning of the self-sacrifice of Jesus radicalizes the relevance of Jesus, fostering dialogue centering on the application of injunctions to love the enemy, renounce coercion, and recognize the dignity of the lowly.

Central to this vision is the idea that meetings must be an open process in which the voices of even the lowest and least educated are valued. Different voices will contribute in different times and places to the shape of a community, which in turn will be continually assessing what is obligatory and not obligatory.

Process itself, even one premised on advocacy of openness to each person, can ossify and cement injustice. Yoder's teachings strive to guard against this outcome not merely by emphasizing the potential of every participant. For gifts to be given and received, some order is necessary. But Yoder warns that for most of history, the principle of order has been given priority to renewing multiplicitous vitality. The need has always been, as Coles, relaying Yoder's viewpoint, writes:

> to renew a radically dialogic and multiplicitous "vitality." Paul *first* said, every-one has a gift; then he said let everything be orderly. We too need the first truth, as Good News, before the second. In the name of the first truth we need to question the concentration of authority in the hands of office-bearers accredited on institutional grounds. One must bend over backwards to give opportunities to and hear the words of the "least comely." Multifarious vitality needs to be reined in only after it begins to overreach itself in deaf and selfish forms of "self-validating enthusiasm." Subverting the way body metaphors have often supported hierarchy by identifying a member as the head, he notes that Christ, not one of the other members, is the head and Jesus was the last priest. There is a certain functional hierarchy in that understandable prophecy is preferable to unintelligible speaking in tongues; Paul said he did not want his readers to have to choose. Both were valid; he practices both and wanted others to do so. Church disciplines must always aim to cultivate both,

the expectation of unanticipatable and often initially incohoate newness and the discerning capacity to renew the orientation, direction, and order of the gospel tradition that faces and works with it.[13]

To my ears the commonsense language of bending over backward and having a gift resonates with and strengthens the receptivity to difference suggested by some deep pluralist genealogies.

Even a church or community body committed to processes of openness internally can find in this commitment reasons to disparage other communities not so committed. Here Yoder argues that the Christian community has and always must expect to be subversive to some other community outside it. Yet this recognition should spur and support receptive encounters with those beyond the church. Most fundamentally, the Church's basic ethical commitments to dialogic vulnerability and a care for difference are not known and generated merely within it. The church gains a better sense of its commitments through encounters with outsiders. Outsiders themselves also play a vital role in reminding the church community when it is not listening to dissident voices either within or outside of itself.[14]

For Yoder, deeper recognition of the unpredictability of God's gifts and of the need for an ethos of care for the world to recognize these might be better perceived within the Christian community if a gift from outside is somehow recognized and engaged. Yoder suggests that just as a proper understanding of the dialogic and caring church can inspire more openness to the pluralism of the world, that pluralizing world can itself bring surprises that deepen our understanding of and commitment to a caring community.

Yoder's own confrontation with outsiders leads him to see in the Gospel something that was not visible before. Babel might be read as an implicit rebuke of those who see moral and geographic boundaries as both codependent and essential. Babel in the myth of Genesis

> places the multiplicity of cultures under the divine will. Restoring His original plan, YHWH scattered them not as an act of angry retribution but in an act of divine benevolence for their own good, as Paul recognized. The renewed multiplicity of particular languages, the need for discourse dependent upon particular communities, was to save humankind from its presumptuous and premature effort at divination by which various particular individuals and groups tried and continue to try in myriad ways to enforce uniformity according to their own self-transparent Truth.[15]

Yoder's is a valuable struggle to evoke a pluralizing and more just social order through retelling of the mystery of God's revelation in history as told in scripture. His celebrates Jesus as the Christ and scripture for their very receptivity to new and neglected styles, concerns, movements, and injustices. Jesus and scripture are the center of his narrative.

Yet as Yoder himself acknowledges, there is no call for generosity that is not without risks against which it must struggle. I agree with Romand Coles's judgment that his work would benefit from engagement with other bodies of work that encourage similarly pluralistic understandings of community.[16]

I have already presented one critique of traditional notions of omnipotence in Catherine Keller's rejection of a God who controls every outcome. One can find within evangelical Christianity itself other perspectives on God's limits. Open theists pray to a limited, loving God who is exemplary in virtue of the fact that He learns as the world turns.

John Sanders, author of *The God Who Risks: A Theology of Divine Providence*, came to Open Theism in the years following the death of his young brother. Fellow parishioners had explained to him how the death was part of God's inscrutable plan. He resisted that story. Later, he read scripture with this issue in mind. Moses convinces Yahweh not to kill the Jews who had sacrificed the calf and Jesus implores his God to listen. Prayer itself may suggest a God who listens, thinks anew, and periodically changes His mind. Sanders summarizes his reading of Scripture at one point: "In wisdom God decided to fulfill his promises through the particular path Jesus took. In wisdom God decides how he continues to fulfill his promises, and the divine wisdom takes the changing circumstances of the world into account... God is free to do new things and so identify himself in new ways."[17]

The politics of right is especially susceptible to forms of celebrations not merely among nationalistic groups but even on the left. Here is a recent letter to the editor of the *Nation*:

> As a Chicano, here are my credentials. Grew up supporting the UFW boycotts, family participated in the East LA walkouts, union family fought in Nicaragua, Honduras against the contras, worked to sue the US at the world court... Enough said. Any illegal alien in this country is a disgrace, a criminal and needs to be sent back to their country of origin. My grandparents came here from Mexico legally. It took many years, but they did not break in and demand services, Spanish etc." (April 2, 2007)

The implication here is that because one fought for an expansion of rights in the 1960s and because that set of rights and the extension of rights to a particular group of formerly excluded citizens improved our politics and eventually became widely accepted, the nature and the contours of the moral universe have become fully established. Those who supported these earlier reform efforts are best qualified to assess who should receive future rights and what those rights should be. There is no sense that the very successes of the 1960s, once established, might create new needs to which more open sensitivities need be applied.

No social or even personal life is possible without coming to terms with the fact of our mortality, our limited knowledge of our circumstances, and the need to frame some common purposes and collective and personal identities. Each of these imperatives interacts with and helps shape the others. But perhaps there might be less suffering on a grand scale if civilizations would not seek revenge against the fact of finitude in absolute claims on behalf of their moral schemes and modes of punishment of rule breakers and dissidents designed to reflect and reassert the certainty of our convictions. We might entertain the possibility that any distinction we draw may well reflect not only timeless and necessary requisites of any sociality but also narrow and conventional rationalizations and glorifications of our own petty prejudices and lifestyles. Or perhaps ethical openness can spring from other sources. Work upon ourselves or confrontations with new cosmologies may even enable us to take delight in new social movements and currents of thought, a capacity some see as already a potential installed in many of us. The best ethics are those that strive always to open themselves to critique, to let as many flowers as possible bloom in a social and material world that may always exceed our grasp and may always be full of surprises.

These suggestions, like Cal Thomas's absolute, are hardly completely proven. Nonetheless, it surely deserves a hearing amid all the fashionable talk of good and evil. If advanced with openness to the limits and contestability of its own foundations, it might counter to some degree the religious rhetoric that so easily resonates with and reinforces our most exclusionary political and geographic boundaries. No advocate of such a perspective can offer promises, but I deem it worth a try.

Beyond Border Wars

Now if we challenge the worst forms of immigrant stereotyping and some of the religious postures with which it resonates, what sorts of cultural and political possibilities might we see? A world without any borders, a la John Lennon's famous song, is not in the cards now. Modern societies cannot be managed without coordination and institutional structures established along some geographic lines. Citizens must understand and at least partially accept these principles. Yet if lines must be drawn and regulations issued, must the principles underlying these regulations be seen as necessarily unitary, or must the citizens living within borders be uninfluenced by those who live outside the borders? A border drawn for administrative convenience is different in both meaning and effect from one that is seen as defining and bounding our identity. What we mean by borders and how we enforce them can certainly be reconsidered.[18] Nations should surely exclude criminals, bearers of terrorist weapons, and so on. And full political citizenship should require some knowledge and commitments to basic democratic rights. The real question is how far beyond such minimal standards we go. Should noncitizens within our borders have only two choices, that they become full citizens or have no rights at all and be able to stay only as suits our economic or moral imperatives? Perhaps far more nuanced, negotiable, and evolving standards can be crafted.

Every one who comes to the United States for a job should have full economic rights. When they have the rights to join unions, receive a just minimum wage, file grievances against occupational health and safety violations, they are creating new products and new demands for goods and services. If they enjoyed a body of rights that all workers should have, wages and productivity would go up. The most significant problem facing many American workers is not the lawlessness of so-called illegal immigrants but the lawlessness of their own employers, who illegally fire fully a fifth of all those engaged in union organizing. In even more cases they resort to illegal threats in the face of even the slightest hint of labor organizing.[19] All workers should have the same body of rights and those rights need to mean something. Workers of all backgrounds would stand to gain from passage of the employee free choice act currently under consideration in Washington.

The question of a road to citizenship raises other issues. Are those who, like myself, seek an easier road to citizenship for those who have worked here, plan to stay, and desire citizenship on the assimilationist side of Honig's dichotomy? I think this depends both on the grounds one cites in defense of citizenship and one's understanding of democratic politics. I also believe that for those who have been in this country many years and will likely stay many more, justice demands access to citizenship.

There is every reason to believe that Mexican immigrants can challenge our cultural certainties in ways that can strengthen and revive this culture. Alternatively, rather than fear, for instance, the effect of more traditional notions for gender relations held (presumably) by Mexicans, a more diverse and multicultural politics is an occasion to engage and challenge these conventions. And honor them in instances where no attempt is made to impose them from an authoritative center. A reading of Yoder might open us to such a view just as the political success of immigrants and the contributions they make could make us more receptive to theologies like Yoder's.

The wave of demonstrations during the past three Mays illustrates the contribution immigrant workers are making to our lives and politics. It is all too easy to say these demonstrators are merely acting in their own immediate self-interest. Yet if the narrow self-interest that characterizes so much of mainstream culture were their sole motive, the May demonstrations would have had far less support.

Millions risked arrest and deportation. Any single individual immigrant could simply "free ride" and let his or her fellows take the risks. Last year, The Black Commentator pointed out: "In the countries they hail from there are traditions of working class militancy and solidarity deeper and more widespread than anything here, and traditions of broad left wing social movements tougher and more enduring than we see here in the U.S." Compare the reaction to the chicanery and irregularities in the recent Mexican election to the ways in which Gore and the Democrats reacted to our own electoral injustices. Looking once again at the Midwestern meatpacking raids, one can find further support of these views. The willingness of unionized workers to challenge abysmal working conditions in the industry was clearly a factor in the raids.

As economic rights are gained and conditions and opportunities for citizenship broadened, there are many positive prospects. And these can and should go beyond notions of a melting pot. Interethnic, international collaboration is both more likely and more productive to the extent that as much difference as possible is accepted and valued.

Earlier generations of immigrants from desperate impoverishment in such nations as Ireland and Italy were much vilified in their time. Nonetheless, they made substantial contributions to our economic growth. Just as importantly, they were vital in the formation of unions and in the fight for the forty-hour week. These contributions lay in large measure in the ways they broadened and challenged a prevailing national identity. Had their concerns been established as a more permanent and legitimate counter to the imperatives of our work- and growth-oriented society, we might all have been the winners.

Having argued the case for domestic citizenship on nonassimilationist grounds, I would also concur with Honig that we might

> redeploy the affective energies of kinship on behalf of a democratic politics that is more cosmopolitan than nationalist in its aspirations...sister cities use the model and the rhetoric of sororal relation to establish affective sights of transnational connection that bypass state apparatuses in order to pursue shared goals and establish relations of long standing...sister cities are not limited to carrying out a single project and this makes them an important complement to more temporary, issue-oriented forms of local and international forms of solidarity that are conditional. Most important,

sister cities interrupt projects of (re)nationalization by generating practices of affective citizenship that exceed state boundaries and sometimes even violate state foreign policy. They are one sight of enacted cosmopolitanism, sites of leverage in national politics, sites at which alternative (non-state-centered) forms of membership and affiliation develop.[20]

I will offer some more specific thoughts on the ways that more cosmopolitan, less state-centered politics and more open identities could address our current range of economic, immigration, and environmental woes in the final chapter.

For now we are far from adopting even the modest suggestions given in this chapter. Broader proposals seem utopian. Yet expelling undocumented workers and forcing employers to accept real sanctions are both cruel and even more implausible.

Robert Frost is often cited to suggest that good fences make good neighbors. But Frost is really mocking this idea. Whether good fences make good neighbors or not depends on what you are walling in and walling out. If you are walling in cows, it makes perfect sense. Frost sees these as easily and profitably domesticated, though Bennett might properly raise some caveats on this point. But both would agree that ideas and human travel are a different story. The neighbor who walls himself off in splendid isolation walks in shade and darkness. Surely we need some boundaries, but brick walls assure only that our walks will be not only in hazes of our own making but monotonous as well. Even worse, like Plato's cave dwellers, we will treat our shadows as the light of the sun.

CHAPTER FIVE

US CAPITALISM'S BUMPY RIDE:
WHERE TO FROM HERE?

Twenty years ago Francis Fukuyama announced that history had ended in the triumph of liberal democratic capitalism. In May 2009, a major retail brokerage firm ran an ad on CNBC lamenting the "economic tsunami" that had unnerved its middle- and even upper-class investors. The ad's choice of the tsunami metaphor is especially apt. Tsunamis represent not only extraordinary destruction but their occurrence is also all the more terrifying because they are notoriously unpredictable. The collapse of the immense housing bubble represents the loss of great wealth. It has also challenged the once widespread faith that markets would deliver steady and predictable progress.

Many on the Left have responded with their own versions of apocalypse. In June 2009, even as some economists began to speak of "green shoots," an economy showing signs of housing starts and corporate investment rebounding, former *New York Times* war correspondent Christopher Hedges proclaimed the end of the American empire and the economic system that sustained and was sustained by that empire:

> This week marks 01 the end of the dollar's reign as the world's reserve currency. It marks the start of a terrible period of economic and political decline in the United States. And it signals the last gasp of the American imperium. That's over. It is not coming back. And what is to come will be very, very painful.[1]

In the light of the last decade, Fukuyama's confident proclamations of triumph and Hedges's prophecies of doom raise several crucial questions. Are crises self-evident, merely a perception of a fact-based world or of a universally shared frame of reference basic to knowledge as such? Is an economy really governed by laws and thus at least in principle fully predictable? Can the "scientific method" determine the answer to this question or does what we take as an appropriate, inescapable method reflect at least in part our gut sense of the answer to that question? Does the faith in predictability itself raise great risks? Are dangerous and disruptive social and cultural tsunamis made all the more likely by various proclamations of history's end? Do prophecies of doom become self-fulfilling? Or do they blind us to green shoots of another sort, not a typical capitalist rebound but new cultural and economic and political prospects that might build a new system? Is there a case to be made for more early attentiveness to the strains and diffuse concerns that lie outside accepted and expected norms and trends? For me these important questions are raised by some of the religious and deep pluralist discourses I have discussed in this book. They inform my reading of the recent history of US capitalism, but these religious and philosophical discourses are themselves clarified, buttressed, and extended by my examination of these economic issues.

From the Golden Age to Reagan

That Fukuyama could proclaim an end to history is all the more startling when one reviews the largely unexpected changes that occurred in the forty years leading up to this famous book. Most Americans of the 1950s could hardly have imagined the economic events of the last decade. Many 1950s Republicans celebrated a "mixed economy." They acknowledged the need for a safety net and modestly redistributive taxes. They embraced banking and security trading regulations aimed at preventing a recurrence of the 1930s. Most major industrial corporations, though not enamored of unions, accepted them as a fact of life and were willing to share productivity gains with them. Daniel Bell, as confident as Fukuyama would later be, announced an "end of ideology."

Nonetheless, under the apparent surface consensus and order of the 1950s, tensions were growing. Workers had security but no voice in the structure of their jobs. Labor writer Jane Slaughter points out:

> The factories continued to be, in [Walter] Reuther's words, "gold-plated sweatshops." The foundry and the assembly line remained an inhuman way to make a living...The mind-numbing drudgery, the high injury rates,...led many workers to hit the bottle—and, in one famous case, led black Detroit Chrysler worker James Johnson to pick up a gun and shoot two supervisors and a co-worker. A jury after a plant tour, found that brutal working conditions and Chrysler's shop-floor racism had literally driven Johnson insane.[2]

The racial tensions and workplace injustices Slaughter's analysis highlights had long-term causes and consequences. The postwar accord between labor and capital extended almost entirely to wages and some measures of security, and even then did not include any commitment to those who were marginal to the manufacturing sector. The UAW, an early supporter of universal healthcare, put aside this issue once the autoworkers received generous health benefits from the Big Three automakers.

Employer freedom to manage the workplace was rarely challenged except regarding seniority and arbitrary discharge. Input into management prerogatives, such as investment decisions, which were part of the codetermination structure in West Germany, were never seriously considered here.

Organized labor, disproportionately white male employees, did make important gains in this arrangement, however, and the United States as a whole benefited initially from foreign investment and resource exploitation.

Yet even as early as the late 1960s it became apparent that workers were dissatisfied at least in terms of the quality of the working experience. In the late 1960s white workers, protected by both a reasonable safety net and relatively full employment, increasingly resented the demands and limits of their jobs. Robert Kuttner points out that the workplace is as much a social organization as an economic one. It cannot function smoothly without some set of common norms. Workplace norms are unlikely to take strong root unless workers themselves have a major, independent voice in articulating and implementing them. Treated by their bosses, supervisors, or fellow employees as mere cogs in a machine, or as irresponsible employees naturally allergic to work, individuals cease to identify with their jobs. The more workers are so treated, the more, in Kuttner's words, they "will live up to their billing as would-be shirkers—and the more the employer will need to follow the economist's imperative to supervise relentlessly."[3]

In addition, even some of their monetary gains were eroded by the inflationary pressures of the Vietnam War. Nonetheless, the only models of economic governance prominent at the time involved either conventional corporate management or state ownership. State ownership was, and always has been, properly a nonstarter in the United States. Populist currents of reform, which were far more democratic than either, tended to write off both large corporations and centralized governments as inherently evil, although they were willing to use the latter to reform the former. And populist notions of the possibility and desirability of self-sufficient communities, of the evils of governmental authority, and the discounting of the importance of corporate efficiencies and economies of scale have blunted the ability of populists in the modern era to contribute to broad-based, national reform efforts.

Other limits of the New Deal consensus weakened its future reach. Major US unions had accepted "open" international markets, thereby endorsing implicitly the principle of unrestricted foreign investment.

Though trade expansion brought initial success for both workers and own-ers, eventually US firms faced major competition, either from their own subsidiaries or from foreign-owned firms once they had rebuilt after the War. Thus industries that the United States had dominated, such as con-sumer electronics, became entrenched elsewhere. The Cold War also com-plicated this equation. Mainstream labor unions opposed any reforms or reformers who espoused any basic change in the structure of corporations or the prevailing ideology. Often with little or no evidence they portrayed anyone who sought changes in the ownership or control of corporations as necessarily communists or even as inspired by a foreign power. Unions thus achieved "respectability," but at a cost. Economic reform in foreign nations, however, would have driven up labor costs, making these nations less attractive for the kind of US capital flight that would eventually weaken severely the bargaining power of American workers.

Social costs grew as well in consequence of demands for some modicum of justice from African Americans and other minorities largely left out of the accord. During the high-employment 1960s, workers all across the board gained, but not all were equal. Full employment and strong unions did not automatically trump race as Thomas Sugrue's study of postwar Detroit suggests. Until the war, most Detroit blacks had been confined to domestic, hotel, restaurant, and maintenance work. Wartime labor short-ages forced the auto industry to open new jobs to them. Yet even amid the boom of the 1940s, they generally received the dirtiest and most dangerous industrial jobs. Many plants remained essentially white as both manage-ment and the union left hiring largely to the discretion of individual plant managers. By the late 1940s and early 1950s, blacks were most heavily represented in hot and dangerous forge work but had almost no presence in the skilled trades.

Housing patterns both reflected and reinforced racial boundaries and racial identities. Sugrue shows how blacks in Detroit were confined to crowded areas of the city and limited in loan sources. They paid inflated prices for very inferior housing. They "could not get loans to improve their property. As a result, their homes deteriorated...Moreover, the deteriorat-ing neighborhoods offered seemingly convincing evidence to white land-owners that blacks were feckless and irresponsible...and would ruin any white neighborhood they moved in to." [4] We can see here the ways in which even housing policy could both reflect and lend apparent plausibility to the widespread (but false) cultural assumptions that African Americans lacked the appropriate work and family ethics.

Unlike previous generations of immigrants, Detroit's black community then had to face the massive deindustrialization that started in the auto industry as early as the 1950s. Concerned about union power and growing worker wages, GM and Ford began automating and moving production both to the suburbs and to plants in the rural South. In order to reduce new hires and control costs, auto manufacturers also started stretching the hours of the most skilled workers through forced overtime.

Most unions themselves were largely uninterested in bringing blacks into the unionized workplace and lacked the will or capacity to extend unionization. Even liberal Democrats were loath to challenge union or management control over workplace hiring policy. The Democratic Party's only recourse was to enhance a governmental noblesse oblige agenda for the poor. Lyndon Johnson's Great Society. Compensation took such forms as improvements in welfare payments, the War on Poverty, and Medicaid. These programs were targeted at the poor and administered on a state-by-state basis. They also imposed severe limits as to savings one could have or income one could receive and still qualify.

As business costs increase while new competitive international pressures grew, profits slumped and with that slump came declines in corporate investment. Job growth and productivity slowed, but unions and corporations still had enough political and market power to drive price increases. Inflation in the early 1970s, exacerbated by oil price run-ups, war-related deficits, and productivity slowdowns, eventually led the government to adopt fiscal and monetary policy that forced severe recession.

Corporate response to the stagflation even under Democrat Jimmy Carter was implicitly to repudiate the postwar accommodation with labor. Carter and Reagan used recession as an occasion to lessen the power of unions and that portion of the pie going to workers, in order to make more capital available to business. Federal Reserve Board chair Paul Volcker's driving up of interest rates led to double-digit unemployment.

Blowback from the very limits of the New Deal consensus had created a powerful dilemma for the Democratic Party, the origin of the "chain reaction" Thom and Mary Edsall have described. At the same time that it had helped secure some—albeit very modest—government charity for minorities, its unwillingness to address corporate power over workplaces and investment left it few options other than to squeeze working-class white wages. It became easy for white workers, trapped in ever more demanding jobs and lacking any alternative ideas about corporate governance reforms from liberals, to fall back on deeply held racial stereotypes. Often working with little evidence besides anecdotes, they portrayed blacks as lethargic, irresponsible, and gaining something for nothing. Republicans eagerly abetted this cause by zeroing in on affirmative action and taxes paid for welfare as the cause of white worker decline. They portrayed urban crime and decay as the fruit of Democratic welfare policy and a sign of black's lack of moral fitness. Many came to regard themselves as uniquely virtuous and under assault from a liberal elite unappreciative of their hard work.

Liberal embrace of many environmental concerns only added to the dilemma. For many personal consumption had become their only opportunity for satisfaction and self-esteem. A liberal agenda that would raise taxes—often in regressive fashion—on their favorite enjoyments only added to the Democrats' dilemma.

These mutually intertwined tensions and anxieties set the stage for Reagan's polished rhetorical contempt for government, taxes, eggheads, "welfare queens," peaceniks, and affirmative action hires. Reagan benefited from other fortuitous events. The seizure of the US embassy in Iran provided the perfect visual symbol of weak, effeminate US policy. These resonating fears and hostilities were in turn redeemed by Reagan's smiling persona and promise of a better day that would restore an idyllic past. Tax cuts would pay for themselves, thereby avoiding any embarrassing discussion of the fate of popular, universal government programs, such as Medicare or Social Security, programs that spent far more than welfare. It was morning in America.

The Rise of Crony Disaster Capitalism

George W. Bush built on his own convenient crises to extend the Reagan revolution. In *The Shock Doctrine: The Rise of Disaster Capitalism*, Naomi Klein suggests that crisis or "perception of a crisis" can become an occasion for elites to impose unjust forms of capitalism; 9/11 is her paradigm case. But as Klein implies through her reference to perception, crisis can be in the eyes of the beholder, and the policies implemented after 9/11 may also be seen as part of a long-term assault on American democracy. Human beings always evaluate the world through some frame of reference. The foundations for crony disaster capitalism were being laid well before 9/11. James Galbraith's *The Predator State* (2009) provides an excellent look at the larger economic context of post-9/11 politics.

Galbraith argues that US politics has been rhetorically dominated by an idealized view of Adam Smith's market, one that in some ways even goes beyond what Smith imagined. The market—not any single business or government—is to set prices. Our greatest freedom is seen as the ability to choose among products. This view has influenced policy at key points in disastrous ways and is no longer an adequate narrative of how the world works. Yet liberals continue to embrace this view, even as the political right and most centrist Democrats know better. They may talk markets to deter forms of government intervention that hurt their interests, but once in power they have long relentlessly used government to advance their interests. That pattern long preceded 9/11.

Monetary policy was used in the late 1970s and early 1980s to kill inflation on the assumption that inflation was simply the result of too much money chasing too few goods. Inflation, however, had more systemic causes, ones that challenged the simplistic market theories. As indicated earlier, it was rooted in the loss of the United States' unchallenged economic and military strength and the challenge to the dollar's role in international finance as well as forms of nonmarket monopoly power, such as OPEC and cost push union contracts. Monetary policy under Volcker led to a huge spike in interest rates. It did kill inflation, but at the cost of nearly killing the patient. Our whole industrial base took a big hit.

To get us out of the stagflation of the 1970s, conservatives advocated more "free market" medicine. Trade among nations should expand and, just as importantly, currencies should "float" and find their own optimal level in currency markets. Corporate management should be forced to immediately realize "shareholder value" through any form of merger or breakup of stock buy back that would maximize immediate profits. Capital and banking markets should be made more liquid through deregulation.

Yet this approach had almost immediate negative consequences. Doctrinaire free trade—at least vis-à-vis the manufacturing sector—further blunted our ability to compete effectively in international markets. Our competitors had industrial strategies, subsidized key industries, even engaged in outright protectionism to get some industries started. US multinational firms did gain through investment abroad, but the profits were concentrated in few hands and the jobs were lost. In practice, even Reagan could not let the auto industry completely collapse and engaged in some managed trade with Japan on autos.

Under Reagan, the United States implemented low personal income taxes as supposedly an incentive to save, but these spurred more conspicuous consumption than tangible investment. They also discouraged firms from retaining earnings, leaving firms more vulnerable to capital markets and short-term fluctuations. Tax cuts did not pay for themselves via an incentive effect on how hard people worked or how much they invested. Eventually even conservatives ended up defending these cuts primarily on the grounds that the wealthy made the money and should therefore be able to keep it. Tax cuts supposedly to promote savings became in effect a form of favoritism of the rich.

Conservative rhetoric and the hemorrhaging of the manufacturing sector led the US economy to become more financialized. By this term I mean that more of total profits come from speculation in financial assets. Banks and financial institutions gained more of a role in corporate governance and insisted on CEOs being able to act independently of boards and workers and even stockholders and also, being able to emphasize short-term profits. Workers' incomes were further eroded. CEOs were paid with stock options, which increase emphasis on short term.

And the success of a few CEOs had a demonstration effect on others. Inequality increased and levels of consumer demand could be maintained only through extensive borrowing by the middle class, also aided and abetted by the questionable forms of financial innovation discussed earlier.

In a world where the demand is for quick results, only the quick-witted can survive. So the high-tech aspects of the traditional corporation separate themselves and start their own small, nimble operations. They develop or claim to develop new patents that would be invulnerable, and solicit funds.

High-tech is often celebrated as a triumph of the free market. Many of their gains, however, are in fact predatory and depended on the exploitation and patenting of government research. High-tech and banking innovation each reinforce the other. But investment banks are really too detached to see what is really going on, and corporate fraud becomes rampant.

Public interest regulation at the federal level, such as occupational health and environment protection lost much of their role in the post-Reagan years, and not merely because of Republican hostility to regulation on behalf of workers. The unions and progressive businesses that might promote such regulations were too weakened. Where regulations have not been abolished, they have been disregarded by the backward business interests. More generally, the predators that have come to economic and political power treat the government as just one more business the assets and powers of which can be appropriated to their purposes.

What has emerged in both the investment banking community and corporations is a new predatory class, and this class has strived to manipulate not only corporations but the government itself. Most of the corporate predators do not want to eliminate government so much as to use it for their own purposes. Some examples: (1) Drug companies do not want to eliminate the FDA. They do want to "streamline" its procedures, but with an FDA approval process they can always say that if a drug fails, it "has been FDA approved." (2) Oil companies benefit from the interstate highway fund and the Pentagon budget. (3) Health insurance companies benefit from regulations requiring citizens to have coverage. (4) High-tech companies benefit from strict enforcement of trademarks and patents. (5) School regulations, like No Child Left Behind, create a market for private test tutoring systems.

Our "market economy" has really been sustained in large part throughout the post–World War II period by a set of institutions Galbraith calls parapublic (chapter 8; The 2001 Federal Law mandating minimum standards for public school students, more standardized testing, and teacher accountability). These include the university system, the earned income tax credit, much of the healthcare system, and the housing industry. All receive both direct subsidies from government and benefit from tax deductibility and various forms of government guaranteed loans. These along with the more traditional New Deal program of Social Security have served to keep consumption going during economic downturns. But because all of them except Social Security are not run directly by government, they are not even perceived as interventions in the market. This system has also created a population willing to go into debt to sustain its lifestyle and in the process keep the economy going. In effect this is a form of private Keynesianism (deficit spending to create economic growth), the Keynesian devolution as he call it. It produces mainly services and is driven by personal and household debt. It depends on the willingness of foreigners to hold that debt, absent discovery of new natural resources. It could be endangered by predation from within and by unwillingness of foreigners to collaborate.

Klein overplays the impact of the mere fact of 9/11 deaths and exaggerates Bush's role in crony capitalism. Just as in the months leading up to the Iran hostage crisis and the election of Ronald Reagan, the attack on the World Trade Towers took on intense symbolic significance because of several interrelated and long-standing political and cultural threads. These included: (1) the growing cultural role of Manichean theologies and moral perspectives anticipating Armageddon and dividing the world into good versus evil; (2) a US society that has always seen both its government and its (imagined) market as exceptional, "a city upon a hill"; (3) part and parcel of these other two beliefs is the conviction that the United States is a uniquely open society, where free markets allow anyone a real chance to become rich; and (4) a sluggish economy and increasing cultural and political challenges to the centrality or certainty of these beliefs. Seen in the light of a perspective attuned to the social and individual propensity to secure identity, 9/11 was as much an occasion to construct a crisis as a crisis in itself. Many individuals were tragically killed and a financial nerve center temporarily disabled, but nothing compared to even a fraction of the devastation of the air war in even one European city during World War II.

Nonetheless, Klein is on to something. The attack on what was symbolically the heart of American capitalism made this event especially fertile for securing a national identity.

The events of 9/11 made and was made into great video. Repeated replays of the apocalyptic chaos, panic, and human suffering served as a tipping point or catalyst that mobilized and intensified a more secretive, internationally muscular, resource-exploiting, and undemocratic form of capitalism. In earlier chapters I have highlighted the role of Manichean worldviews and the United States as a uniquely moral society. Here I want to emphasize the way the economy unfolded in response to perceived crisis. Policy and rhetoric limited economic opportunities and thereby helped entrench dire scenarios, further transforming the structure and ethos of US capitalism. But whether Bush era crony disaster capitalism is sustainable or not is itself a vital question. The system is inequitable and unstable, but its future course is hardly assured. The left itself may not be served well by embracing its own version of right apocalyptic scenarios.

Under Bush, capitalists embraced more tax cuts for the wealthy, further attacks on unions and wage standards, a rollback of environmental laws, demonization of Arabs and Islam under the inflammatory rubric of "Islamic Fascism," and an indefinite foreign occupation. A climate marked by increasing militarization and secrecy, in turn, helped to reinforce a welfare culture—for the well positioned. Along with the demonization of the poor and selected minorities went a glorification and celebration of the rich. Government, rather than being hollowed out, was further outsourced to private corporations. Deals often took the form of contracts, many offered secretively, with no competition and little oversight, to a sprawling network of privileged firms and industries.

Bush also built upon and intensified the Keynesian devolution Galbraith describes. He entered office committed to extending home ownership to working-class and minority families as part of his vaguely defined ownership society. But rather than extend to working-class citizens the fruits of their increasing productivity, the emphasis was on how new financial products could make more home loans available. A shadow banking system emerged. Mortgage companies, unlike your local bank, are not depository institutions and do not have the same rules.

Since mortgage companies are not depository institutions, they could borrow a larger percentage of the funds used to make loans. In addition, investment banks bought large numbers of these loans, combined them in complex ways, and sold them to other wealthy investors, hedge funds, and so on. Hedge funds and investment banks eagerly bought such securities because rating agencies, paid by the issuers of these securities, endorsed their credit worthiness and the rate of return was greater than could be gained in the low interest environment of the day. The existence of this vigorous secondary market allowed even small banks to make risky loans, knowing they could just sell off the loans.

The capital and expertise available for such complex instruments was increasingly global and fluid, thanks to computers and global capital markets. European banks themselves had become convinced of the US miracle and were highly leveraged and major purchasers of the new mortgage-backed securities. The very success in extending mortgages widely and the consequent steady rise in housing prices seemed to justify and strengthen the already strong faith in "deregulated" capital markets, homes as key to the ownership society and future wealth, technology, and globalization.

The pool of capital was also greatly enhanced by one of the most sophisticated derivatives, credit default swaps. The financial world is constituted by three products, speculative investments, depository banking, and insurance. Credit default swaps were created by investment banks but marketed as a form of insurance. These are instruments like futures contracts that airlines, for instance, buy to hedge themselves against increases in the price of jet fuel. But investment houses marketed these not only to holders of mortgage-backed securities but also to third parties who simply wanted to speculate on the future price of these assets. And because investment banks had convinced President Clinton not to regulate them, no one knew if the investment banks could back the possible insurance claims. Investment banks, for their part, had now also often merged with commercial banks, meaning that if any of this structure started to collapse, ordinary citizen's accounts would be endangered. The Federal Reserve, under Alan Greenspan's leadership, neglected the rapid rise in housing prices and eulogized the wisdom of the market. The culture and the major media celebrated the wizardry, success, and wealth of the new kings of finance in both enriching themselves and making homes affordable. Rather than a system that managed risk, modern finance became a theater of risk itself and an intensifier of risks for the entire market economy.[5]

Commentators on left and right describe the modern financial system as deregulated, but that is not fully accurate. Regulations that protected ordinary citizens from crass exploitation were eliminated, but new regulations and monetary practices were enacted to protect the masters of finance. Bankruptcy regulation was amended to protect credit card companies in the event of bankruptcy. And when an early hedge fund with many systemic ties seemed likely to go bankrupt in the mid-1990s, the Fed arranged bailout funds and new consolidations. Crony capitalism did not start with 9/11. The Fed had implicitly changed regulations on banks during the mid-1990s and financiers got the message: you are more likely to be shielded from the consequences of your behavior if you are systematically interconnected with other vital sectors of finance. In this environment, once a few stressed consumers can no longer make payment on mortgages, investment banks holding securities tied to this debt and often having little backup capital become at risk.

Levels of debt and deregulation of small fry protections have not only destabilized the financial system, they have also reshaped work life. Debt is the modern indentured servitude. Individuals in debt are locked into long working hours—often at lousy jobs. Private consumption outlets become more entrenched. Having sacrificed family and leisure time for work and consumption, other interests cannot develop. Many workers also become bitter toward those "elitists" who challenge one of their main pleasures in life, especially one for which they have given so much. Of course, overwhelming corporate and personal debt is now the eight-hundred-pound guerilla in the living room.

Predicting the Future: Scientific Laws, Social Evolution, and Revisiting Darwin

What is the future of capitalism? To answer so sweeping a question it helps to distinguish among three levels: the process of buying and selling goods in individual markets, the macrolevel problem of balancing total employment and total demand for goods and services, and the larger political, institutional, ethical and even aesthetic settings in which the micro- and macrodimensions are entangled.

Since the late 1970s, US politics has been dominated by a faith that a free market cannot just solve the microlevel problem of maximizing consumer utility (e.g., providing optimal levels of cheerios versus frosted flakes) but that it also solves the macroproblem of keeping demand for all products high enough to assure full employment and steady growth. If anything were needed it would only be a little tweaking of the money supply by the "nonpolitical" Federal Reserve. Finally, Americans generally, if not always happily, viewed privately held and managed corporations as the institutional vehicle to achieve those ends.

On some levels faith in the microlevel's ability to function in predictable fashion remains, and probably correctly, pretty much intact. If the price of oranges goes up, consumers will buy fewer of them and substitute other drinks or sources of vitamin C. Nonetheless, even here cracks can be discerned. Even neoclassical economists admit that free exchange in the market produces predictable and optimal price and quantity only in purely competitive markets. In markets with a few large firms and great economies of scale, the effects of any major exogenous change will not produce automatic and fully predictable alterations in price or quantity. What firms do will depend on what other large competitors do, concerns about long-term consumer attitudes and government policy. In addition, some product markets are so heavily regulated and subsidized and so central to the economy that they hardly behave in the classical fashion. The housing market is affected by numerous subsidies, Federal Reserve interest policies, and consumer and bank expectations regarding all of these.

On the macrolevel confidence that pure free markets can secure relatively full employment and satisfactory growth has been shaken. By late 2008 and early 2009, a wide spectrum of business and political elites agreed that a one-time government stimulus package was needed to restore the economy. But even the belief that the stimulus need only be one time and that it will surely work implies that the system can be fixed without larger changes in the economic institutions and mores that brought on these problems. It also suggests that at least over the long term the system is predictable.

The scenario of the financialization of US capital set forth in Galbraith is one that Keynes had witnessed in the 1920s and 1930s. And the instability it fostered was the backdrop for one of Keynes's key insights. Keynes distinguished between risk and uncertainty. Life insurance policies are written based on risk analysis. Insurers do not know whether a particular fifty–year-old nonsmoker will live to eighty, but based on prior experience and statistical models they can establish probabilities with fairly certain accuracy. But in modern times, financial markets have started to provide forms of insurance on such matters as legal risk, regulatory risk, and shares of stock and financial instruments are based on "risk analysis" of interest rate futures. But the applicability of the insurance actuarial model to these matters is suspect. In his exhaustive study of Keynes and financial crisis, Robert Skidelski puts this clearly:

One cannot apply insurance models to non-insurable products. Although both...actuarial and microforecasting...models rely on historical data, the analogy between actuarial models of life, property, and casualty insurance and insurance of complex derivatives is false. Although there have been failures in insurance markets,...insurers in general have not suffered the same losses as investment banks, because the risks they take on are generally measurable. Life assurance companies can correctly price they need to cover their payments because they have reliable, up to date statistics of life expectancy. For them, the future is a statistical reflection of the past. But insurers, relying on a false analogy with life expectancy, have been spreading into a world beyond actuarial risk. They started offering insurance on every type of risk—credit risk, liquidity risk, market risk, legal risk...regulatory risk, political risk...all of which they claimed were actuarially calculable in exactly the same way as life assurance...We talk about "political risk" when we should talk of political uncertainty. We simply do not know what the probability is of the future direction of Russia's economic or political policy. The use of the word risk to cover uninsurable contingencies conveys a specious precision, which comforts the markets but has no basis in science.[6]

In the light of phenomena where one simply cannot make predictions with any degree of certainty, certain "irrational" forms of behavior become quite rational. Thus Skidelski, following Keynes, argues that if there is no real basis to predict what interest rates will be in thirty years or whether the Russian government will expropriate oil millionaires, following or trying to anticipate the crowd or sticking with old habits becomes sensible. I would add that the deeper existential need for some sense of order or identity also impels such behavior. Unfortunately, it can also push it to extremes, where conventions become unassailable. These factors introduce the possibility of vast and rapid changes and even fluctuations far above and below any reasonable price line for the asset in question.

Uncertainty cannot be eliminated from life. But Keynes and Skidelski argue that economic policy can "reduce the scope of irreducible uncertainty." The corporate CEO can be allowed to return to the position of risk manager when he or she can focus on assessing the likelihood that a new technology or product will work, will be more efficient or appealing than competitors. He or she should not have to think in such terms as whether current corporate assets could be pedaled for a high return now or whether stocks as an entire asset class are "overvalued." And he or she should surely not have to worry about vast changes in the value of the national currency or whether unemployment in three years will undermine all consumer markets.

Thus Keynes was more than the technocrat that even many of his US defenders turn him into. Yes, government should stimulate when necessary. But long term, it should engage in institutional reforms that reduced the scope of uncertainty, such as changes in the understanding of what it means to own stock, assuring more patient capital, and stabilizing world finance. And since an advanced capitalist society may soon produce more than it needs, he anticipated a gradual reduction in the hours of work.[7]

As Skidelski argues, Keynes addressed a fundamental epistemological problem, the inability to foretell the future. There may be a gap between our cognitive capacity and the world "out there" or the very nature of things may embrace elements of randomness or agency. Whatever its origins, Keynes sought to cordon off an economic realm that could function in relative stability and provide the conditions for future cultural change. The case for reforms along the lines he suggested seems as clear today as when he wrote, but there remains a question for me as to whether

Skidelski or Keynes adequately acknowledge that the boundary between risk and uncertainty, which must be drawn, can be drawn only provisionally. Rules and institutions that cordon off capital markets are needed and have worked, but can be gradually or rapidly undermined. The very workability and stability certain restrictions provide may spawn new behaviors undreamed of by regulators or even bankers and capital markets. So recognition of the role of uncertainty may entail a chastened, tentative orientation toward even our most thought out reforms. I will have more to say on this in connection with the Consumer Protection Finance Bureau, an agency whose approach may be more important than any specific reform.

Will American Keynesians Raise their Game?

The best liberal Keynesians remain in many ways tethered to the neoclassical assumptions. Human beings rationally maximize their own interests, but information asymmetries or sticky prices prevent markets from working as fully optimal. So limited and specific intervention is called for.

In another sense, they do so as well. If we can simply present a clear case for the failure of the laissez faire approach and present tested, statistically validated alternatives, voters will go along. But economic policy "preferences" and narratives are closely tied up with—though not reducible to—one's personal, social, and national identity. There is an uneasy, shifting, and never fully predictable mix and set of evolving interactions here. Some of the best and smartest Keynesians, disturbed by the obvious failure of their prescriptions to win popular ascendance even in the face of a slew of failures of the classical school (the bubble, interest rate predictions, stimulus, etc.), have begun to consider how complex identity politics shapes and is shaped by the evolution of the political economy.

Brad DeLong, favorably cited by Paul Krugman, is a hopeful exemplar of a new interdisciplinary openness. Thus consider his Nietzschean take on the Tea Party:

> Let me mention one last hypothesis—one that may get my economist union card revoked and get me transferred to a department of rhetoric, or perhaps cultural studies.
>
> Friedrich Nietzsche talked about the losers, or about those who thought they were losers. He discussed their tendency in various ways to transvalue their values—to say that what was thought to be bad was in fact good precisely because it was thought to be bad.

Three weeks ago I was talking to some activists from the California Tea Party. I was trying to explain the Keynesian perspective: Shouldn't we keep public employment from falling...because...the government can borrow at such extraordinarily good terms, and if we keep our teachers at work then they educate our students and our students can earn more in the future— and if teachers have incomes they spend money and that employs more people in the private sector?

And they said no. They said we have lost our jobs in the private sector. It is only fair for those who work in the government to run some risk of losing their jobs as well. They are unionized. They have pensions. It is not fair that they should have jobs too. They need to lose their jobs as well.

The unemployment becomes something to be valued. The fact that government austerity will increase unemployment becomes a transvalued virtue of the policy.[8]

Nietzsche of course also presented aesthetic and rhetorical counters to this transvaluation. He also spoke to the limits of linear causal models, models that represented a kind of frozen time. Keynes too worried that econometric models assumed without proving that patterns in one era would simply replicate themselves in another era.

In referring readers to DeLong's talk, Krugman jokes:

It seems that I have to raise my game: Brad DeLong manages to bring Friedrich Nietzsche into a discussion of the failure of macroeconomic policy.

Let's see...there must be some way to invoke Wittgenstein here...

By the way, Brad's essay is excellent.[9]

I hope Krugman and DeLong will continue to point to the inadequacies and contradictions of the classical model. But I also hope that economist as talented and thoughtful as these two will raise their game by taking a closer look at the broad epistemological assumptions they share with their neoclassical adversaries.

Here is my attempt to help them raise their game. When I was writing the first draft of this chapter, fall 2008, little attention was devoted to the question of why many Americans wanted the smallest package possible or might even be unwilling to accept any stimulus. The move from the capitalism of Eisenhower to that of Reagan-G. W. Bush entailed major changes in institutions and social mores, ones that were not widely foretold at the time and have had serious implications for future government initiatives.

These considerations raise the issue of to what extent market crises or large changes in economic institutions are predictable. Mark Blyth et al. sketch three types of world and the accompanying forms uncertainty can take:

A type 1 world is one in which directly observable generators produce predictable risks. A six-side die, for example, does not generate "17" as an outcome. A type 2 world, by contrast, is one in which generators are only partly observable and past patterns draw a more volatile curve with fat tails. Here risk shades into uncertainty. For example, in a stock market we see outcomes in the movement of shares, but we do not see the generators of those movements: a monetarist theory of inflation or a belief in the "new economy." Such generators are not directly observable and are interdependent with the beliefs of the actors themselves. A type three world is even more unsettling. Here highly complex, unobservable generators produce patterns that shift in unexpected direction. Such distributions may look stable and regular over certain periods until a major unexpected shift invalidates the theories developed from sampling past data. The end of the Cold War seemed to bring such a shift in IR broadly, and as the latest subprime mortgage debacle shows all too clearly, many financial crises seem to do so with unexpected frequency in IPE. The simple fact that there are three "generators" of economic models that seek to understand three different currency crises strongly suggests that highly complex generators produce inconstant causes. That is, the causes of one currency crisis at "time-1" change institutions and expectations such that the causes of the next crisis at "time-2"cannot be experienced or caused the same way.[10]

It seems to me that the crash of the housing market requires a model attuned to a type 2 world. We could observe the movement of the housing market and some, but far from all, of the key actors. In particular, the role of derivatives was almost entirely hidden and the "shadow banking system" was just that—in the shadows. Contrary to the assertions of Alan Greenspan and other leading conventional economists, a number of economists who were not true believers in market optimization and smooth equilibria, did suspect that a housing crash was coming, though none claimed ability to predict when or how deep the fall would be. But when housing debt burdens severely outpace income or when the gap between the costs of ownership and renting become extreme, something has to give.

Though there was a possibility of predicting the collapse of the housing bubble, predicting the full institutional, political, and legal response to that collapse may not have been possible. In particular, though there is good reason to believe that labor and consumer markets will still respond in relatively predictable ways to a stimulus, whether political leaders would pass such a measure may be highly unpredictable. The beliefs and biases of politicians and the media constantly shape and are shaped by the ongoing evolution of the political and economic crisis. This process is best viewed from the lens of a type 3 world.

I will begin with a possible model of indeterminacy in a type 2 world, a model that I believe sheds light on the housing market collapse. Yet that type 2 model, despite its recognition of the wide areas of uncertainty, may not be adequate to the full scope and depth of uncertainty when major crises converge. Then I will discuss developments in neuroscience and complexity theory that would seem to lend plausibility to a type 3 worldview. If the process of institutional change contains elements of type 3 indeterminacy, how can or should citizens prepare and adapt?

Models of Uncertainty

Even today, all too few market participants, especially investment bankers and brokers, seem interested in the large question of whether and to what extent economic crises and major collapses can be predicted. One very conservative wealth manager John Mauldin has had a long-standing interest in the topic and one that predates the collapse of the housing bubble. His weekly newsletter dated April 22, 2006, caught my attention at the time. I quote him at length:

> In Ubiquity: Why Catastrophes Happen, Mark Buchaanan describes the work of scientists at Brookhaven lab whose attempts to explain difficulties in predicting avalanches led them to computer simulations of kids dropping grains of sand on a beach as they build sand castles. They learned that there is no typical size of an avalanche. To find out why Bak and colleagues next played a trick with their computer. Imagine peering down on the pile from above, and coloring it in according to its steepness. Where it is relatively flat and stable, color it green; where steep and, in avalanche terms, "ready to go," color it red. What do you see? They found that at the outset the pile looked mostly green, but that, as the pile grew, the green became infiltrated with ever more red. With more grains, the scattering of red danger spots grew until a dense skeleton of instability ran through the pile. Here then was a clue to its peculiar behavior: a grain falling on a red spot can, by domino-like action, cause sliding at other nearby red spots. If the red network was sparse, and all trouble spots were well isolated one from the other, then a single grain could have only limited repercussions. But when the red spots came to riddle the pile, the consequences of the next grain became fiendishly unpredictable. It might trigger only a few tumblings, or it might instead set off a cataclysmic chain reaction involving millions. The sand pile seemed to have configured itself into a hypersensitive and peculiarly unstable condition in which the next falling grain could trigger a response of any size whatsoever.

These scientists are not suggesting that the world of sand grains is chaotic. In situations before the extreme disequilibrium has set in, there is orderliness to the consequences of dropping more grains of sand. They also identify conditions that predispose systems toward dramatic and unpredictable occurrences. They can specify, at least in rough terms, a range of intensities and the probabilities of different degrees of intensity, but what they cannot do is foretell exactly when such will occur, their specific intensity, or the exact course they will take.

One cannot of course rule out the possibility that scientists could develop a fully predictive model of avalanches, perhaps by closer specification of the speed and direction of the sand falling as well as closer determination of the position of each grain of sand in the pile and the winds affecting the downward course of the sand. Yet whether our capacity to measure such variables would ever be equal to the task and how measurement itself might affect outcomes remains a troubling question.

The view of avalanches presented here is both a metaphor and a schematic oversimplification of a market economy and a market crash. It does give us some tools for assessing the probability of a crash and the degree of such an event. But markets are the creation of human minds and exist within and help secrete particular moral and institutional foundations. How will institutions and mores change in response to a crash? Can the evolution of these be predicted with any degree of assurance? In chapter two we reviewed modern evolutionary biology's skepticism regarding hard predictions in the natural systems and the implications of related concepts of indeterminacy.

Predictability becomes even more problematic when we move to human society. Contemporary neuroscience increasingly rejects the passive, information-processing model that encouraged views of human thought and action as potentially susceptible to law-like regularity and predictions. Knowledge emerges from a complex, multilevel process of interaction with the world. Humans possess gut-level drives and fears that are too crude and too rapidly transmitted within the neurological system to be fully comprehended by the higher levels of the brain. Nonetheless, these gut-level fears and drives have an effect on and are crucial to our actions and the emergence of consciousness. These interactions are hard to encompass in any closely specified causal model of human thought.

Let's say we wanted to predict the effect of a major swine flu epidemic or even fear of one on our severe recession. Since swine flu carries the possibility of massive deaths via pathways not fully understood by contemporary science, it touches very deep fears and human aspirations on the cultural, conscious level that I will explore further later. At this point, drawing on William Connolly's *Neuropolitics*[11] I will content myself with some general comments on the pathways involved in reacting to such a traumatic event or fear.

Neuroscientists know the amygdala is involved. It is a speedy little brain nodule communicating with slower, higher levels of the brain. It triggers vague but intense feelings of fear, caution, and anxiety. Though we know it is involved, its effects on thought and action are inherently hard to predict. For one thing, the amygdala in individual persons may have different levels of physical health, and second the amygdala will have had a different experiential history for different individuals. Though it is simple in linguistic capacity and must engage other regions of the brain, some cultural learning is inscribed in it. And the intensities it sends to other regions of the brain must, in turn, be processed by these regions in terms of their own speed, intensities, and conceptual schemes. Slippages, free-floating material that is not fully integrated into concepts, may surely remain and offer the possibility that these will self-organize or themselves be organized in ways that redirect thought in unpredictable ways. Such notions need not invoke Freudian repression in the interests of a superego.

The brain's higher level schemes and concepts in turn develop within broader cultural debate and discussion that are notoriously hard to predict. Conscious thought and purposive action can in turn alter these crude drives and even in some instances the architecture of the brain. In the cute phrase, neurons that fire together wire together.

The problem of constructing a fully predictive model of human thought is further complicated because our evolving understandings of these connections will in turn enter our thought patterns and influence how events play out. Once again with the slippages between levels of the brain and the indefinite expansion of possibilities at the level of the natural and physical environments in which we act it would seem unlikely that the feedback loops among the levels of the brain, the culture, and the natural world would ever be so tight as to lead to law-like regularities. And even in the unlikely case that such exist, we humans are unlikely to gain it.

A professor of physics and mathematics with whom I have raised this issue maintains that in the example of such exogenous events we don't need to be able to predict the reactions of an individual brain. The vast number affected will cancel themselves out and yield the usual normal distribution.[12] Yet such a response once again assumes the idealized free market where everyone has equal access to information and an equal ability to affect outcome. But if we put aside textbook markets, some individuals at key nodal points may control or limit the flow of information. Certain targets and forms of anger may survive the corporate and media censors while others are filtered out. If we imagine a situation of extreme fear and uncertainty and few contrasting messages, the mere reaction of a few of one's well placed and symbolically significant compatriots may induce a kind of herd effect.

But we need not always be victims of violent swings. Neuroscience's growing understanding of the functions of various nodules in the brain and the way they are connected does suggest areas and means by which to intervene in the relation between drives and fears and the higher regions of the brain. Meditation, visualization, drugs both legal and illegal, and targeted neurological stimulation have been able to reduce damaging fears and open new forms of creative potential. These techniques are, however, trial-and-error interventions. They don't work on everyone, have different effects both in intensity and quality, and must be subject to continual revision on an individual basis. But building the time for and an inclination to employ such techniques can be important, as I will suggest later.

On an institutional and policy level discussions of the possibility of a type 3 world are vital. Following every major crisis of US capitalism economic elites have endeavored to escape the consequences of a type 3 world. After Depression and World War II, the compromise of military Keynesianism, a modest union movement, and the Bretton Woods international monetary system was inaugurated. When that system broke down, US capitalist leaders moved to restore a fuller measure of corporate control of wages and prices. By the 1990s, the role of finance capital had greatly expanded, all on the promise that complex and largely hidden financial markets would work as smoothly as farmers' markets.

Financial reform has been weak and limited. The modest fiscal stimulus has served pretty much as predicted, but the institutional and political support for more has been inadequate. If the combined crises of joblessness, war, and ecology continue to destabilize, expect major sectors of capitalism to renew demands for a larger IMF role in structured debt relief, to reassert the virtues of deficit reduction, and to once again tell us that the Phillips Curve prescribes a tradeoff between unemployment and inflation. Progressives attuned to the possibility of a type 3 world need to remind our citizens that these laws have often been broken and that they are human creations that have enjoyed predictive and normative power only in certain circumstances and domains. They impose and shore up an economic reality they purport to describe. The possibility, indeed the necessity, of intervention at the level of corporate governance and cultural mores is there.

Blyth et al. put this point quite well:

Mainstream materialist and rationalist approaches view the IPE [international political economy] as a type 1 set of interactions: with enough rolls of the dice we should be able to work out the distribution. Constructivists who take the route of uncertainty, however, see the unpredictability of IPE outcomes over time and space as suggesting that the IPE may actually be a type-three arena. Their working hypothesis is that agents inhabit type three worlds of great uncertainty, have a hard job living in such a random world, and thus construct stability through the development and deployment of governing ideas, institutions, norms, and conventions.[13]

Can we prove that the world we live in is in some ways a type 3 world? Can we resort to the scientific method? The problem is that our choice of method is in some ways inflected by our large ontological commitments. Some scientists assume from the very start, indeed declare it as a condition of inquiry itself, that the world must be explainable. And by explainable, they mean that cause and effect are separate, that the dichotomy between analytic and synthetic propositions is sacred, and that the world is law-like. Connolly appropriately criticizes these rules of inquiry:

> To the extent that it is advanced as necessary, practices of inquiry which encounter and even appreciate a modicum of mystery are demeaned from the start. Such an injunction could well rule out, for instance, a conception of emergent causality in which the interplay between disparate factors in producing a new formation is said to exceed our capacities for detailed knowledge and prediction.[14]

In my estimation, an emergent causality explanation of the triumph of Reaganism and crony disaster capitalism both sheds important light and offers new political possibilities. Did racism, economic decline, and more welfare for blacks "cause" the rise of the Reagan Democrats? From an emergent causality model that would be simplistic, long-standing racial feelings surely existed, but for many these were barely conscious gut forms of fear and disgust. It took a particular concatenation of events and a degree of self-organization for the phenomenon we call Reagan Democrats to emerge. Gut-level fears about blacks and disdain for the elites who seemed insensitive to white working-class male strains at work built on and intensified each other. The smooth persona of Ronald Reagan gave these concerns and tales a human face, an articulate expression, and a degree of social acceptability. In a climate of work internsification, declining rewards for work, and black protest, Ronald Reagan was able to successfully coin and politically deploy the epithet "welfare queen." He filled it in with picturesque tales of black women on welfare driving Cadillacs. Anger toward work, liberal elites, and blacks had all resonated together and intensified but now could crystallize and focus on a definable target. A specific rhetoric and policy agenda emerged, thereby further entrenching the key concepts of lazy welfare cheats and queens. Concern about the social issue of welfare queens then became part of the definition of the Reagan

Democrat, though that concept can be seen as present in nascent form in the process that produced the Reagan Democrat. As I read the phenomenon of Reagan Democrats though immanent naturalism and immanent naturalism through such historical examples, it is clear to me that there was nothing inevitable about this outcome. Interventions at several levels attuned to simmering discontent might offer even more chance for constructive alternatives.

Whatever the truth status of the suspicion that the world is not fully predictable, the belief has political and existential consequences. Advocates of a type 3 worldview do not deny that there are realms and periods when linear causality and relatively predictable risks prevail. The uncoupling of systems of different speeds and intensities can issue in such periods. Nor are they opposed to efforts to find and articulate regularities. Indeed the very nascent currents they seek to nurture would gain little staying power apart from construction of laws, rights, and institutions that both solidify and clarify them. But denial of a realm of uncertainty discourages receptivity and experimental responses to the vague and emerging discontents that might blossom in proper circumstances or cause institutional avalanche and cruel destruction in others. Of course, that claim itself reflects a stance on the very issues at play here.

Immediate Reforms and the Hazards of Left Apocalypse

Issues respecting the long-term predictability of the system in the face of intersecting health, environmental, and cultural crises do not, however, rule out immediate policy interventions. There are systems that are relatively closed and stable and for which fairly predictable interventions may be made. Unfortunately, some on the left may be overly convinced of the futility of even short-term relief of sagging markets and even more convinced that such failure can lead only to dangerous institutional change.

Some micromarkets seem to be the most closed and predictable systems. Cash for clunkers did lead to junking of older cars and purchases of more environmentally suitable alternatives. Carbon taxes or cap and trade will change production technologies.

On the macrolevel, Obama's modest stimulus package does seem as of this writing (December 2010) to have slowed the pace of economic decline. Keynes argued that relief for the poor and unemployed had a relatively high and predictable multiplier because the money had to be spent on bare necessities. Yet Chris Hedges remains convinced that this recession will crush the traditional Keynesian faith that domestic fiscal policy can act as a predictable stabilizer. Hedges cites in particular the continuing costs of the American empire. He also cites the desire of newly emerging economic powers China, Russia, India, and Brazil to control more of their economic destiny and to become less willing to fund the US balance of trade deficit. A US currency collapse could precipitate a burst of inflation, followed by Federal Reserve efforts to uphold the currency with high interest rates, thereby choking off any recovery and sending the economy into a deep depression. Hedges pictures most factories closing, even more vast disparities between classes, and a new autocracy.

Hedges scenario is surely not impossible, but even empires in decline can suffer less severe fates—witness Britain. And as several commentators noted soon after Hedges's article, despite the fact that Brazil, India, China, and Russia shared a desire to lessen US economic influence, they presented no clear consensus on a positive agenda and also lacked the deep capital markets to sustain a complete alternative to the US dollar. Nor had China lost all interest in a US export market. Talk of China as willing to engineer or even accept a complete collapse of the dollar seemed premature. As Dean Baker has pointed out, China has no interest in US dollar devaluation now as it would only crush its own export market.

Finally, talk of empty plants and social violence seems to completely bypass the possibility that Americans might recognize the very strength and potential they have in those plants and the skills of the men and women who work in them. Talk of empty plants leading immediately to repressive politics may neglect the creative possibilities implicit in the complex and indeterminate processes of institutional change.

Confident forecasts that Keynesian interventions won't work even on a limited basis squares with the current right-wing attack and may discourage creation of the very breathing spaces that might give progressive institutional change more of a chance.

In the near future, the best way to avert wild currency swings might be for all major capitalist economies currently in crisis to devise cooperative stimulus packages. Such ideas have been briefly considered, but policymakers need to be more attuned to the possibility of such volatility and willing to consider and periodically reevaluate ways to achieve such cooperation.

The deepest levels of unpredictability lie at the institutional and political levels. Obama has staked his administration on a stimulus package that pales in comparison to the bank bailout. That bailout has taken the form of loans and stock purchases of some of the largest investment banks. These banks have a greater interest in survival than in increasing new loans to the private sector. What they are doing with these vast sums is largely hidden from the public and even most Democrats have resisted legislation that would force more public disclosure.

Doomsday scenarios played a major role in the passage of the bank bailout. Some on the left, including this writer, were so worried about the instability of the system as to easily buy the argument that something must be done—right now—to shore up banks lest immediate runs on even healthy banks destroy the whole economy. Yet as Dean Baker has pointed out, there was ample evidence that even at the height of the crisis many local banks had funds to lend.[15] And had large corporations been unable to sell commercial paper, short-term loans so vital to big business—the Fed already had authority to buy the paper. Banks were not making loans primarily because few businesses wanted to borrow money or the banks were unsure of future markets for their products. We are properly critical of the system and its risks and dismissive of those who always see light at the end of the capitalist tunnel. Nonetheless, we must not be seduced by the rhetoric of inevitability to the point we don't take even a brief pause for further reflection.

In retrospect, it seems clear that a stronger stimulus package, which might have saved more jobs and more mortgages, would have been a better use of our funds. Obama's package was large enough to make up for only about a third of the fall off of demand already experienced in the current slide.

If and as environmental and economic crises deepen, it becomes especially imperative to push a larger and more adequate economic reconstruction program. Timothy Canova has commented that:

> The Greatest Generation was able to invest on a scale much greater than today, spending billions of dollars on the Second World War, the Marshall Plan...and the G.I. Bill of Rights that housed, educated, and integrated more than sixteen million returning war veterans. As a percentage of GDP, the US government spent more than twice as much and borrowed more than fifteen times as much as today.[16]

Canova's specific historical example should, however, carry a caveat with it. The GI bill extended college and home ownership benefits to returning veterans but discrimination within the banking and college admissions systems kept most blacks from availing themselves of these. As I suggested at more length in chapters two and four concerns about ethnic, racial and gender biases cannot be put aside simply through enactment of an egalitarian class-based agenda. Nor can such a broad stimulus package be adopted without attention to a range of social issues.

Economic Democracy and Social Issues

Some whites of all classes and many media pundits still need to be reminded that racial profiling and discrimination still scar some sectors of American life. But one must also note that dramatic gains have been made in other areas and any specially targeted program requires continuing scrutiny. Fifteen years ago, Joanne Barkan made an important point still relevant today. Progressives should "drop the defensiveness about scrutinizing individual programs. Affirmative action begs for democratic management—for careful design and monitoring by the people who live with it. When a fair evaluation shows a program to be ineffective, fraud-ridden, wasteful, or unjust, the left should endorse revamping or dropping it."[17]

Yet part of any rethinking of affirmative action should also include broadening our understanding of historic disadvantage and its implications. One way to blunt the divisive politics of race would be to focus on harms and burdens shared by working-class whites and African Americans. Socioeconomic class also acts as a barrier for many poor and working-class children. Rather than scrapping affirmative action, it may well need reforms that would assess and redress the advantages over their poor and working-class peers middle- and upper-class students and workers enjoy.

In addition, some forms of racial discrimination that have become more apparent in recent years, such as new voter identification laws that in effect are similar to the poll tax, also impose inordinate burdens on poor and working-class whites. Recognition of the shared nature of these barriers can open up more opportunities for cross-racial, class-based politics.[18]

Crony capitalism, however, is wary of any effort to address economic distress through democratic politics. It is not accidental that once crisis is acknowledged, they turn to the Federal Reserve, our least democratic and most secretive body. Despite their manifest failures and manipulations, the titans of the financial world are still often treated with some degree of awe by a media that itself has continually denied or underestimated the crisis.

The consequences of banker-friendly financial reform and inadequate stimulus packages may touch culture and institutions. Obama has treated modest legislative successes as triumphs that will jumpstart the economy. If economic distress grows, more cynicism about a political system already in crisis will follow. Democracy may take a hit even if our least democratic institutions have occasioned this crisis. The result may be more authoritarian forms of crony capitalism. Even an adequate stimulus package would merely restore the kind of inegalitarian corporate order that produced the unsustainable debt economy. That would soon require further stimulus, which may well be impossible in a world that several years from now will be so heavily laden with debt.

Other alternatives, however, are possible. The obviously manipulative and even corrupt practices of our major banks have also managed to open up broader questions of corporate governance. But for such openings to amount to more than momentary doubt, progressives must address one legacy of the 1970s, the fear that proactive government or more active and powerful labor within the workplace necessarily means a return to stagflation or social turmoil.

Corporate Governance and 1970s Fears

Though we cannot predict, our job is not to sit around and be pessimists or optimists. We can advocate some general direction for new capitalist forms. But in both Europe and the United States, one specter continues to haunt prospects for progressive capitalist transformation. In both, memories of the inflation haunted 1970s and its resultant cultural turmoil are strong.

Unionized workers in the 1970s were often accused—sometimes accurately—of demanding raises that went beyond productivity growth, thus fostering inflation. Yet, as I have noted, such one-sided analysis neglects the role played by OPEC and the oil companies, monopoly pricing power, and the Federal Reserve in creating asset bubbles. In addition, more broadly it disregards the social damage that occurred when the Fed cooled inflation by fostering double-digit unemployment.

With the continued ineptitude, if not outright fraud of the banking sector, there may be more inclination to question reliance on central bankers and to reexamine the structure of enterprise. One reason the Employee Free Choice Act is so controversial may be that corporate management recognizes that the future structure of corporate enterprise is now more up for grabs than at any point in a generation.

Polls indicate majority repudiation of capitalism among those under thirty. These numbers, however, do not mean that younger citizens necessarily want government bureaucracies running the economy. Such polls may, however, point to the need for other enterprise models.

The corporation is a creation of government and law. The corporate form in the United States took on such importance because it offered considerable advantages over private partnerships in a world in which new technologies had arisen.[19] Libertarians like to suggest that property is natural, but in fact it has evolved often in response to technological possibilities and problems that markets and earlier forms of property had created. The firewall between government and the market is not possible, not merely because markets concentrate power and with it the temptation to use government for private gain but also because of the technological and social changes markets foster. From its inception it has been the recipient of privileges not granted to other forms of enterprise. Corporations can raise capital far more effectively than business partnerships because government grants them limited liability. The owners of the corporation, its shareholders, only stand to lose what they have invested in the stock. They are not personally liable for any debts if the company goes bankrupt.[20]

Government allows individuals to form corporations in order to facilitate economic growth that modern technology and economies of scale made possible. Without corporations, a market society could not take full advantage of these possibilities. Nevertheless, government will be less effective in promoting this goal if it does not impose the right rules for corporate governance.

Lax antitrust enforcement, contempt for labor laws, persistent, no bid contracts now enhance corporate power. Within the corporation itself, CEO compensation is determined by boards often chosen by the corporate heads. A strong union movement can provide the countervailing force that sustains equitable wages, fairer CEO pay, and a more stable economy. A strong union movement could also be important not merely for economic justice but also to keep alive the possibility of different forms of economic enterprise. Although the leadership of mainstream unions in the United States has generally shown little interest in worker control issues, dissident caucuses within unions such as the UAW have begun to explore such alternatives. They have asked why, if the Federal government can bail out the auto giants and in effect fire a CEO, it cannot give workers a greater voice in product priorities and design. If the financial crisis deepens, more direct action by employees to seize plants, as has happened in several well-publicized European cases, may raise these issues in more dramatic terms.[21]

Corporate lobbies claim they oppose the EFCA out of concern for workers' democratic rights. Unions and progressives should welcome the opportunity to discuss just how democratic past union representation elections have been and to present models of more truly democratic workplaces. But in both the United States and Europe there are nonstatist models of economic enterprise. Workers can have board representation, a say in major financial and enterprise planning, pay scales, and an ownership stake. These enterprises can create a context where workers demand and receive fair wages but also have incentives to assure their company enough profit to finance further business investment. Full employment in such a context would not necessarily lead to major inflationary pressures.

Shortening Hours: Coping with
Depression and Preadapting to a New World?

Finally, it is important to talk about immediate strategies that cope with depression while also preparing the way for an alternative economy. Hours reduction was developed as a strategy to deal with immediate job loss in the 1930s. It has an equally interesting rebirth among some dissident unionists as long ago as 1951. It could be considered a social instance of the Darwinian preadaptations I discussed in chapter two. In 1951, workers at UAW local 600, Ford's giant River Rouge facility, recognized that deindustrialization was a threat to all workers. And they knew that shortening working hours through curbs on overtime would create more jobs and improve the quality of life for all. But UAW president Walter Reuther had insisted that the union focus on organizing workers in the new rural locations and seek continual wage growth rather than hours reduction. Recalcitrant leaders were purged. With tacit support from company and government, his case carried the day, especially in a climate poisoned by McCarthyism.[22]

Recently, Dean Baker has suggested that government could both foster job growth and promote the long-term goal of work reduction. In a recent online piece he advocated: "a tax credit to employers for giving workers paid time off. For example, if employers offer paid parental leave or paid vacation,...then the tax credit would cover the lost work.....Suppose that employers of 100 million people give their workers an amount of additional paid time off that is equal to 5 percent of their work time. These employers would suddenly have demand for 5 percent more workers, or 5 million workers. I can't think of a quicker, less bureaucratic way to create jobs..."[23]

Troubled businesses, either voluntarily or under worker or community pressure, could reduce hours across the board rather than lay selected workers off. Hours-reduction strategies serve the economy better than layoffs. Workers on 80 percent normal income will need to spend most of what they earn. In the typical layoff scenario, the workers earning full time salaries will save more, especially as they see colleagues being axed. In addition, all workers retain their skills and are less demoralized.

Even as, or if, more prosperity returns, hours reduction could serve broader and more enduring purposes than simply getting us through one recession. More free time, as leading corporate executives worried in the 1920s (see chapter three) could be genuinely subversive. Emerging as a dissident current within the ordinary life of work and consumption, its realization offers time and space for further reconstitutions of a more egalitarian but not statist economy. With a shorter workweek employees and employers could jointly restructure the workweek to reduce commuting and child-care costs. Finally, and most importantly, shorter workweeks, and more countervailing power within workplaces provide the time and the space to adapt to and assess continually the geological, atmospheric, economic, and even virological challenges we are likely to confront. Once some of these reforms are put in place, time plus a cultural sensitivity to the limits of prediction and the social sciences could encourage a willingness to step back and see how this all works.

In the long term, regular hours reduction pegged to productivity increases would blunt surges of overproduction and provide more leisure time, allowing a range of cultural activities to displace some consumer drives and reduce environmental impact. Yet even in a just economy, overproduction and recession are possible. Productivity grows and large segments of the population become satiated. Government programs or renewed bursts of advertizing could then boost spending. But alternatively, workers can and should have the opportunity to take productivity gains in the form of shorter hours for the same total compensation.

Finally I offer a thought on the political and cultural perspective that guides my work. This perspective flows from acceptance of the flux and infinite potentiality of the human and natural worlds as well as the myriad ways in which we humans connect and repel each other. I have argued in several ways that a new capitalism may also entail and be encouraged by exploring understandings of God, truth, history and morality that challenge widely prevalent notions of truth, morality, and causality today. Conventional religious and moral currents resonated and interacted with events like 9/11 to catalyze the international economic, social, and environmental crisis we now confront. I have developed some possible replies to these perspectives. But how do these countervailing abstractions become part of the daily practice and wisdom of a critical mass of the culture?

A start is to recognize that we are more than actors in a formal political practice of elections or lobbying for particular bills. We are consumers who can enact at least modest changes in consumption habits. And we are community members who can find ways to share not only rides but lawnmowers, snow blowers and much of the other expensive paraphernalia of middle-class life. The decision to join with others to share lawnmowers as well as rides is made possible by and in turn enables changes in our sense of ourselves, our relation to things, and to our world and is in turn enabled by these changes. These changes in turn affect and are affected by perspectives and policies we pursue in the more formally political, more purportedly "powerful" world.

Surely there are risks both existential and practical, in premising reform in constructive engagement across many lines of politics and culture. Nonetheless, there are risks in not taking such steps and in living or pretending to live the life of splendid isolation with "dominion" over nature. We can participate in community planning that gives pride of place to walkers and transit vehicles. In daily discussions, those of us who reject the Christian right's literal interpretations of scripture as a license to sanction harsh judgments and punishments need to speak up and assert that there are other Christian views.

It is, however, equally incumbent on us to acknowledge both the contestable nature of our own faiths and recognize that even within the evangelical community there are many who are not captivated by revenge and punishment sagas. It is fully possible for one to believe in a Second Coming and a Day of Judgment and yet to feel sympathy for and a willingness to work with those one suspects may face divine judgment. Working with such groups around a set of specific issues even as we differ on others may both advance agendas in which we believe as well as open minds to further exploration of their fundaments. It is easy for intellectuals to assume that political differences can be most easily handled or consensus reached when participants share a moral or ideological foundation. But the process for many, even perhaps at some point for the intellectuals themselves, can work in the opposite direction or in a more interactional way. A concern over a closed school, the loss of a park, a dangerous intersection may have no solid grounding in any particular moral agenda, and it may be shared. Collaboration on such a problem may in some instances lessen demonization of those who are ethnically or morally different and open a willingness to engage in broader discussions. In politics one should strive for help where it exists, not merely because of the tactical advantage one may gain but also for the surprises it may open up.

These seemingly mundane activities can be a vital form of politics. Social organization is not arboreal, flowing as branches from one central tree trunk. The attempt to view it as such and act accordingly has had disastrous consequences. Dumm argues:

> Drawing vocabulary from [Deleuze and Guattari] regarding the distinction between arboreal and rhizomatic linkages, we may respond to formulations that absolutize the boundaries between something called the political and the rest of life by shifting a concern for the political to a concern for politics and by suggesting an alternative though less succinct aphorism to the one so favored by serious thinkers. To the claim where "everything is political, nothing is," we could respond: where politics is arboreal, institutions hierarchize and colonize meaning, establishing zones of legitimacy for privileged kinds of politics. Where politics is rhizomatic, institutions disperse meaning and pluralize the dangers and powers of politics. In all cases, politics exists as a capacity and as a yearning.[24]

In a forthcoming book, *A World of Becoming*, William Connolly reminds progressives today of the damage that some on the New Left did by pushing a radical agenda in very provocative ways on a constituency little prepared for it. He suggests, correctly in my eyes, that we are still paying a price for it. To avoid the same mistake, the kind of micropolitics advocated above may play a vital role.

In addition to that, however, one can learn some lessons from a neglected aspect of prophetic Christianity. Romand Coles distinguishes between prophetic voicing and prophetic listening. The former speaks truth to power and is the more usual understanding of prophetic Christianity. Yet as Coles points out: "Were not Jeremiah and Jesus most profoundly astonishing listeners before they spoke their first unwonted and unwanted words?"[25] In an illuminating interpretation of Ella Baker, he points out:

> One of her chief objectives was to participate in building an organization in which teachers would above all "teach their capacity to learn," and leaders would aim to engender more leaders. Hence Baker sought to cultivate a profound "openness to experience" on the part of the organizers she helped teach: a strong sense that this was a chief quality that they themselves should seek to practice and engender in their efforts to organize radical-democratic communities of struggle. First and foremost, to change the world meant developing a practiced culture of people with discerning eyes and ears for present-yet-subordinated possibilities—for hopeful latencies—in self, in others, and in the surrounding world, possibilities that might be explored and refigured toward the "beloved community." Baker enjoined organizers to learn to see and solicit latencies: to "be able to look at the sharecropper and see a potential teacher...a conservative lawyer and see a potential crusader for justice." Yet to see, solicit, and nurture such latencies—and a sense of hopeful possibilities as such—SNCC organizers had to strive to exemplify a mode of engagement that was receptive and vulnerable to the manifest as well as to the latent specificities of the others one faced, rather than to seek to bend the world to fit rigid ideological frames.[26]

As Coles knows and points out, the concern about imposing rigid ideologies can go too far. In a world drenched in fundamentalist religious and economic ideologies and apocalyptic discourse amplified by a singular media, social change movements need alternative multicentered discourses and visions to address the very forces that discourage and repress grievances. Without some theoretical development and articulation to combat the status quo, listening and listeners can become co-opted into little more than personnel and strategies that reinforce and legitimize the status quo. Even the process of looking is not independent of theory. Baker could see the teacher in part because of a religious perspective that recognized the uniqueness of every person and was attuned to forces of repression and their effects. But a theory imbued political practice blind to the reservations of those they aim to help or to how theory plays are also unlikely to discover the teacher. Such practice yields bad theory and politics. These are tough balances to achieve, both for theorists and activists.

In this regard, Coles's comments on Harry Boyte's efforts to nurture and build more responsive and participatory workplaces are suggestive. There is much to commend in Boyte's emphasis on the workplace and his commitment to respond to and build on workplace grievances and frustrations. Nonetheless, an organizing focus that eschews systemic critique in an effort to be close to the people has major limits. It fails to address the larger market and macropressures that can make such endeavors less likely and sustainable. I agree with Coles that

> we need to proliferate critiques and constructive alternatives (across a variety of scales and time frames) that are offered *not above* the fray but *in the fray*; affirming contestation; soliciting the work of independent criticism and imaginative reconstruction from those newly drawn to practices of grass roots democracy; relentlessly striving to link far-ranging transformation to more immediate political challenges and engagements...we must articulate theoretical analyses, practical political work, and local and larger-scale experimentation that demonstrate ways in which the freer space it is possible to *open* in the midst of bureaucracies and markets can survive and *proliferate* in ways that transform currently hegemonic practices until the "powers that be"—that render them so vulnerable—are no longer dominant.

Coles adds that at the very least, the future of democratic engagement requires a more open and reflective conversation between proponents of a politics of inclusion, patient discernment and receptivity, and the politics of disturbance.[27] Encouraging such debates must be part of the theory and practices of deep pluralism.

Doomsday and the Left

Finally, everyday politics on the left needs to avoid its own doomsday scenarios. I have spoken of the limits and possible problems with predictions of inevitable ecological and economic catastrophe. But overarching many of these visions is a kind of political doomsday scenario in need of careful scrutiny.

It remains to be seen whether the Geitner/Obama bank bailout will restore health to the banking system. I doubt that it will, and I fear the political and economic consequences of that failure. In any case, the plan will be extraordinarily costly and is exceptionally unpopular. The early Paulson versions of the plan elicited a nearly 99 percent rejection. Geitner's plan to subsidize purchase of toxic assets was only slightly more popular—in part because it was more opaque.

Seldom has our democracy been as dysfunctional. On the eve of the 1960s turmoil, C Wright Mills spoke of a "Power Elite" controlling the nation's vital policy choices. More recently, Senator Durbin wondered if banks "don't own the place."

If by elite we mean a tight coterie of executives who collaborate to control outcomes, such a claim is too simplistic now. But the current triumvirate does have two traits in common. They have made immense profits from government in recent years and they have channeled much of this money back to both political parties. It is thus not surprising that big banks are treated differently than local banks or that Medicare for ALL is off the table.

Nonetheless modern capitalism as a system is not locked in place or suspended from one pivotal point. It is a looser assemblage of laws, institutional practices, and social mores that do not consistently or fully cohere. Faith in markets can easily be mobilized to fight the minimum wage or unions, but it can also be used to inspire greater resistance to banker bailouts. Bashing immigrants divides the working class, but can also focus anger on the companies and bosses who break the law by hiring them. Many businesses want tight borders as symbolism but not at the cost of their own hiring decisions. They cannot, however, be sure to get the former and avoid the latter. Aspirational politics, the dream that anyone can become rich, can drive many to resist proactive government, but it can also lead others to ask if the United States has any real equality of opportunity. How these cross-cutting and never fully coherent currents, laws, and practices evolve cannot be fully predicted or controlled, even by the most powerful capitalist agent or coterie of the powerful. Whether these potential strains can be mobilized to foster more justice and space for all citizens depends on another variable, the kind and quality of our politics.

This leads to another sense in which power elite talk is simplistic. Citizens are not absolutely powerless. They can pass the broad public campaign finance that states as different as Arizona and my home state of Maine have done. They can also demand media reform so that more voices are heard. The breakdown of the conventional press, the problems with digital piracy, controversies over access and control over the Internet create both problems and opportunities. Perhaps we can construct through our proliferating digital technologies many new ways to highlight issues and concerns neglected by the mainstream. That all of these goals remain aspirations for a large subset of the population shows that the "power elite's" domination is much less than complete.

In the long run, a new democratic capitalism is likely to be more politically as well as environmentally sustainable to the extent it becomes attentive to early, emerging rights claims and injustices such as hours reduction that are often off the radar of existing standards. If we are fortunate, progressives today may face the risk that the very success of their reforms in easing current distress and bringing new stability may force new rights claims on them. These may amount to more than extensions of existing rights. In 1930, who could have imagined discussions of the second shift? In the 1960s hardly anyone contemplated claims of a right to die.

Jane Bennett provocatively wonders how our politics might change if matter inorganic as well as inorganic, were regarded as having an active claim on our attention.[28] Perhaps in a world with more time and security we can learn to be enriched rather than automatically threatened when such claims confront us or even well up in our own consciousness.

I cannot predict the future shape of capitalism. The system is shaken and its current leaders are neither as monolithic nor all powerful as some of the Left portray them. Nonetheless, some remain dangerous. In uncertain times, many of these leaders will demand a restoration of that uneasy mix of market fundamentalism for the masses and crony welfare support for elites, perhaps coupled with further ways to insulate their decisions from accountability. Too many others, including some small business leaders, professionals who benefit from special privileges, and white and blue collar workers who have been able to hang on and even more deeply resent "liberal elitism" or who identify with the rich and with the possibility of becoming rich may support them. In a world of uncertainty and flux, however, our task is to press ahead with a different vision, to appeal to those who are alienated and even to try to open up communication to those who remain tied in varying degrees to the old order.

What might a new and more humane capitalism look like? Americans have traditionally seen upward mobility, becoming rich, as the answer to the injustices and frustrations they feel. This aspirational politics is hard to uproot, even in the face of statistics that show how increasingly improbable that journey is. Nonetheless, the cultural forces may be shifting and positive alternatives are as important as demythologizing. In a world where obscene wealth and those who had pilfered and manipulated markets had been discredited, Americans might be less likely to canonize the rich or to aspire to be like them. They might discover more value in sharing a life of mutual creativity with their pluripotential world.

A new capitalism would include some traditional corporations, some unionized ones, but also a mix of many cooperative and worker-controlled ventures. Both the United States and Western Europe already have seen experiments along these lines. The survival of such efforts and sustainable capitalism will require national and international standards, such as limitations on toxic substances or child and prison labor sanctions. On the positive front, a deep pluralist capitalism requires strategies to gain more control over the use of social capital in the form of pension funds so that the surplus created by the public goes to foster both more democratic and environmentally sustainable production. It would include a safety net that reflected a society marked by less aversion to work because work itself had been reduced and restructured. A guaranteed annual wage and job retraining programs might replace the unemployment compensation and welfare mixes in established welfare states. More would be spent publicly to reduce the need for private consumption.

A deep pluralist suspects that such rights will only emerge and be effectively enforced through collaboration across states and nations on the part of environmental, social justice, and immigrant rights communities. But a deep pluralist will also be attentive to the role such rights claims can and must play in fostering greater economic diversity. Diverse communities can experiment with different modes of economic development and different understandings of the good life and the balance between private and public consumption. A bevy of federal or international rights claims that are exclusive, centrally defined, and enforced can become tools of power.[29]

Consider occupational safety as an example. One battle deep pluralists should fight is on behalf of the right to a safe workplace. This is hardly even acknowledged as a right today, but one can imagine a circumstance in which it was given priority. How shall that right be defined and enforced? One model, an idealized version of the present system, would involve a government agency drawing up standards, publicizing and seeking comments on these, and then sending inspectors to see that each workplace abides by those. Alternatively, the right cannot be merely insisted upon through grassroots coalitions but further developed and enforced by workers at the plant and industry levels. Workers can directly shut down unsafe workplaces, and businesses must have independent workers' safety teams whose members cannot be easily fired. The second model has advantages that are both practical and moral. Even a strong and committed federal government will be hard put to find and fund enough good inspectors for every workplace. But second, a bureaucratic centralized approach would tend to freeze workers' understandings of what a safe workplace is and how to achieve it. Workers can become rote followers of procedures that may keep them safe, but at the cost of innovative approaches. And the understanding of safety cannot evolve. Where workers at the plant level are part of the process of defining and implementing the right, one can imagine understandings of safety broadening to include a whole set of psychological questions, with further implications that would be hard to predict.[30]

The contested career of Elizabeth Warren provides another example of an expansive politics of regulation.

During a mid-September CNBC "Squawkbox," Bernie Marcus, the retired CEO of Home Depot, lovingly recounted his small business past and lionized his small business friends. They are all petrified by Washington. They hold government at fault for rising healthcare costs. They do not even blame insurance companies for raising premiums. These companies were also victims of the DC bureaucracy. Obama is imposing unions on business and is rewriting fifty years of labor law. Economic life would be better if DC just shut down for a year, with the exception of funding the war.

The business offensive resonates with an earlier populism. Nonetheless, it omits a crucial theme of the populist movement. Though populists, like Americans generally, have been suspicious of "big government," another major concern has always been the power of the large corporation. Today's corporate lobby is highly selective in its attacks on big government. Talk of the beauties of unregulated markets is used to forestall consumer or worker protection even as big business then reshapes regulations and subsidies to feather its own nest.

Would we be better off reverting to a truly unregulated market economy, as libertarians advocate? This is an economy where modern technology enables vast economies of scale—and also power abuses by market players—where technology has many spillover effects, and where economic and natural systems are in complex contact. Regulation of the competitive process, products, and technologies is imperative. Government has always played a large role in establishing markets. With every crisis the extent and intensity of government intervention grows.

Rather than romanticize small business, or fantasize about perfectly competitive, self-regulating markets, progressives should highlight the one-sided nature of government intervention and fashion more compelling paradigms of government regulation.

Let's ask the questions the sycophantic CNBC hosts probably never even imagines: (1) If small business is a big job creator, isn't it also, as Dean Baker has pointed out, the largest job destroyer? Though public policy should not tolerate unfair competitive pressure on small business, should these businesses be given a pass on occupational or environmental regulation? (2) With DC shut down and no food and drug regulations, would our drugs and food become more or less safe? Would "consumer confidence" grow? (3) If drug and medical costs are rising, what role has government subsidy to the health insurance and pharmaceutical industries played? As Baker has asked repeatedly, what role has government patent protection played, a market intervention that worried even Adam Smith? (4) Who has rewritten fifty years of labor law? Didn't Bush II's NLRB turn a blind eye to firing workers who even suggested an interest in unionization?

Of course, had this been a genuinely open conversation, the discussion might well have turned back on me. Current drug and food regulations failed to prevent the salmonella outbreak. And with regard to the larger financial crisis, deregulation and repeal of Glass-Steagall played a major role, but progressives must ask a deeper question. If markets are not as simple and self-regulating as some business ideologues imagine, can simple regulations or regulatory methods provide a one-time fix or guarantor of economic justice?

The United States follows a familiar pattern. When financial or public health crises erupt, there is a widespread demand that government clean up the mess and regulate. But the mess is often cleaned up at taxpayer expense and regulations often defended as permanent fixes. Mission accomplished! The world, however, changes over time and regulations come to be seen as archaic. The market is then valorized as dynamic.

Especially during crises the default position in the United States remains faith in markets. Corporate elites and the media sing a song of market flexibility and innovation to repel minimum wage laws and federal job creation even as they quietly use government to buttress their own position. Many middle- and working-class citizens, dreaming of becoming rich, join in celebrating the market. Then when corporation corruption of regulators or the cost and beneficiaries of bailouts is exposed, regulation gets a bad name.

To change this dangerous dynamic, the regulatory paradigm itself needs to be altered. Elizabeth Warren's role is significant not merely because she is unlikely to be captured by the industry but also because she understands the need for and possibility of a different kind of regulation:

> This is an agency that will be the first to be born digital. ..It will have the capacity to communicate with millions of Americans by just hitting a send button. It will also be an agency where millions of Americans have the capacity to communicate with the agency by hitting a send button...The notion that part of how one comes to understand and define the problems in the credit area will change if...this agency...hears from people who are experiencing it...it can be built into the research function of the agency...It changes the concept of how regulations work, of how regulations are tested, of how regulations are communicated and how they are enforced. So, I think of this as a real opportunity...to try a whole new model, to think about this agency from a different perspective.[31]

Stay tuned—or plugged in—to see whether Warren is given a real chance to launch the first digital regulator.

In this regard, I agree with Rom Coles's further suggestion that redistribution and investment of the community surplus occur at a variety of temporal as well as geographic sites. Thus hyper efforts to spur solar technologies could be coupled with "archaic efforts of radical slow-time agrarian practices..." What is envisioned is a "commingling of a multitude of different practices operating according to different traditioned teleologies and different paces of development and/or conservative stewardship."[32]

In my own thinking, I give pride of place both in the immediate context and in transformational potential to hours reduction and free time. All across the social spectrum citizens are concerned about the lack of time. Free time provides some break to reflect on the pace of life and the established social norms. It could inspire more individual creativity and more self-production of goods and services and that might in turn reverberate back on the more formal markets by giving a consumer more knowledge and making companies less inclined to manipulate. Advertising, at least of the manipulative type, might be scorned. Free time would also give citizens more opportunity to appreciate vibrant matter. That appreciation in turn might further elevate the interest in free time. A virtuous circle, albeit one likely to elicit surprises of its own.

CHAPTER SIX
NATIONAL SECURITY AND APOCALYPSE

In earlier chapters I have sketched ways in which existential anxieties played into both Manichean, apocalyptic understandings of contemporary issues and constricted policy debates. I have argued for broader religious dialogue, altered patterns of consumption and energy use, more leisure time and different modes of relating, as well as policy changes as a way of addressing not only the crises but the mindsets and ways of being in the world that inflect these crises.

But isn't national security one area where the threats are clearly "real," the dangers overwhelming, and the risk of apocalypse clear and present?

It is hard to dissuade many citizens from such a perspective, but with the occupation of Iraq and Afghanistan so clearly a failed, unnecessary, unjust, and expensive undertaking, there is space to probe the underlying motives and driving impulses of our foreign policy. Consideration of this policy, both as feeding and fed by the domestic policy and religious narratives I have discussed throughout the work, can suggest new foreign policy narratives and possibilities.

Global Conflict, the Nation State, and Fragile Identity

Conventional international relations theory has been dominated by two models, realism and idealism, or liberalism, to employ the terminology of some introductory texts.[1] The former assumes that each nation pursues its own interest. War is likely or inevitable in a world with no hegemon. Peace can be achieved—if ever—only through a balance of power among nations. Idealists view world peace as springing from a set of universal principles or procedures that nations can and will eventually adhere to. The prospects for peace can be improved by trade and economic development among nations. International organizations and collective legal and moral standards can enhance the process.

Despite their differences, both theories assume that nations are stable, natural entities and that the world is, or at least is capable of being, understood. Recent events, however, have given pause to such perspectives. With the end of the Cold War, several theorists speculated on the ways a peace dividend, the end of nuclear standoff, and the growing prosperity of market societies and free trade could create new possibilities of global peace and prosperity. Today, however, the "winner" of the Cold War finds itself beset by anxiety about terror. Its economy and the international economic system it sponsored are near collapse. Neither established IR theory even remotely predicted such a transformation. This failing is an especially hard blow for theories that place such value on the possibility of prediction. Perhaps the deficiencies of these two established traditions should open some space for consideration of alternative perspectives.

In politics, several of our most pressing global problems now cross national boundaries in ways that seem to challenge the solidity of the national state and the notions of an orderly world. Hundreds of billions of dollars are traded in world currency markets at the touch of a computer key, destabilizing domestic currency markets. Pollution and deadly bacteria circle the globe. Millions of families are displaced by famine, war, and economic hardship. Nations depend on and fight over far flung resources.

More basically, nations are complex nodal points of divergent ethnicities, histories, religions, and modes of being. National anthems, flags, and World Cup soccer rivalries help fashion—often destructively and imperfectly—a core collective identity. Epidemics, economic cycles, mass media in turn each operate on their own time scales. Each interacts with the others in complex ways that further destabilize domestic identities and cultures, which are themselves rapidly disseminated across borders. All of these trends are unsettling and often provoke defensive reactions. Though it is a crude oversimplification, one could counter the current invocations of "a dangerous world out there" by suggesting that, rather than nations making wars to defend their interests, constructing threats and their attendant wars help establish the nation as a "real" collective entity. Finding a "dangerous world out there" can also encourage casting aspersions on domestic dissidents whose commitment to national ideals is viewed as incomplete.

In the face of these global contingencies, some theorists and politicians strengthen their commitment to the nation state and its borders and values. Boundaries must be enforced against immigrants, diseases and drugs more strongly quarantined, economic protectionism endorsed. Religious and ethnic fundamentalisms are strengthened. Other theorists fall back on a belief in international markets as a way for interests to be balanced in order to encourage orderly progress. A few others endorse the need for new instrumentalities of world government.

But a dissident group of IR theorists have questioned the adequacy of both the nation state as absolute and the epistemological realism that often accompanies it. These deep pluralist IR theorists assert that we have no unvarnished, utterly independent lens to view the events of world politics. We are interpreters of the texts of global politics, which are themselves interpretations put forward by government leaders and major media.

Deep pluralists are fascinated with the issue of identity. This is the frame that they use to interpret world events. "We" make war on "them," but just who we and them are and come to be defined as such is the vital question. I have already discussed the strategies by which identity is established through everyday domestic practices and politics as well as the dangers and injustices implicit in the propensity to convert difference into otherness.

International relations play an equally vital role in the process of establishing identity. Indeed these relations are an inseparable aspect of the process. Briefly put, conflicts among nations cannot be explained solely by reference to "objective" fights over land or resources. Thus opposition to the Soviet Union, though in part a matter of control over land, was also a struggle over identity. Some formerly classified National Security documents suggest that the very example of the Soviets, with a differing economic system that did not honor private property, was what disturbed and energized policymakers more than the possibility of military defeat at their hands. These documents show an emphasis on the Soviet Union as a "communist" nation rather than on its military prowess. And that system was readily associated with other reviled character defects. Communism equated with or encouraged free love and perverse sexuality. The Soviets were characterized in terms of the hated behaviors and beliefs attributed to earlier revolutionary or even precapitalist economies such as those of the Native Americans. Much of the language used to condemn the Soviets was the same as that used to denounce nineteenth-century socialist movements such as the Paris Commune, which certainly did not constitute a military threat to the United States.[2] Pushing our identity outward to include reference to the Soviets as a dangerous national countermodel (dangerous by its mere success even if it did not wish to invade us) was one part of affirming that domestic identity. The connection, however, also moved in the other way. Viewing domestic radicals as "inspired" or coerced by the Soviets diminished the legitimacy of any dissent against reigning US values.

A world governed by conflict is fostered through other linguistic and cultural techniques as well. We have video games making war into a game and we have other practices that make our games into war. Consider the way that sports in this society is militarized. The quarterbacks of our football teams and point guards in basketball are "field generals." Quarterbacks "throw the bomb." These tendencies are even more reinforced when, as now, wars are fought by drones through distant control rooms, insulating technicians from the direct human costs of war. From a deep pluralist reading, turning games into war and war into games eases any anxieties that war is unnatural or to be fully questioned.

Deep pluralist theorists view idealism and realism as theoretical tools that have the same aim as Cold War discourse. Their emphasis on fixed national identity, on laws, and on the possibility of neutral observers and discourse aims to buttress the process of building comprehensive identities and seal off consideration of gaps in that identity.

Both liberal idealists and realists place national security at the top of their agendas and differ primarily in their means. But in addition to treating as unproblematic the concept of nation, they are equally suspect for their treatment of the notion of security, which has an ambiguous heritage seldom recognized today. James Der Derian comments: "Coeval, however, with the evolution of security as a preferred condition of safety was a different connotation, of a condition of false or misplaced confidence in one's position. In Macbeth, Shakespeare wrote that 'security is Mortals cheefest enemie.'"[3]

As I write the final draft of this chapter (December 2010) political elites are outraged by the release of classified US Army intelligence cables regarding Afghanistan. They worry about increased risk to US soldiers and informers, but thus far no specific examples have been produced. That these cables will embarrass the United States and hurt its reputation abroad is also claimed, though not emphasized. From what has been revealed so far, a stronger case can be made on these grounds. But notice that this is exactly the kind of security about which Shakespeare worried, the smug belief that with us all is okay and above reproach.

The Quest for Winning Wars and Definable Moments

The current "war on terror" is governed by a rhetoric of security, but the complex history of that concept invites a question seldom asked. Are we seeking safety or a more hubristic denial or exclusion of modes of thought and being that challenge us merely by their existence?

From 9/11 on, US foreign policy can be viewed less as a succession of just wars and more as an effort by elites and many anxious citizens to find a war that could forge or renew a strong sense of national identity.

In the beginning, it was Afghanistan. Then it was Iraq, to be followed a few years later by threats to Iran. Now with Obama as president, focus has once again returned to Afghanistan. In each case, we were warned that the target du jour was the central source of dangers to our nation.

These serial invocations of threat have one clear lesson. However much Obama may wish to focus on the present and put aside recrimination over torture or lies about weapons of mass destruction, similar mindsets continue to govern US policy.

This became especially clear to me when, early in the Obama administration, Robert McNamara's death provoked a series of commentaries on Vietnam.

Robert McNamara's life sheds a new light on contemporary tragedy. Just weeks before his passing President Obama was pressuring reluctant Democrats to approve a strange hybrid measure that increased Afghanistan war funds while ponying up more for the IMF. It looked like war funding pared with a compensatory offering to the gods of peace, much like McNamara's career. The ultimate war technocrat shed his armor and morphed into a World Bank president supposedly committed to the developing world. He then capped his career by admitting how sorry he was for Vietnam.

Unfortunately, Obama appears hell bent on following McNamara not only in unjust wars but also in employing global financial institutions as the velvet glove to complement the iron fist of military power.

Resemblances to the domino theory and Viet Cong fear mongering could hardly be stronger for those of my generation. Earlier this spring the president proclaimed:

> my greatest responsibility is to protect the American people. We are not in Afghanistan to control that country or to dictate its future. We are in Afghanistan to confront a common enemy that threatens the United States, our friends and allies, and the people of Afghanistan and Pakistan who have suffered the most at the hands of violent extremists.[4]

Yet as the president spoke, even the mainstream media featured reports that should lead us all to worry about military involvement in the region. *New York Times* reported that the Afghan and Pakistan Taliban are burying their differences and uniting their forces in response to US military escalation.[5]

As for the power of the Taliban, Middle Eastern scholar Juan Cole wondered why "the Taliban...are considered such a big threat that the full might of NATO is needed...They have no air force, no artillery, no tanks. They are just small bands, apparently operating in platoons, who, whenever they mass in large enough numbers to stand and fight, can just be turned into red mist from the air."[6]

And as in Vietnam, the United States is supporting reactionaries in order to prevail in the dire conflict it has fanned. Cole points out that

> The US has actually only managed to install a fundamentalist government in Afghanistan, which is rolling back rights of women...In a play for the Shiite vote (22% or so of the population), President Hamid Karzai put through civilly legislated Shiite personal status law, which affects Shiite

women in that country. The wife will need the husband's permission to go out of the house, and can't refuse a demand for sex.[7]

Can we imagine Robert Gates someday confessing his mistakes? And then heading the World Bank or IMF to repent by "fighting poverty"?

McNamara hardly modeled even genuine penitence, which involves abrogating some power and wealth, something the United States has never done. McNamara's World Bank fought poverty by making huge loans to Latin America, leaving these nations with very unequal social systems from which American elites profited, and with unsustainable levels of debt. When world oil prices skyrocketed in the 1970s, he loaned more money—with harsh restrictions preventing government aid to the poor.

Obama now gives the secretive and insulated IMF more money to bail out European bankers. Western European bankers and governments, their own economies floundering, are unwilling to take the political risk of aiding Eastern Europe. Instead of the difficult but potentially more rewarding task of US-European collaboration on bigger joint stimulus packages, international banking regulation, and reform of the IMF and the World Bank, bankers will be bailed by international banking institutions as secretive as ever even as the European economy stagnates.

If there is a lesson in McNamara's passing even as the United States follows his dangerous military and fiscal course, it is one I take from Amherst College political theorist Tom Dumm's early critique of Obama's presidency. Dumm points out that recent US presidents have had a limited window of opportunity in which to accomplish major goals. Globalization and the attendant inequalities it has fostered have exacerbated fierce partisan divides. Obama did achieve some gains, such as a modest stimulus package, but in most instances he has followed the lead of the Bush administration.

President Obama's rhetoric is softer, but he continues to evade the requirements of habeas corpus and he has opposed efforts to examine abuses of the Bush administration. Why, Dumm asks, has this been the case?

He goes on to point out that every president since FDR has violated the Constitution in ways that are serious enough that if one were a stickler, these presidents would merit impeachment.

These violations have been connected to foreign policy, but they are also very much implicated in the politics of globalization and the Cold War. In all cases, presidents felt frustrated either by statutory constraints, or by the slowness of Congress to approve, or by the need to wave bloody flags in order to get Congress to move. What am I suggesting?

We believe in the Constitution, and we believe in the special fate of America. But we've not necessarily been well served by either belief during the past half-century. Obama,...may well need to imitate another great leader from the past. We need to look for a leader who has managed the decline of an imperial power, without destroying the world. I am referring to Mikhail Gorbachev, the last leader of the Soviet Union, who spoke the truth and led the Russian people past a system of government that no longer could be imagined to serve them.[8]

In the US case,

if we do not learn to live more humble lives, in diminished circumstances, and replace our foolish dreams of a return to the American century past, we will suffer a lot more than we will if we finally face the truth about the damage we have done to ourselves, the obsolete character of our governing institutions, and the failure of democracy that we have suffered in order to acquire this strange empire we are now losing.

The Politics of Cold War and Globalization

Thus far under Obama, despite some positive rhetorical flourishes, US policy continues to demonstrate the very lack of humility that contributed to and was reinforced by the Cold War. Obama remains beholden to the policy logics of his predecessors.

Even torture retains its viability. Conservatives decry the Obama administration's disavowal of torture, not merely to clear their names but to lay a foundation for future power. We are at greater risk of a terrorist attack because Obama has tied our hands, they claim. Obama has properly pledged to eliminate torture, but still retains indefinite detention of those enemy combatants the US government deems dangerous. Efforts to close Guantanamo have thus far fallen victim to Congressional opposition, even from many Democrats.

And should some such attack occur, they may have more leverage. All the more reason, both politically and morally, not to bury the past and to take a closer looks at the mindset that governed policy under Bush and has hardly gone gently into the night.

That the actual or documented possibility of attacks on one's citizens explain why this draconian approach remains viable is questionable when we examine the actions of other governments far more vulnerable to domestic terrorism. Glenn Greenwald pointed out:

While the US continues to debate whether it must imprison accused terrorists without charges or trial—and now even refuses to say whether it will release those who are given trials but then acquitted—numerous other countries are, with their actions, adhering to the values and principles which we, with words, righteously claim to embody.

Greenwald goes on to cite cases involving charges against terrorists in extremely bloody attacks in Turkey and Germany where defendants received expeditious hearings. Many were cleared for lack of evidence. He goes on to add:

> Giving real trials to people whom the state wants to imprison—even accused Terrorists—is what civilized, law-respecting countries do, by definition. By contrast, lawless and tyrannical states—also by definition—invent theories and warped justifications for indefinite detention with no trials. Before the U.S. starts talking again about "re-claiming" its so-called leadership role in the world, it probably should work first on catching up to the multiple countries far ahead of it when it comes to the most basic precepts of Western justice—beginning with what ought to be the most uncontroversial proposition that it will first give due process and trials to those it wants to imprison. Shouldn't the claim that the U.S. cannot and need not try Terrorist suspects be rather unconvincing when numerous other countries from various parts of the world—including those previously devastated by and currently targeted with terrorist attacks—have been doing exactly that quite successfully?

Greenwald's comments are commendable. In light of Dumm's comments, however, they suggest a further line of inquiry. To the extent Americans are convinced, and hold as part of their core identity a sense of exceptionalism they will be less inclined to address Greenwald's questions and more inclined to deny that we torture or at the very least to blame reported abuses on a few, low-level bad apples.

From Iraq to Iran—In Quest of Demons

Why some of the worst practices of the Bush administration persist is further illuminated by another look back at the Bush administration's 2007 attempt to shift popular focus to Iran.

In 2007 the press was full of reports that the United States might soon attack Iran, perhaps with nuclear "bunker buster" bombs? American planes were patrolling the border between Iraq and Iran, US forces were authorized to kill Iranian agents in Iraq, and two US aircraft carriers and missile defenses were in the Gulf.

These actions were accompanied by a rhetorical bellicosity not equaled since the invasion of Iraq. During a mid-February 2007 press conference the president asserted that an Iranian paramilitary group, the Quds

> was instrumental in providing these deadly IEDs to networks inside of Iraq. We know that. And we also know that the Quds force is a part of the Iranian government. That's a known. What we don't know is whether or

not the head leaders of Iran ordered the Quds force to do what they did. Either they knew or didn't know, and what matters is, is that they're there. What's worse, that the government knew or that the government didn't know?...What's worse, them ordering it and it happening, or them not ordering it and it happening?[9]

The way the Iran debate unfolded, especially in light of the failure to unearth any weapons of mass destruction in Iraq, leads me to believe that many Bush critics let themselves off the hook too easily when they blame Iraq on the president's lies. I have never been comfortable suggesting that the president was lying, not because that is a harsh accusation but because lying touches on questions of individual knowledge and motivation.

It has become popular now even in mainstream circles to charge that presidential lies about Iraqi weapons led not only to the war but also to widespread initial support for that war. Blaming the Iraq invasion and occupation on presidential lines takes the press and opposition political leaders off the hook. In the months leading up to the Iraq invasion, even the mainstream press contained occasional articles contesting the plausibility of the administration's claims about Iraq weaponry and Saddam's ability or desire to invade his neighbors, let alone to launch any direct attack on the United States. The mainstream treated the evidence even in their own papers with eyes wide shut.

Bush may have been lying about Iran as well as Iraq, but as I watched his February 2007 press conference, my impression was of an embattled man deeply convinced of the righteousness of his mission, a cause so good and noble that only a powerful and singularly wicked nation state could stand in its way. Iran has always been part of Bush's axis of evil. If the noble Iraq venture is collapsing, the fault must lie with powerful outsiders. The role of Saudi Arabian dissidents in aiding Iraqi Sunni attacks on US troops seems not to fit the president's Manichean view of the world.

A president on a mission, especially one who views that mission as inspired by God, may be singularly blind to counterevidence. Self-deception, at least in its practical implications, may be more dangerous than lying. Former *NY Times* war correspondent Chris Hedges has captured the ways in which financial and ideological/moral views may come together in a dangerous push toward ever-expanding war:

> What they've done is—or what Karl Rove has done—is essentially adopt a corruption of Leon Trotsky's notion of a permanent revolution—only, it's permanent war. Now, you know, the military-industrial complex, which is making huge profits off the war in Iraq, let's not forget, is essentially driving this administration. I think these people live in an alternate reality.

I think they really do believe that they dropping cruise missiles...against supposed sites that they've targeted in Iran...will bring the Iranian regime down...But a strike against Iran would be, in the eyes of Shiites throughout the Middle East, a strike against Shiism. You have two million Shiites in Saudi Arabia, many of whom work in the oil sector...and, of course, most of Iraq is Shia. And I think that that kind of a hit...has the potential to unleash a regional conflict.[10]

Hedges greatest fear is that the resulting economic and political instability would expand the opening to cultural and political currents in the United States committed to imposition of their Manichean worldview. The Patriot Act and the repression it has encouraged would be only a pale foretaste. Most disturbingly to Hedges was the relative quiescence of the 2008 Democratic candidates on the possibility of an Iranian invasion. He cited with horror Hillary Clinton's blank check to the president to take whatever steps regarding Iran he deemed appropriate.

Hedges was careful in his articulation of these as only possibilities. He was not presenting a left-wing version of inevitable Armageddon, though in subsequent work on the economic collapse he has verged on that. There is, however, ample reason to take action. A possible war on Iran, like the Iraq occupation, may well be driven as much by a persistent, often religiously based, impetus to divide the world into good and evil states and people and may lead to a chain of events that helps intensify the very divisions upon which the policy is based.

Unfortunately the Obama administration demonstrates how pervasive this worldview is among elites and much of the population. Though somewhat less bellicose, it feels compelled to remind us that no options are off the table. As the world's most heavily armed nuclear power, that language is ominous.

Cold War history may provide perspective on a world often defined as currently dominated by one superpower, but where that superpower sees itself as threatened and beleaguered and seems to need such a self-image.

State Funerals and Court Historians

State funerals in Western European monarchies have always been an occasion for court historians to spin lyrical sagas of a nation's many triumphs. Lacking royalty, the United States still has the corporate media. Increasingly dependent on government favors, they eagerly fill the void. The passing of Ronald Reagan was an occasion to trumpet once again the proudest claim of the Reagan hagiographers: The fortieth president's iron will, firm sense of right and wrong, and steady reliance on US military power won the Cold War and ushered in a new era of political freedom and prosperity.

A less sycophantic media would not take this claim at face value. The changes in the Soviet Union and Eastern Europe and in their relationship to the West were the work of many leaders, grassroots dissidents, and intellectual currents Reagan neither controlled nor understood. Reagan often impeded rather than advanced those changes, and the military and ideological excesses of the Cold War bear some responsibility for current global crises.

Reagan is famous for his stinging repudiation of the "evil empire." The line was purportedly a wake-up call not only to Soviet leaders but also to a US foreign policy establishment that had become too comfortable with their Soviet counterparts. Yet repressive and authoritarian as the Soviet bloc was, by the early 1980s it already had become little more than a paper tiger. In an *LA Times* op ed, Andreas Szato, director of the National Arts Journalism Program at Columbia and a former Hungarian conscript, characterized a 1983 military training exercise as

> logistical disarray and utter ineptitude. We were dropped off in a valley somewhere; old trucks dressed up as enemy targets awaited our attack. But the ammunition supplies were late in reaching the artillery units behind us. Hours later, when the cannons unloaded their ordnance, they hit everything but their intended targets.[11]

Well before the end of Reagan's first term, the Soviet bloc was in deep crisis. Many Eastern block dissidents did value market freedoms, but few wished to dispense with all safety nets. The crisis was also indebted to something Reagan admirers hardly ever celebrate—the culture of the 1960s and its pluralistic vitality. Historian John Patrick Diggins points out that the overthrow of the Soviet block represents

> the three great antagonists of conservatism: the youth culture, the intellectuals of the '60s generation and the laboring classes that still favored Solidarity over individualism. American neoconservatives like William J. Bennett are haunted by the crisis of authority at home and see knowledge threatened by skepticism everywhere. In *Why We Fight*, Bennett claims that we are in Iraq to take a stand for truth and to rescue "moral clarity" from the quicksand of liberal "pseudosophisticated relativism." But in Eastern Europe, intellectuals took a stand for courage without certainty... The playwright Vaclav Havel, associated with Charter 77 and the Prague Spring, took his bearings from the metaphysical anxieties of Martin Heidegger and the existential meditations of Franz Kafka and Samuel Beckett. Against totalitarianism such writers stood for skepticism, irony, uncertainty, and a refusal to believe in and yield to an authority that prefers to possess truth rather than pursue it. Soviet communism ended the way American liberalism began: "Resist much; obey little," as Walt Whitman wrote.[12]

Gorbachev and a new generation of Soviet leaders became convinced that high levels of military spending and political and economic repression were counterproductive. They offered political and economic reforms and disarmament initiatives. Yet as William Blum, author of *Killing Hope: U.S. Military and CIA Interventions since World War II* points out, Reagan impeded this process. Blum summarizes and corroborates charges by former Soviet ideologue Georgi Arbatov and George Kennan, the foremost US architect of containment, that Reagan's refusal to negotiate slowed reforms and weakened Gorbachev's internal leverage. Only after the Iran Contra scandal was Reagan willing to engage in substantive negotiation with the Soviets. That belated change of course, whatever its motive, was the one bright spot of the Reagan presidency.[13]

In the light of the Iraq War, one would think that even our mainstream media would recognize that talk of an evil empire is more than catchy rhetoric. The Manichean impulse to treat all opposition to US interests and policies as communist-inspired left an ugly and destructive residue. As Diggins points out, "Thus the fall of the shah in Iran in 1979 was alleged to be as ominous as the fall of the czar in Russia in 1917—not because it presaged a religious fundamentalism that one day would become America's mortal enemy but because it signaled the 'prelude' to communism's inevitable march into the oil states." The Reagan administration "saw nothing wrong with America arming Osama bin Laden and Saddam Hussein and establishing a covert alliance with the House of Saud, which would turn out to be the financial angel of al-Qaeda."

Before we cheer "victory" in the Cold War, we would do well to examine the meaning of victory and the price paid for it. Burdened by a half century of fruitless efforts to match US military escalation, Russia is economically eviscerated, and its democracy is flawed and tenuous. Yet it remains armed to the teeth. In an op ed for the *LA Times* in April 2007, Robert McNamara and Helen Caldicott reminded us that Russia still has over eight thousand nuclear weapons targeted at US cities and that its

> early warning system is decaying rapidly. As always, the early warning systems of both countries register alarms daily, triggered by wildfires, satellite launchings and solar reflections off clouds or oceans. A more immediate concern is the difficulty of guaranteeing protection of computerized early warning systems and command centers against terrorists or hackers.[14]

The world is awash with terrorists, many of whom regard the United States as their mortal enemy. Terrorism has more than one parent. It would be as misguided to attribute terrorism solely to the failures of US policy as to evil foreign empires. Nonetheless, as our citizens mourn President

Reagan's passing, a more nuanced assessment both of the Cold War and the former president might be in order.

Dissent and Security at Home

The Cold War may suggest other lessons and questions as well. That war may have been as much about the containment of dissent at home as about physical security from either domestic or foreign incursions. We must resist the assumption that dissent is disloyalty and the accompanying notion that greater surveillance of dissent brings greater security at home.

A relative of mine, an ardent Bush defender, took comfort in President Bush's no-holds-barred pursuit of terrorists both at home and abroad. To concerns that warrantless wiretaps represent a threat to valued personal liberties, she responded: "There are dangerous people in our midst who are out to destroy us. Law abiding folks, even those who disagree with the President, have nothing to fear from the President. I have nothing to hide; the President can listen in on my conversations if he wants to."

Perhaps the administration's suggestions that opponents of its policies are aiding and abetting an enemy (treason) may be instances merely of rhetorical overkill. They should be condemned, but as with all citizens action should be taken more seriously than words. It is in the area of actions, however, that concerns about the violation of civil liberties should be the strongest.

The Bush administration found itself increasingly on the defensive in both domestic and foreign policy. It viewed itself and this country in a protracted battle against evil agents. Both electoral concerns and its very sense of its purpose and worth gave the administration incentives to find ever more dangerous threats to our health and safety.

Skeptics and administration critics pointed out that news of many suspected plots come at suspicious times. The purported plot to explode liquid bombs on overseas flights to the United States came when Bush's top Democratic apologist, Joe Lieberman, had just suffered a stunning loss in a primary. The president's party appeared to be headed to defeat into the fall election.

Some of the suspects in several purported planned bombings have been released. But what is more disturbing is that the major media rarely did much follow-up reporting on much ballyhooed plots. A plan by al Qaeda to fly a hijacked plane into a LA skyscraper, revealed in early 2006 by the president, proved to be a hoax. A purported plot in Britain to unleash deadly ricin, revealed by Vice President Cheney in January 2003, was almost immediately proven false, but British authorities withheld this finding for another two years.

Other terror alerts have proven to be inflated at best and may have amounted to nothing beyond idle speculation on the part of disgruntled citizens. These might be placed in the category of "I wish my boss were dead," sentiments that if taken seriously might make many American workers economic terrorists. Blum reminds us of George Orwell's cautions about thought crimes. Most of these suspects

> haven't actually DONE anything. At most, they've THOUGHT about doing something the government would label "terrorism"... perhaps just venting their anger at the exceptionally violent role played by the UK and the US in the Mideast and thinking out loud how nice it would be to throw some of that violence back in the face of Blair and Bush. And then, the fatal moment for them that ruins their lives forever... their angry words are heard by the wrong person, who reports them to the authorities.[15]

Worse still, there is reason to worry that some of the agents being asked to defend us encourage the disgruntled to express their anger. Agents often go beyond monitoring or reporting on such conversations to suggesting violent tactics to the aggrieved. Such tactics, known as entrapment, are illegal but are often employed.

Authorities may not merely entrap, but now often file away information for highly questionable use at a later date. Mainstream media report that law enforcers now act so swiftly against al-Qaeda sympathizers that they often grab idiots whose plots amount to little more than pipe dreams.[16] Add to these practices the concern that some of the noncitizens with whom one speaks may be reported to or detained by foreign states that practice torture. When the administration warned Americans shortly after 9/11 to be careful about what we say, it evidently was issuing sound advice, advice made prudent by its own agenda.

The Bush administration marketed itself as the only viable defense against terrorism. Yet its tendency to equate differences in thought and lifestyle with threats to physical security in fact make us ever less secure. In this respect, it mimics the least savory aspects of our heritage and gives lie to the claim that the United States is a model of freedom.

Democrats, like almost all Americans, are repulsed by terrorism. It is the role of preemptive wars, like Iraq, in eradicating terror that at the very least must be subject to a debate free from demonizing charges of disloyalty. As early as 2004, reports by The International Institute for Strategic Studies in London suggested a different view: "A rump leadership (of al Qaeda) is still intact and over 18,000 potential terrorists are at large with recruitment accelerating on account of Iraq."[17]

Opposition—even well founded—to US policies on Iraq, Palestine, Israel, and Saudi Arabia does not justify terrorism. Nonetheless, terrorism is not merely a random and totally inexplicable act. Unwillingness to examine the depth of political opposition, even among many secular Middle Eastern groups, severely limits our ability to address the condition in which terrorism is more likely to thrive. It leaves us in little position to lay the educational, economic, and political foundations that help citizens understand and support civic norms and nonviolent means of expressing grievances. Even in the short run, many secular political leaders in the Middle East who opposed bin Laden will be less inclined to share their knowledge and their resources. They will fear collaboration with a government that casually jails Arabs, treats all disagreement as a threat, and reduces terrorism simply as "hatred of us for what we are."

Here at home, the Patriot Act continues the tradition of legislative initiatives that judge the threat to national security by the degree of dissent expressed. Today many look back in shame on the 1940s and 1950s, when membership in left-leaning organizations could disqualify one for a job. But scrutiny went even beyond mere membership. It was not uncommon for congressional committees and J. Edgar Hoover's FBI to treat advocacy of racial equality or women's rights as presumptive commitment to communism and thus as disloyalty.

Hoover's mindset seemed firmly entrenched in the Bush administration. An FBI memo leaked in November 2003 both codified and make explicit the administration's practice. It suggests the government now intends "a coordinated, nationwide effort to collect intelligence" on the antiwar movement. The memorandum singled out lawful protest activities.[18]

Rather than fighting terror, the Bush administration was engaged in a cultural war to validate and secure its own conception of ethics, politics, and economics. Its efforts to limit democracy's proudest moments—when we have forged more space for disparate ways of life and political perspectives to coexist—are making us ever more fearful and less physically secure.

One of the most shocking revelations was that president Bush authorized the National Security Agency to conduct warrantless wiretaps on American citizens. Media should not have been surprised. In the months following 9/11, the Justice Department itself documented extensive violations of the rights of immigrant Americans summarily arrested and detained without formal charge or trial. That same Justice Department also conceded that videotapes of prisoners taken to assure humane treatment and minimal due process had been destroyed, contrary to the Department's own standards.

Why are these dangerous and draconian procedures needed? In the case of the warrantless intercepts, existing law already allows the president

to seek retroactive approval for such surveillance. Law enforcement officials can move as quickly as circumstances require. It is hard to avoid the
conclusion that the Bush administration simply wanted to be able to act
without any challenge or accountability. An administration that treated
criticism of the war as unpatriotic and that also deemed scholarship assessing the precursors or motives for terrorism as sympathetic with terrorism
was as afraid of dissent as of violent acts.

Our history suggests that restrictions on political freedoms or rights of
association have hardly enhanced our security and may even be counterproductive. Jeff Milchen of Reclaim Democracy, a project devoted to restoring
constitutional rights, suggests that "allowing officials to spy on citizens
based on their politics or to search property without judicially scrutinized
evidence typically wastes resources. Martin Luther King Jr. was the target
of countless federal agents' investigations that produced mountains of files
but no evidence of dangerous activity." He also points out:

> the most dangerous terrorists tend to keep a low profile, rather than advo-
> cating publicly for social change. The Sept. 11 attackers, for example,
> evidenced little or no public political or religious activism. Government
> security agencies did have evidence that should have led to the investigation
> of some of the Sept. 11 hijackers, but that crucial evidence apparently was
> lost in an information overload.[19]

Congress needs to push for hearings not merely on the NSA scandal
but on the Bush and Obama administration's broad civil liberties record.
Who has been tapped, toward what ends, and with what implications for
democratic debate?

If physical safety is our real concern, full debate and access to information are vital. Terrorists have many ways of learning about the source and
nature of our chemical and nuclear repositories, but access to information
is a key resource for citizens concerned with evacuation plans and long-
term safety decisions.

Perfect physical security is unlikely ever to be attained, and much of
the modern technological progress we most admire may also paradoxically
increase our risks. The 1984 Union Carbide catastrophe in Bhopal, India,
killed far more people than any domestic act labeled as terrorism. A private corporation cut corners on basic safety and denied the public access
to vital information. Rather than face the implication of such dangers, the
administration prefers to live in an intellectual cocoon. Protecting corporate prerogatives and limiting public debate is the real subtext of this
administration's "war on terror." Both security and democracy are the losers
in this process.

As for torture, perhaps the saddest legacy of the Bush II years, there
is need for a much more complete debate. There are more noble reasons

to oppose torture, but torture almost always leads to false or misleading information that takes the police up many blind allies. Entrapment, surveillance, and torture, often focused on distrusted populations, also multiplies suspicion among the very groups whose cooperation is most needed in order to root out the real terrorists.

There is, of course, no guarantee in a world of some flux and uncertainty that honest and principled police work concentrating on cases where there was probable cause to suspect imminent violence will forestall all terrorism. But even if absolute freedom from terrorism could be achieved only by the president's methods, I will opt out of his war. A world where one cannot practice thought experiments at home, express one's anger or frustrations free from concerns about how an unknown and unpredictable third party will distort or manipulate these thoughts, or endanger those with whom we speak, is a world that has lost much of the joy and expressiveness that make life worthwhile.

In the anxious world fostered by declining economic security and the rapid and seemingly uncontrollable movement of capital and stateless immigrants, the so-called terror war has become reminiscent of the worst moments in our heritage. Its defenders remind us of ticking time bombs and hint at or openly defend torture as an antidote. Yet the horrible scenarios of which they speak reflect as much the dangers of modern technology as the demonic minds of terrorists. And scenarios of salvation from terror through torture of an evil and omniscient terrorist may reflect as much nostalgia for a controllable world as realistic strategy to overcome terror. So too may be Barack Obama's vision of a world where terror is "directed" at the United States from small cells in Afghanistan or Pakistan. Bin Laden had suggested that the US view of the world is analog whereas al Qaeda is part of a digital world. Resistance springs from many centers and takes different forms. As James Der Derian puts the case so succinctly:

> The international danger posed by failed states exists largely in relation to the transnational insurgency movements (TIMs) housed within those nations, and the conflict that ensues between TIMs and sovereign states. These transnational non-state actors may be referred to as "digital" states in light of Osama Bin Laden's argument that the United States is forcing nations like Saudi Arabia, Egypt, Iraq, and Sudan into "paper statelets" to further the "crusader-Zionist alliance." "Paper" is an apt adjective in that it is an analog form of communication/inscription, and thus a traditional means of conveying and systematizing authority. What is meant here as traditional, is a notion of sovereignty conceived of by Western sources. The opposition to a paper state would be a digital state, something ephemeral, mobile, and non-national, which unlike paper, can be reconstructed and reconstituted by the user. It is apparent that Bin Laden has no desire to acclimatize his Islamist cause with all other movements and beliefs. Nonetheless, al Qaeda has gone to great lengths to accommodate

and support a variety of Islamic fundamentalist causes, both Shi'ite and Sunni, ethno-nationalist movements, and separatist groups throughout the world. The threat also has become digital in that individuals and groups, not directly associated with al Qaeda, are committing attacks in its name. A virtual brotherhood has emerged, which allows individuals to identify with the struggle while not physically connected to the movement.[20]

The Bush administration sought to assure the rest of the world that it was not engaged in a war against Islam. But indiscriminately jailing Middle Eastern males made that an impossible sell. The FBI has a sorry history of equating opposition to US foreign policy with espionage. The administration's constitutional coup increases the likelihood of terrorism. Legitimate dissent is quashed and willingness to cooperate with police diminishes among suspect and victimized communities.

Yet as I write this chapter (December 2010), the Obama administration's refusal to disavow preventive detention and to abide by habeas corpus continues to arouse concern not only among civil libertarians but also among many of those whose cooperation is needed.

An effective antiterrorism campaign—through collaborative international intelligence and law enforcement—is ill served by the blatant denial of civil liberties to populations marginalized here at home and under attack abroad. If we are genuinely concerned with our physical survival, the four best steps we could take would be to enhance and modernize our nation's transportation, energy, manufacturing, and health infrastructures, reaffirm our commitment to basic civil liberties—especially for marginalized members of our society—end the war in Iraq and Afghanistan, and adopt a more even-handed posture toward the Palestinians. As for terror itself, international police work—collaboration with governments with whom we may not share economic or political ideals over a common concern with the safety of our citizens—may be the best digital response to the digital threat articulated by Bin Laden. Yet the current sanctification of one more war and continued support for an expansionist Israel drains us of the funds and goodwill so badly needed.

Private Wealth and Peace of Mind

Progressives complain that economic gains during the 1990s went disproportionately to the rich. As government's tax and regulatory role diminished, wealthy Americans achieved unprecedented growth in their relative and absolute affluence. Poor and working-class citizens witnessed economic stagnation or even declines in their net worth. Nonetheless, however accurate this picture is—and I have endorsed it—it begs an important question. Has the quality of life and physical security for wealthy Americans improved along with their wealth?

Wealth may not buy happiness, but at least private wealth ought to enhance one's ability to travel, to obtain state of the art health care, and to rest secure in one's home. Yet even before the terrorist onslaught, immense wealth may have been losing some of its capacity to assure these goods. Indeed, terrorism may have inadvertently exposed growing gaps in a public sector vital to the security even of the wealthy. These deficiencies may constitute little reason to pity the wealthy, but they should encourage us to take a closer look at the motives for and defenses of the acquisition of wealth.

In an outstanding piece in the August 5, 2001, *LA Times*, Peter Gosselin commented that the boom of the last decade, unlike that of the 1950s and 1960s, left us with no "public monuments." The earlier era brought the interstate highway system and universal phone service, but after the last decade of growth, "Americans are twice as likely to own a personal computer...But they're also more likely to run short of the power needed to operate it. They can purchase the most technologically advanced health care on Earth but face a rising risk of being unable to find an emergency room...They can buy Perrier but can't always get clean tap water."[21]

Gosselin's focus on how the wealthy are now affected by these trends is distinctive. Years ago, the *Nation Magazine* reported that realtors in Los Angeles marketed properties based in part on the quality of the neighborhood's air. Some parts of a metropolitan area still are more polluted than others, but smog now increasingly blankets whole regions. In addition, vacation hideaways frequented by the rich, such as Mount Desert Island, Maine are at the end of the pipeline for noxious urban air. I wonder how many wealthy visitors were unable to enjoy mid-afternoon tennis or golf during the days coastal Maine was under a smog alert this summer.

Gosselin's example of Perrier is revealing. Years ago wealthy summer residents here dug wells to avoid the chlorine taste of "town water." Yet with the proliferation of large lot suburban developments and individual septic systems, well water itself became problematic. Bottled water then became the apparent answer for those willing to spend what it takes to obtain safe water. Nonetheless, the bottled water industry itself is unregulated. Consumers are putting their trust in a corporate logo.

The search for paradise through private affluence and free markets has ended up tainting not only air and water but even vacation travel as well. Suburban sprawl makes inter- and intracity travel increasingly time consuming and dangerous. States now face the dual problem of ever more roads to maintain and a reluctance to fund the public sector. The American Society of Civil Engineers reports that: "One-third of the nation's major roads are in poor or mediocre conditions," which contributes to "as many as 13,800 highway fatalities annually."

Wealthy citizens have historically minimized delays and dangers by hopping on airplanes. The health of the ambient air on airplanes, however, has now become a concern. An adequate response to new epidemics may well depend on the resources and training of state-level public health personnel. Nonetheless, the rabid budgetary fundamentalism discussed in chapter four includes continuing opposition to the Federal assistance needed if states, which face the greatest fiscal crisis since the Depression, are to avoid further massive cuts in many essential public services.

Even now, when injury or diseases strike in the course of travel, the wealthy may face unaccustomed challenges. They are not turned away from an emergency room because they lack health insurance, but emergency room capacity has itself often been downsized in response to the relentless pressure for profit maximization.

Wealth can mitigate every one of these problems, but it is hard to argue that the decay of such "public monuments" as quality medical centers, public transit, clean air, and pure water doesn't take a toll even on the most affluent. Might not their quality of life improve with the tradeoff of a little more in taxation for improvement in public amenities? If the answer is yes, then one can only conclude that for some resistance to taxation and the public sector is rooted in something more than economics. Private affluence and freedom from any publicly imposed limits have become the core of personal identity and ends in themselves. Sadly, an obsession with these private liberties may trump even one of their best historic justifications, enhancing the quality of life.

On Wars, Reunions, and the Politics of Everyday Life

Just as more effective security will require attention to the politics of our daily public spaces, so also will it take an end to the war that increases threats to our lives and robs us of the treasure needed to rebuild that infrastructure.

In June of 2007, I attended my Amherst College (1967) reunion. It was an occasion to catch up with old friends, but I was also saddened by a recitation of the names of too many classmates who had passed away before their time. This reunion, however, was notable for its distinctly political focus on the many other men and women who are being killed well before their time. The organizers had scheduled a symposium on the political evolution of our generation, which graduated from college with eyes fixed on Vietnam. For most students today, however, Iraq seems at most a distant distraction. These generational differences constitute a special challenge to those of us whose early political commitments were so heavily shaped by Vietnam.

Commentators remind us that military strength in Vietnam peaked at about half a million men, whereas US troop strength in Iraq may reach only 170,000. These figures, however, are deceiving. The US presence in Iraq now also includes approximately 125,000 employees of private contractors, most of whom are performing functions once carried out by active duty military personnel.

With nearly two-thirds of the highest Vietnam era military presence in Iraq, with occupation expenditures topping one hundred billion a year, and with daily reports of substantial US casualties, comparisons with Vietnam era politics are irresistible. Two years before my graduation, Amherst gained national notoriety when five graduating seniors publicly walked out on Defense Secretary Robert McNamara's commencement address. By the time of my graduation, President Johnson faced the prospect of an antiwar challenge to his own renomination. Months later he stepped aside.

As noted earlier, President Obama has recently been granted funding to continue to expand the Afghanistan War even as withdrawal for Iraq remains partial and credible reports suggest that the military presence there will remain substantial for at least a decade. Why is there no political movement that might give the Democrats the spine to provide more than a temporary inconvenience to the president?

The increasingly incestuous relationship between mainstream media and the incumbent administration is one factor. The Bush administration was clever enough to embed reporters during field operations and forbade pictures of caskets. The US media have always been cheerleaders for war, but today it is even harder for them to jump off the ship. By 1968, longtime CBS Evening News anchorman Walter Cronkite had become disabused of his government's portrayal of the war and presented footage that challenged prevailing Pentagon reports.

Today star media players, such as Dan Rather, seem able to express dissent—if ever—only after leaving their positions. Media as institutions are just as embedded as their correspondents. TV networks are part of vast conglomerates and depend on administration approval for new mergers and acquisitions. They also rely on direct government subsidy, license renewals, and trade treaties—all of which exert a huge impact on the bottom line. The very definition of journalism has become altered, with journalists viewing success in terms of access to high administration officials. Inside gossip and personal style trump issues as subjects of media attention.

For their part, Democrats have allowed the media to define the boundaries of the possible. Most are shameless triangulators. Since most Americans still get the bulk of their political information from television, media labels count for a lot. The trick for politicians is to appeal to their base while finding subtle ways to reassure the media as to one's conventionality and thus avoid the most damaging labels in US politics, radical or unelectable. Thus many Democrats today suggest they oppose the current course of the war but "support the troops" and defer management of the war to the president.

But perhaps the largest reason that presidents rests easy on the throne is the absence of a full-blown student movement. Though many college students are involved in antiwar protests, their efforts lack the numbers and the intensity of an earlier generation.

This absence has several causes, including the rise of consumerism and a quarter century attack—permeating all sectors and demographics—on the very possibilities of politics. Foremost, however, in framing a 1960s student movement was the draft. Facing the strong possibility of being drafted in 1967, most of my classmates and I spent endless hours calculating how a choice of jobs, graduate schools, ROTC, and so on might allow us to avoid being drafted into a war most of my friends and I did not support. A high-school teaching position won me a "national security" deferment from my local Detroit area draft board.

Although virtually none of my friends served in Vietnam, the war was continually part of our consciousness—if only because the inequities of the draft did require some skill to navigate and the steps taken to avoid the war forced dramatic shifts in life plans. Should we conclude from this, as some on the Left have done, that one way to ramp up opposition to the occupation of Iraq is to restore the draft?

Today college students need not fear a draft. Only those middle-class youth who are ardently committed to the war will choose to serve. The war is fought by professional soldiers who need active combat on their resumes and by the economically marginalized. The latter "choose" military service for its advertised—and exaggerated—economic opportunities. A few on the political Left seek restoration of the draft, both for the sake of equity and in the hopes of reigniting a vigorous antiwar effort.

In our political economy, however, any "universal" draft would probably contain even more loopholes than the Vietnam-era draft. Rather than seek restoration of the draft, which might also encourage further adventurism, or lecture fortunate middle-class youth that they are not doing enough, my generation might remind ourselves of the benefits we received from an inequitable draft. A young inner-city Detroit black man may have died because I avoided service. I can't restore that life but guilt could take a productive turn. We can ask if there are other steps we might take to spur new activism and save the lives of today's youth both here and in Iraq.

We all need to consider whether and how to reinvigorate such older strategies as civil disobedience, campaigns to defeat prowar Democrats in primaries, letters to the editors of local papers, and so on. But in addition to such an approach, we might broaden our sense of political discourse. Politics occurs in our churches, over our back fences, in our dinner table conversations, in our emails. When friends or acquaintances suggest that the occupation of Iraq or Afghanistan is needed to prevent terrorists from invading our shores, we can reply by asking them to read the news summaries of the leaked government cables from Afghanistan, clearly indicative of the havoc the war has wrought and its role as a recruiter for the Taliban. In addition, one hundred billion dollars a year squandered in Iraq is money we do not have to better secure our ports, our chemical plants, our levees, and to build the forms of transit that might make us less dependent on a turbulent Middle East.

For the Democrats and the media who reiterate mantra-like the notion that the Constitution makes George W. Bush or Barack Obama commander-in-chief, we should remind them that the Constitution clearly gives Congress the right to defund even declared wars. As Alexander Hamilton points out in The Federalist Papers, and even George Will agrees:

> The legislature of the United States will be OBLIGED, [by the constitutional provision that Congress has the power to raise and support armies] once at least in every two years, to deliberate upon the propriety of keeping a military force on foot; to come to a new resolution on the point; and to declare their sense of the matter, by a formal vote in the face of their constituents.[22]

Politics also occurs in our churches—and not just when religious leaders endorse causes or candidates. Every Sunday, my wife and some friends read the names of that week's war dead at her local church. Just seeing or hearing these names and ages in the company of those who share this grief makes the deaths seem more tragic. Like my reunion, it reminds me of the painful reality of the death of friends and colleagues, but the names of men and women at the formative stage of their lives also evoke another thought. We pass on to our children a given name and a surname. The human capacity to name is a fascinating and fortuitous aspect of social and biological evolution. For me names evoke a sense of both continuity and change. Parents invest much creative energy is naming children, whose lives in turn may flow in many different ways. With every dead young soldier, that individual promise has been snuffed out well before its time.

Let's find more daily acts to bring this war to a close.

Epilogue: Lessons from Lysistrata

Women as war opponents is hardly a surprising theme today.[23] Cindy Sheehan, the mother of a soldier killed in the Iraq War, is the most conspicuous antiwar voice in the United States today. Mainstream commentators and even some versions of feminism assume that women are "by nature" more pacific or even more noble. Yet one of the first great literary celebrations of the case against war by a woman, Aristophanes's play Lysistrata, shows that the choice of a woman as an antiwar voice can rely on other, often not so positive, stereotypes about women. The choice of women can draw on a sense of women's ordinariness, their narrow daily burdens, and even their earthly passions. That women, who were thought to be confined to and thoroughly absorbed by the realm of blowing noses, could manage to coordinate and argue for a comprehensive antiwar analysis and strategy carried surprise and shock value in a culture where only men were regarded as capable of rising above passion and having the knowledge to participate in serious affairs. But just as the Montgomery, Alabama, activists I discussed in chapter one drew on existing social stereotypes even as they challenged conventional forms of racism in other arenas, Aristophanes must first draw on and even reinforce some demeaning stereotypes about women in his quest to receive a hearing for his antiwar views. There is in this a lesson. Neoconservatives and even many liberals like to speak of national security and the peace and antiwar movements of international peace. But security, in its literal sense of freedom from care, and peace, in the sense of a quiescence above conflict in any form, are both ethically problematic. When the Romans, or any empire, make the world a desert and call it peace, it inflicts great harm. And faith in any set of international procedures, immigration regulations, environmental caps, financial regulations, or trade and nonaggression agreements as final antidotes to conflict can impose subtler but equally significant damage.

Let's start with the text of this classic. Athens is locked in a bitter and costly war with Sparta. The play's heroine, Lysistrata, calls a meeting of the women of Athens to propose that they withhold sex from their husbands until the latter agree to pursue peace initiatives. Just as surprisingly, she advocates an occupation of the treasury by older women to erect fiscal barriers to continuation of the war.

Aristophanes begins by replicating in amusing language the usual degrading stereotypes about women's normal trivial pursuits, a strategy sure to hold the attention of his all-male Athenian audience. When Lysistrata calls the meeting to present her plan, few women show up. She complains, and Calonice responds by citing the seemingly trivial tasks that are limiting these women: "It is not so easy getting out this early. We've got to do our husbands' little favors, we've got to get the servants out of bed, we've got to wash and feed and burp the kids" (I say seemingly trivial because these tasks don't seem to strike Aristophanes as important, but care of children is in fact vital) (lines 16–19).

Calonice also reinforces reigning sexual stereotypes about women. When Lysistrata suggests the matter for which she has called them together is very hard, Calonice responds in a way loaded with coarse sexual undertones: then why aren't we all here (line 24). A few lines down, Aristophanes bats us over the head with the stereotypes by having the women react with horror to the suggestion that they give up sex with their husbands in order to pressure them to end the war: "Through fire I would even walk. But as for fucking, no. There is nothing like it, dear Lysistrata" (lines 133–135). This leads Lysistrata to despair "We're nothing but a diaper and a bed."

These women also retain their acceptability to a male audience by sustaining other social conventions as well. They are upper-class women who express disdain for their own slaves. They fear they will arrive late at the citadel. They were "delayed by slaves and pushy bitches" (line 330).

But once having gained some sort of legitimate perch for their views by reinforcing degrading class and gender stereotypes, they then move to challenge other conventional views. A male magistrate threatens to grab one of the antiwar women. Old woman B responds: "By the goddess, if you lay a fingertip on her, you'll need an icebag for both eyes" (443–444). As always, Lysistrata then broadens the point: "But what did you expect? Did you imagine that we were slaves, or did you think that women can't show courage?" (463–464).

The play's discussion of reasons for opposition to the war also builds on traditional stereotypes about men's and women's role in a way that also serves to give new importance to the once demeaned role of manager of the household. The women argue that war is fought to make money for generals and weapons contractors. By preventing access to the citadel and thus stopping the war, the women portray themselves as being fiscally responsible. When the male magistrate charges that the women merely want to keep the money, Lysistrata responds that they will save it. She adds "what's so strange in that, don't we manage household money?" (495). By implication, the role of household management is elevated. It is not merely a matter of changing diapers, and its monetary aspects are portrayed as good preparation for statecraft.

In their quest for ways to end the war, the women also draw on their daily knowledge about household management and use the social recognition of their skills in this realm. Spinning wool becomes a metaphor for ways to end the war. The use of this particular metaphor is perhaps one of the most provocative turns of this play:

First you wash the city as we wash the wool, cleaning out the bull shit. Then we pluck away the parasites; break up strands that clump together, forming special interest groups; here's a bozo: squeeze his head off. Now you are set

to card the wool: use your basket for the carding, the basket of solidarity.
There we put our migrant workers, foreign friends, and minorities, immigrants and wage slaves, every person useful to the state. Don't forget our
allies, either, languishing like separate strands. Bring it all together now,
and make one giant ball of yarn. Now you're ready: weave a brand new suit
for the citizens. (573–586)

The language of foreign policy and statecraft is, shall we say, skillfully
woven together with the language of home crafts.

When the magistrate complains that war is not the same as wool balls,
Lysistrata responds that women know a lot about war. They make the children and then send them off to war. Once again she draws on the stereotypical
picture of women and uses it to gain purchase for her antiwar views (588).

The play also builds from and yet subtly challenges another related
stereotype of women—that they are flighty. It is the purportedly flighty
women who hold to their determination even as they remain tempted by
sex. In the characteristically vulgar language the play employs to describe
sexual acts and desires, Lysistrata describes women as desperately wanting
to find some means of sexual gratification, but she pulls them back to the
task at hand (see 717–727).

Duly chastened by Lysistrata, the women stand to their principles and
suggest that if the men sue for peace, it is possible to have lasting friendship: "You seem to understand this, but still you keep on fighting. It is
possible, bad men, to have our lasting friendship" (1016–1017).

The play's well-orchestrated resistance to the war, the women's continued if at times farcical or degrading picture of their containment of sexual
urges, and their persuasive invocation of their skills in running the household lay a fine foundation for Lysistrata's speech in the presence of ambas-
sadors from Sparta and Athens late in the play. Such lines carry more weight
because the play has subtly reversed to a degree stereotypes about men and
women. At the end of the play, it is the men who seem so consumed by sexual urges that they can't even concentrate on Lysistrata's line:

Both parties, listen. I'm female, yes, but still I've got a brain. I'm not so
badly off for judgment, either. My father and some other elders too have
given me a first rate education. In no uncertain terms I must reproach you,
both sides and rightly. Don't you share a cup at common altars, for common
gods, like brothers at the Olympic games, Thermophylai and Delphi? I
needn't list the many, many others. The world is full of foreigners you could
fight, but it's Greek men and cities you destroy. (1122–1134)

Lysistrata has rightly been a powerful symbol for our time of the active
political role that women can play in the quest for peace. But several of its
key metaphors should provoke as well as inspire.

Is building coalitions for peace like carding wool? The wool is washed, the parasites plucked out. Surely an antiwar effort must curb its war profiteers, but even these will deserve some justice. Migrant workers and wage slaves are all integrated into the task, but on what terms? Are they asked to forego concerns about justice in the interests of opposition to the war? Part of the proof Lysistrata cites as to her own brain power is her education at the hands of her father and other men. In all the Greek city states, what education a woman received was through men and thus controlled and limited in important ways. And the case against this war is not based upon some general commitment to pacifism or nonviolence but on the claims of a higher form of patriotism, the need for Greeks to reunite on behalf of their larger shared culture against the foreign Persians.

And just as in Lysistrata's day, issues of international and domestic justice are not easily separable. Her quest for peace requires integration of migrant workers on terms not specified. Any international agreement to stop armed struggle will require that grievance be put aside. Any resolution of borders, no matter how broadly based, is likely to embody compromises based on earlier injustices and inequalities. If these neither can nor should be eternally repressed, what is the alternative to war?

In another text on women and war, political theorist Jean Elshtain suggests that rather than seeing peace, or the perpetual peace of the Kantian vision as the alternative to war, we regard politics as the key.[24] Part of her excellent critique lies in the observation that peace is often conceived of merely as the absence of war. To define merely by what something is not is not only vague, it hardly inspires except through the evocation of the horrors of war and death. Necessary as this task is, it is not sufficient and it can often backfire by inspiring more defensive and aggressive forms of nationalism and fundamentalism both to resist perceived aggression or to give meaning to death. If part of our identity is as peacemakers, we need both to fill out some understanding of the complementary identities that we hope to sustain and to keep alive the play of differance regarding war. The point is not to tolerate infrequent war or war on a small scale but to acknowledge that war has on some occasions been the only way certain groups have had to express persistent and serious grievances and injustices. The task is to fashion alternatives to silence or violence.

A politics among nations can both foster proximate solutions to boundary issues and major human rights abuses even as it also opens up opportunities to pursue inequities that remain or are clarified or become more severe as a result of new settlements. For such a politics to have a chance of working it must be inspired by and in turn help to build an ethos of openness to difference. Paul Woodruff, author of *Reverence: The Forgotten Virtue*, has suggested that:

> one of the most devastating ways to be irreverent is to think that you know the literal mind of God and that you are carrying out God's will... Oedipus and the other tyrants are not in trouble because they didn't sacrifice enough chickens... It was about their attitude towards themselves and their failure to realize that they were not truly godlike... [25]

But a concern about or aversion to hubris along the lines of Greek tragedy may not be enough to sustain an ethos and politics of openness to difference. Just as Aristophanes's Athenians look forward to peace as an entre to the renewal of their erotic lives, a politics of openness has the best chance of survival if it invokes and helps further to evoke a latent human desire for newness and variety in our lives. A broad participatory politics is the key to forging modes of accommodation that can allow different nations and groups to thrive, but such a politics is most likely to be true to its mission and to sustain greater enthusiasm if politics is also celebrated for its responsiveness to the new currents and issues that emerge from any prolonged settlement. Politics can then become one key to enhanced social and personal variety and can have its own erotic appeal.

The root to such a politics must be as pluralistic as the substantive politics itself. By this I mean that just as the procedures and agreements that are fostered must be seen as open to revision, so too must we be attuned to more than one institutional source of movement toward these ends. Negotiation between states at the level of the UN surely plays a role, but is hardly adequate by itself either tactically or morally. Negotiation between NGOs, including labor and environmental organizations, and often growing out of widely discrepant moral notions regarding the nature of the relation of human beings to the natural world can work to open new frontiers of consciousness and put new forms of pressure on national governments to arrive at commonalities that increase our survival options and open new avenues for future politics.

Aristophanes of course also makes his pitch for peace on the grounds of a new nationalism and heroism, the emergence of a broader Greek consciousness. That should be unacceptable to progressive antiwar forces today. But there would be no lack of challenges for a world in which cross-border and cross-cultural politics have replaced the winds of war and nationalism. Natural disasters, from tsunamis to droughts to AIDS, both threaten whole communities and challenge the conscience of an increasingly globalized community. These events can become a cause for despair and should they become sufficiently widespread and disruptive, they may cause a reversion to the most divisive fundamentalisms. But viewed from a perspective that accepts nature's ugly moments as part of a splendid multi-plicity that is the source of life itself and that finds sustenance in the new compromises and lifestyles nature and cross-cultural negotiation require, such events may be viewed as an opportunity for life-affirming heroism and their dangers may perhaps be reduced. There are no guarantee here, only the hope that a life spent doing more than merely waiting for individual death or social doomsday offers both practical rewards and personal satisfactions.

CONCLUSION
ADDRESSING A WORLD OF RHIZOMATIC CRISES

As I prepared a final draft of this manuscript, four issues dominated the airwaves: the Muslim who attempted to bomb Times Square, the BP oil eruption, the draconian anti-immigrant agenda symbolized by Arizona's legislative initiatives, and an increasingly urgent push to cut government budgets and restore balanced budgets. Though media generally treated these as separate issues, I could not fail to be struck by the ways they intermeshed and intensified a general sense of apocalyptic distress and an exclusionary, self-defeating politics. Anti-immigrant groups and terror warriors often had different targets, but fears that built on each other. And both climate change deniers and ardent environmentalists spoke with intense levels of fear, albeit at different targets. Fears and intensities connected even as the targets and programmatic agendas varied.

No crisis seemed to govern discourse for any extended period. In the face of uncertainty and seemingly broadening challenges to core values, large segments of the population, the media, and political leadership seemed eager to reassert their own favored form of fundamentalism—keep the immigrants out, live within your means, drill, baby drill, ramp up terror surveillance. Each fundamentalism fed off and reinforced the other and seemed to encourage a dogmatic and exclusionary form of politics. Both by way of summarizing and further developing my themes, I will provide a reinterpretation of these issues, their connections, and a multidimensional approach appropriate to these.

The connections among these issues might best be seen as rhizomatic rather than arboreal, to borrow terms from Deleuze and Guattari. A tree's many branches spring from a common root. A rhizome is a variety of plant life without deep roots, connected by multiple nodes. There is no central issue or ideological or world view effectively uniting all constituencies and legitimizing the political order. Yet this rhizome, American style, is hardly nonviolent.[1] Paradoxically and tragically, one overarching view does govern modern politics—the need of and quest for an authoritative center. The sense of this need, coupled with the inability to attain it, drives an angry, exclusionary politics with each fundamentalism asserting its primacy or at best seeking coalitions based on a sense of shared superiority. Such a politics may demand a rhizomatic response more attuned to current injustices, one that recognizes the legitimacy of multiple issues and their bearing on if not reducibility to others. This perspective envisions multiple ethnic, religious, and moral sources for such a politics. A spirit of openness to a range of issues and underlying perspectives among those working in different issue areas may spread and inflect the whole polity, a counter to the way anger and fear do today. Through this discussion I hope to catalyze a different form of politics and a passion for justice rather than revenge or exclusivity.

Is BP an Environmental Terrorist?

"Extremist Muslims" here and abroad are readily suspected of violent acts, termed terrorists, and denied minimal rights. BP, however, is treated as a person entitled to full protection of the law. Even in the event of an indictment, BP need not worry about the status of its Miranda rights or its ability to mount the best defense money can buy. Both Faisal Shahzad and BP should be indicted and given fair trials, but crime and terrorism, like all central political concepts, have complex baggage, carry limits, and should start a wider debate. Why are BP executives not designated as environmental terrorists? Corporate PR often brands nonviolent opponents of ecologically destructive mining, drilling, and forestry practices as ecoterrorists. The term, however, better fits BP's behavior. Even had Shahzad succeeded in his plot, far fewer would have died than will perish from the Gulf oil eruption. Toxic fumes are already disabling some clean up workers, and over many years pollutants will kill many of our youngest or most vulnerable.[2]

Since BP did not intend such a catastrophe, shouldn't it be exonerated? As Rand Paul says, accidents just happen. Nonetheless, because accidents do happen, corporations are obligated to avoid riskiest sites, to maintain all possible means of accident remediation, and to follow strict precautions. This company knowingly violated vital regulations. It risked countless lives for the sake of economic power. It has a history of retaliation against internal whistleblowers. Even now it prohibits its temporary cleanup crew from bringing their own respirators as protection from toxic fumes. In defiance of an EPA request, BP spreads a dispersant banned in Europe. It major goal, says one environmental writer, is "to hide the body."[3] Despite a reckless past and inept and high-handed management of the current crisis, the company continues to call the shots. By spending a mere 4 percent of its profits on alternative energy BP rebranded itself as a can-do corporate friend of both economic growth and the environment.

If BP were owned by the Taliban, however, its every past deed, ad, and utterance would be scrutinized and ridiculed. Religiously and often ethnically different from the US mainstream, Muslims here and abroad are often automatically cast in one light. Some of our religious leaders charge that Islam is fundamentally a violent religion. These extremist Christians have a language and rhetorical style that often resembles that of the radical Islamists. Pat Robertson doesn't speak for all US Christians, but his views always command a hearing.

The sacred texts and sects of Islam, like those of Christianity, include some violent rhetoric and violence-prone agendas, though the bulk of both traditions condemns violence. Even Islam's most rhetorically violent sects, as with the Christian right, have varying targets and don't always resort to violence. Nonetheless, those political and media figures that are willing to acknowledge Islam's divergent currents still often paint any Muslim cleric who criticizes the United States with the same brush. They "hate us for our freedom" and seek to destroy us, as President Bush says. Viewing this rhetoric through the lens of one who worries about the propensity of reigning identities to establish themselves by diminishing difference leads me to other concerns. Portraying those who oppose our policy even rhetorically as vicious and out to destroy our way of life, itself a concept ill defined by Bush, may reassure us as to the worth of our own values and policies and give us a sense of common purpose. It does, however, play upon and reinforce an attitude toward US Arabs that long antedated 9/11. Bush I, Bush II, and Obama have all taken very different conflicts as occasions to present war as an opportunity to fashion and restore a proud, enduring identity that would match or exceed that of an idealized World War II generation. Here is Obama's take:

> Now this generation faces a great test in the specter of terrorism. And unlike the Civil War or World War II, we can't count on a surrender ceremony to bring this journey to an end. Right now, in distant training camps and in crowded cities, there are people plotting to take American lives. That will be the case a year from now, five years from now, and—in all probability—10 years from now.[4]

Obama's apparent pessimism is laced with a hidden sugar coating, the promise of an enduring purpose, something many Americans now find lacking in turbulent times and for which they feel a desperate need.

Radical Islamists have not of course attacked Sweden where cultural freedoms, especially for women, exceed our own. And just where, in what numbers or frequency, or why people are plotting to take American lives is hardly specified nor is evidence provided.

One careful study by the establishment-oriented Rand Corporation, little discussed by the mainstream media, suggests that domestic terrorism is grossly exaggerated. Rand pointed out:

> Since September 11, 2001...the problem, while serious, was wildly overblown. There have been...46 incidents of Americans or long-time U.S. residents being radicalized and attempting to commit acts of terror (most failing woefully) since 9/11. Those incidents involved...125 people...about six cases of purported radicalization and terrorism a year...[In comparison} From January 1969 to April 1970 alone, the U.S. somehow managed to survive 4,330 bombings, 43 deaths, and $22 million of property damage.[5]

If the rate of such attacks does increase, does this constitute proof that Taliban or Osama is stirring up US Muslims? Our political leaders seldom contemplate the possibility that US citizen terrorists such as Shahzad might have been disturbed by US drone attacks on Pakistani or Afghan civilians rather than inspired by Taliban leaders. Despite some press reports about Shahzad's anger regarding drone attacks, Obama's top counterterrorism adviser, John Brennan, brushed such reports aside and insisted the suspect was "captured by the murderous rhetoric of Al Qaeda and TTP that looks at the United States as an enemy."[6] Perhaps closer scrutiny of the suspect's own words isn't needed if one doesn't want to confront problematic aspects of his or her own ideals and actions.

Though BP has a full say in our media, we seldom hear Muslim extremists themselves. Even ordinary, nonpolitical Muslims who have contributed to our safety hardly receive a mention. Steven Salisbury reminds us of: "Alioune Niass, the Sengalese Muslim vendor who first spotted the...smoking SUV...If it were not for the Times of London, we would not even know of his pivotal role in the story. No mainstream American newspaper bothered to mention...Niass,..."

Documenting Niass's role might blunt prevalent monolithic stereotypes of Muslims and also plant the notion that getting the cooperation of minority communities is more effective in curbing violence than generalized surveillance or racial profiling.

And when violence is wreaked on Muslims in this country, few mainstream media conclude that Americans are uniquely violent or dare suggest that Muslims too can be victims of terrorism. Pierre Tristam comments:

> Few of you know that 10 days after the [incident] in Times Square, an actual terrorist attack took place in Jacksonville when a firebomb exploded

outside the city's biggest mosque,...60 worshippers were praying inside when the bomb went off...The bomber is still at large. The Jacksonville Times-Union [and other local media] did an admirable job of covering the story...But...that terrorist attack drew almost no attention from the national media...the terrorists-from the Oklahoma City bomber to the Fort Hood attacker to the Times Square bomber to, most likely, the Jacksonville bomber-are American. There's convenience in creating a false sense of security by identifying Islam as the evil and Americans as the good guys. But it's demonstrably not true.[7]

Quoting or discussing the particular motives of extremist sects is especially suspect and often harshly attacked. The radical and often rhetorically violent social right generally escapes scrutiny—and certainly faces no prospect of assassination by the CIA—because it is white and Christian and its goals and aspirations often are too close to the mainstream for comfort.

Discussion of the specific motives of radical Islamist groups is off limits because it is taken as excusing terrorists. This exclusion is one that both deep pluralist and prophetic Christian traditions might encourage us to interrogate. Placing discussion of motives off limits is an odd position when we consider our justice system. In murder trials, part of confirming guilt lies in establishing motive. Showing the motive of a murderer hardly excuses the crime. Motives may partially exonerate, but they can also suggest how despicable some crimes are. In any case, if our goal is safety rather than buttressing our own sense of righteousness, shouldn't we want to know as much as possible about the criminal? To combat BP and Taliban crimes, we need to understand both the cultures of predatory capitalism and various radical religious sects both here and abroad. The concept of crime must be applied as carefully to corporate actions as to those of extremist religious sects. The Left must avoid a double standard. If we are willing, as we should be, to assess the motives and context of the Times Square bomber's actions, we must adopt the same breadth in our examination of other Manhattan reprobates. There is little to admire in Goldman Sachs's Lloyd Blankfein or Tony Hayward, BP's CEO, but an immanent naturalism like Bennett's would ask us to assess more critically the nature of their responsibility. Both are part of a corporate culture and worldview that idolizes wealth, has celebrated deregulation, disrespects government, regards fines for law violation as a cost of doing business, and places a premium on immediate rewards. And both strive to control volatile ocean currents or financial markets whose dynamism may at times exceed any human capacity.

A generation ago the corporate culture emerged amid the crisis of liberalism. Following the sharp run up in oil prices in the wake of the oil embargo and late 1970s stagflation, Republicans ran on a plank of economic deregulation and bashing of government. Many Democrats followed close behind. Not surprisingly both regulation and regulators easily got a bad name.

More broadly, the sense of cheap oil as a right has become built into the culture and is part of the context in which BP operates. One former oil executive is not far off the mark in suggesting that one reason BP operates in deep water is that coastal residents abhor rigs but want the oil. Out of sight, out of mind.[8]

Car culture is one of the core values of American life. And corporations such as BP, while held in a more ambiguous light, are often deemed part of a market economy seen as a major tool of that life. A close look at recent media sheds some light on the centrality of car culture. And the current controversies over deficit spending and immigration demonstrate how an uneasy blend of racial and social tensions along with market fundamentalism blunts efforts at corporate and environmental reform.

BP's Accomplice: Car Culture and American Life

This TV commercial (herein condensed) did not make the SuperBowl roster, but Sarah Palin probably likes it:

> My name is Ram And my tank is full. I'm fueled by optimism. Driven by passion and stopped by nothing. I'm a can-do spirit in a get-it-done body. All brawn. All brain. I'm built not to last, but to outlast. Not to achieve, but to overachieve. I'm built to reward the doers who climb behind my wheel every day by working even harder than they do, I carry reputations. I carry livelihoods. I deliver the goods without fail. The road ahead of me is long but I know my destination, I will not downshift. I will not coast to a stop.[9]

Michael Klare, author of *Rising Powers, Shrinking Planet* (2008), remarks that plentiful oil spurred the development of an auto culture that is one of the defining characteristics of US society and an example to other nations. We feel we are entitled to cheap oil and gas-guzzlers. The risk of violent energy conflicts, however, is growing as more and more nations compete for diminishing reserves. Nationalism is intensified, making energy conflicts even more intractable.[10]

David Campbell, author of "The Biopolitics of Security," agrees Americans regard cheap oil as a birthright, but he suggests that oil's iconic status cannot be explained merely by its historic abundance. Oil became one of the ways by which we have sought to define ourselves as a people and to validate that definition. Oil is crucial to one of the central values of this culture—mobility. Mobility is a consequence of and contributor to another key US value—technological prowess.[11]

These values have been validated by viewing as threatening those who appear to have different values or who often been characterized in terms of central markers of danger. Thus in the seventeenth and eighteenth centuries, Native Americans, perceived as having no concept of private property and no interest in technological betterment, were portrayed as shiftless, lazy, and aggressive. Today environmentalists who have qualms about at least how we achieve mobility are often portrayed as effeminate, soft, and so on, even as they are sometimes also viewed as violent. These portrayals in turn have often encouraged and been sustained by bellicose nationalism. Critics of rapid natural resource exploitation are viewed as dupes of foreign influence. Recently, nonviolent protestors of energy exploration have even been vilified as "environmental terrorists."

Well-guarded geographic borders express and reinforce the sense of the mighty and self-sufficient US machine, but these borders are breaking down. Immigration is widely highlighted, but capital goods, money, diseases, media messages, and financial capital all cross geographic borders even more rapidly. Climate change and energy wars, perhaps nuclear, loom as the ultimate cross-border challenge. All limit our options and reshape our expectations. We are, as Campbell says, part of complex networks.

In the face of flux, many strive to reseal our geographic borders. But others seek to shore up conventional identity through various cultural means. The auto, the way it is advertized and even designed, is an attempt to secure new boundaries. The SUV is portrayed as security in a world of crime, dangerous traffic, a reminder of US military triumph, and thus an antidote to the "Vietnam syndrome," and a means to and expression of individuality. Like gated communities, the Ram and the SUV are capsules that appear to seal us off from challenge but actually increase international oil conflict and risks at home.

Thus we can't stop Alaska drilling merely by pointing out that little of our total needs can be derived from there. "Drill baby drill" has a compelling, cheerleader-like resonance, speaks to a visceral anger toward environmentalists from a squeezed working class experiencing flux. Drilling now bespeaks a take-charge mentality.

Ending this vicious circle requires willingness by environmentalists and social justice advocates to engage the core values and identity anxieties central to car culture. One counter is to ease immediate economic burdens and foster jobs that recognize the talents of displaced workers. We might also address critics in more respectful ways by acknowledging that car culture does speak to deeply held views that we cannot simply disprove and for which some space must be accorded. We might tap and respond to other interests that working-class critics themselves may find undervalued in this materialistic culture, such as time with family or enjoying the wilderness rides those SUVs were supposed to enable.

This is a task that involves attention to the most immediate occasion of working-class stress, an economic crisis that has left a large portion of the electorate jobless or feeling in immediate danger of job loss. The refusal by political elites, especially Republicans, to commit to the countercyclical spending and a media that seems often hostile can and should be blamed.

Nonetheless, popular attitudes are ambivalent. The complex legacy of race and 1970s stagflation have left a mark, and effective reform would entail addressing these broader issues. Economic distress itself curbs any willingness to address global climate change. Even in the Gulf states, many citizens are ambivalent about new curbs on offshore drilling. Conflict over immigration is now also a central aspect of this mix. Immigration politics increases the urge to retreat to capsules and provides a scapegoat for job loss. Movement on both fronts, the domestic economy and on immigration are each essential to the other and to progress on energy politics.

The Retreat to Budgetary Fundamentalism

"Runaway government spending" is an easy target now. It is not the cause of our problems. Government spending will not "crowd out" private investors. It is essential in stimulating the demand on which the private sector and even our ability to sustain healthy debt to GNP ratios depend. Further cuts in domestic job creation, sure to result from Congress's unwillingness to add new stimulus and its slow and miserly extension of unemployment benefits, will even be counterproductive. It will lead to more unemployment, more welfare expenditures or prisons, emergency healthcare, domestic violence, and further declines in government revenues—a true death spiral.

That message, however, hardly ever gets a hearing. CNBC anchors regularly proclaim: "only the private sector creates wealth." I wonder what these anchors would be using for their research and communication but for massive government subsidy and R&D on computers and the Internet.

Critics also claim that the Obama stimulus did not work. Using carefully sourced data the nonpartisan Congressional Budget Office shows that the stimulus package created jobs and saved others that would be lost. The problem here is political. As even some business economists pointed out at the time, the initial Obama package was far too small. Dean Baker points out the Federal package amounted to less than half of the trillion-dollar hole caused by the housing bubble collapse.[12] Government stimulus was reduced even further by cuts in state government spending. Perhaps Obama could not have achieved more, but he should have chastised

Congress and made clear the country would need more and soon. Obama's inflated claim on behalf of that modest legislation is a major reason that more Federal job creation is so politically difficult.

The deficit mania has other deeper roots. A core within the business community, especially financial services, never accepted the New Deal. Social Security has always been especially offensive. It is a universal program that worked and became very popular. It constitutes the major reason poverty rates among the elderly declined dramatically. Had George W. Bush privatized Social Security, our great recession would likely have become Great Depression II.

Unable to go after the program directly, conservatives attacked Social Security through fallacious arguments that the program, which its bipartisan trustees certify as fully funded through 2044, is a fiscal time bomb. As Baker points out, the real fiscal time bombs are the exploding private sector dominated health costs, the bank bailouts, and war costs of a trillion and counting. Concern about deficits has never prevented the business press or our senators from supporting these corporate behemoths.[13]

Paul Krugman also provocatively argues that more than immediate monetary interests drive this issue. Ideological and even identity issues are in play. Krugman cites Keynes's powerful aside on classical capitalist culture:

> The completeness of the [the notion that government can do nothing] is something of a curiosity and a mystery. It must have been due to a complex of suitabilities in the doctrine to the environment into which it was projected. That it reached conclusions quite different from what the ordinary uninstructed person would expect, added, I suppose, to its intellectual prestige. That its teaching, translated into practice, was austere and often unpalatable, lent it virtue. That it was adapted to carry a vast and consistent logical superstructure, gave it beauty. That it could explain much social injustice and apparent cruelty as an inevitable incident in the scheme of progress, and the attempt to change such things as likely on the whole to do more harm than good, commended it to authority. That it afforded a measure of justification to the free activities of the individual capitalist, attracted to it the support of the dominant social force behind authority.[14]

The antideficit mania has tangled roots both in immediate monetary interests and in the broader political culture. It has surprising support among some working-class citizens, who stand to lose from its implementation. They are led by and in turn sustain the so-called Blue Dog Democrats. Nonetheless, its deep and tangled roots constitute no reason to treat it as inevitable. Why deficit mania cuts across class and how to construct a culture and economics that sustain full employment are among our most pressing political tasks.

Recovering from Deficit Obsessions

The politics of private and government debt provides an occasion to contest both conventional economic theory and related moral narratives. The old story is that a profligate working class and indulgent governments spent themselves into deserved ruin. Others maintain that liberal government do-gooders through the Community Reinvestment Act forced banks to make inappropriate loans to poor citizens. Yet most of the subprime mortgages were issued by banks not subject to CRA, and government support for such mortgages through Fannie Mae began only long after private banks were heavily involved. In addition, as the *New York Times* reports, the wealthy are now defaulting in disproportionate numbers on investment housing loans.[15] But as Robert Reich points out,

> working class Americans went into deep debt because their wages didn't keep up. The median wage dropped between 2001 and 2007. Workers could keep spending at the rate necessary to keep themselves—and the economy—going only by borrowing, primarily against the value of their homes. The borrowing, however, ended with the bursting of the bubble. Only government can fill the void left by a consumer who is now so debt burdened as to be unable to buy more than mere necessities. And in the longer run, more recessions are likely if working class incomes are not bolstered. Yet the same authorities who told consumers to borrow and spend now argue against any role for government either in job creation or redistribution.[16]

Contemporary deficit mania has a curious, occasionally quarrelsome parentage. It includes fear of full employment, disdain for the poor and leisure, dreams of rags to riches for those who combine self-denial and luck, and a blind—albeit selectively applied—faith in markets.

Some wealthy have reasons to fear full employment. Even more than redistributive taxation, full employment narrowed gaps between the rich and the poor substantially during World War II, the late 1960s, or the final years of the Clinton administration. Full employment and steady productivity growth funded Social Security, private pensions, and gradual reductions in working hours, so crucial to family and to wider ranging interests.

The very success of full employment has also been its undoing. In the late 1960s, Lyndon Johnson's guns and butter economics gave us full employment. As I pointed out in chapter five, corporate pricing power, workplace and racial conflict, and productivity problems, however, drove inflation higher. OPEC and automatic cost of living adjustments (COLAs) embedded inflation. Business and government highlighted inflation and social turmoil to force Jimmy Carter to appoint a conservative banker, Paul Volcker, as Fed chair. He drove interest rates and unemployment sky high.

These problems might have been addressed—and often were in Europe—through wage and price guidelines, labor/management negotiation of codetermination, or profit-sharing schemes. Except in war and briefly during Nixon's administration, however, such an approach had been rejected as inefficient and intrusive by politicians. Ever since the Carter years, tales of the turmoil of the 1960s and the stagflation of the 1970s have been trotted out to blunt enthusiasm for any government initiative. Just as importantly, academic economists have constructed laws such as the Phillips Curve and the nonaccelerating inflation rate of unemployment (NAIRU) to suggest the impossibility of achieving unemployment as low as in the late 1960s. These "laws" blunted consideration of the possibility that with different institutions and social mores, full employment would not lead to vicious inflationary spirals.[17] In recent US experience, only very high levels of employment in the last years of the Clinton administration led to even modest wage gains— probably because unions had been so beaten down and workers were so traumatized. But on a more positive note, various forms of profit sharing and joint labor management collaboration in Europe can also curtail inflation under full employment circumstances. The inefficiency of curbing inflation through chronic working-class layoffs engineered by government is seldom considered.

The private debt economy's unprecedented crash gave Obama a brief window to redress these economic and moral narratives. Once his feeble stimulus disappointed, however, it became easy to revert to familiar narratives. Pundits celebrated a return to government and personal austerity, scapegoated African Americans and immigrants, and magnified the dream of rags to riches.

That cultural attitudes play as much a role in this debate as narrow economics shows in the willingness of "deficit hawks" to save elite bankers and subsidize our parasitic private health insurance industry. And though the public generally hates bankers, this hostility does not sufficiently convert itself to willingness to grant broad regulatory authority to the Federal government.

Congress also seems reluctant to consider inexpensive—albeit unconventional—ways to reduce unemployment. A German work-sharing program extended tax credits (less costly than unemployment compensation) to firms that shorten worker hours while retaining wage and salary levels. It held unemployment constant even with falling GNP.[18]

Much polling data suggest Americans are also ambivalent about public debt. Depending on the question, some suggest jobs are more important than the deficit. Polls and economic arguments probably won't by themselves carry the debate.

Rather than reflexively blame economic troubles on individual moral failings, the United States has also periodically demonstrated deeply democratic moral commitments. In fights for unions, jobs, voter rights, and shorter hours, the Catholic social gospel, the civil rights and labor movements, and various strands of secular liberalism have collaborated. They questioned work without end, challenged gaping inequality, and broadened democratic participation. Like all such efforts, they had their triumphs and their blindspots. Efforts to build on these examples would do well to attune themselves more fully to a pluralizing world where moral and social foundations are more shifting and varied and where new rights claims emerge.

Such coalitions today must include a cross-border effort to address the politics of immigration. The days when, if ever, social justice or environmental sustainability could be built on a unitary culture are likely gone. Liberal columnist Paul Krugman agonizes over the topic in recent blog posts:

> Democrats are torn *individually*...On one side, they favor helping those in need, which inclines them to look sympathetically on immigrants; plus they're relatively open to a multicultural, multiracial society...today's Mexicans and Central Americans seem to me fundamentally the same as my grandparents seeking a better life in America...Open immigration, [however] can't coexist with a strong...safety net; if you're going to assure...a decent income to everyone, you can't make that offer global.

Furthermore, Krugman has argued in a prior column: "Countries with high immigration tend...to have less generous welfare states than those with low immigration. U.S. cities with ethnically diverse populations...tend to have worse public services than those with more homogeneous populations."[19] Open immigration seemingly either overwhelms our scarce resources or undermines the consensus on which the safety net must rest. Both arguments are problematic.

Even as he worries about open immigration, Krugman commends the United States for generally welcoming immigrants. But following Bonnie Honig [*Democracy and the Foreigner* (2001)] I read our traditions as more ambivalent. At times immigrants have been treated as advancing the American dream and worthy of citizenship. The other side of that coin, however, is that when the dream falters—either because it seems unattainable or less satisfying than promised, bashing immigrants becomes a means to preserve our commitment to and reverence for that dream.

Economists disagree about the effects of undocumented immigrants on unskilled worker wages. No study, however, puts their impact anywhere close to that of such variables as minimum wage laws or the Federal

Reserve's manipulation of interest rates and employment levels. All workers advance in a full employment economy. Yet despite overwhelming evidence about the weaknesses in our deregulated banking system, the vast joblessness occasioned by the housing bubble collapse, and crude and illegal union busting tactics, there is, other than from Michael Moore, no movement to deport bankers or corporate thugs.

I do not favor deporting either group. The current crisis is a reflection of the structure of our financial institutions, a culture of greed and exploitation that goes far beyond individual morality, public policies, and the enforcement or nonenforcement of laws already on the books. These need to be fixed, but building a consensus to reform these also entails reflections on the origins of and alternatives to immigrant bashing.

Arizona's draconian law has very recent predecessors Honig cites:

> the English only movement,... blaming immigrants and ethnics for the fragmentation of high culture (perversely enough at a time when the homogenizing powers of American popular culture are at their height) and the identification of enclavism with immigrants... at a time when the propensity to withdraw from public services... is most characteristic not of foreigners but of the wealthy.[20]

More recently, immigrants have been blamed for lawlessness at a time when rates of violent crime are actually falling. Why is this persistent denigration of immigrants so pervasive and how are we to respond?

Arizona and the Politics of Immigration

Arizona, a US state for only about a century, serves as microcosm of our national experience. Most of our ancestors are from away, do not share a common heritage, and have seen ourselves as God's chosen. We experience an especially strong need and temptation to affirm the unity and simplicity of a set of core values.

Paradoxically, portraying ourselves as uniquely open often serves to strengthen our sense of ourselves as a chosen few and to justify new forms of repression of those who are different. There is a long tradition in the United States of treating even domestic dissidents who suggest the limits to or the difficulties in attaining that dream as "foreign inspired."[21]

Obama's tepid and overhyped stimulus package, leaving unemployment at extraordinarily high levels, occasions poverty, insecurity, and scapegoating. Democrats must return to a vigorous jobs agenda. But building support not only for job creation but long-term safety nets requires addressing scapegoating directly.

Krugman maintains ethnic diversity must be limited to maintain support for the safety net. But perhaps the very repetition of such regularities
reproduces the phenomenon and is part of the problem. It may give undue
solidity to the very murky notion of ethnicity and freeze existing group
boundaries.

In addition, Krugman assumes that enactment of a just safety net
depends on what is happening within the society. Even if that were true
in earlier eras of slower pace and reduced mobility, the dynamics between
internal and external may play a more vital role now.

Undocumented immigrants can be a catalyst to transformations—
precisely because they are less rooted. Coming from a variety of Christian
and indigenous perspectives, many value cultural, religious, and family commitments more than endless material growth. Many also share
a greater appreciation for the centrality of political participation both as
a value itself and as a means to a more dynamic pluralism. Many have
engaged at great personal risk in public demonstrations. They may help us
enact a more generous society. Social gospel and prophetic Christian and
postmodern perspectives encourage greater awareness of historic injustices
and more efforts to work with these groups to constitute a more inclusive
politics.

If a commitment to extend worker rights is to grow in the United States,
it will require the active participation of Latino, African American, and the
white working class. But harsh exclusionary tactics applied to the undocumented will encourage repression of both the so-called legal and illegal
Latinos and fracture possible broad-based working-class coalitions. Rather
than build commitment to the safety net—especially in our globalizing
world—on cultural or ethnic homogeneity, the best foundation may be far
more pluralistic.

Giving undocumented workers here freedom from deportation and full
workplace rights enables all workers to report employer safety and wage
violations and thus benefits all workers. And when workers collaborate
here across national and ethnic divides, it can also encourage international
collaboration to reform the corporate trade policies that drive major population shifts.

If Mexican—and US—workers could form genuinely independent
unions, they would be in a better position to demand wages that reflected
their growing productivity. Such an agenda would improve economic
circumstances in Mexico, foster more full and remunerative employment
in the United States, thus providing the revenue to finance a generous
safety net in both countries. More broadly, it could demonstrate at a
practical level that identity need not be centered on the self-contained
nation state.

In the absence of harsh exclusions of immigrants, other coalitions might spring from multiple ethnicities, concerns about gender justice, labor, and social gospel and secular sources, all of whom recognize or can be induced to see the danger to each from repressive agendas. Minimally, they develop a greater appreciation for civil liberties. More broadly, they might develop greater willingness to entertain rights claims regarding other forms of diversity. On this basis, some cultivate among themselves and others a willingness to risk challenge to the certainty of their identities in an effort to have a fuller life together.

The most alienated will likely reject such overtures, but others confused and disturbed by the drift of our politics may respond. In Arizona even as activists oppose the new law both through the courts and boycotts, they can reach out to some police officers who see the cost and inequities in the law. Not all supporters of the new law are racist or unmovable. Collaboration between sympathetic members of the police and Hispanic community leaders can show how community cooperation has already reduced crime. And within the Hispanic community itself, new alliances may be built as some who have shared opposition to the undocumented (perhaps because they or their parents came legally) come to see that demonization boomerangs back on them.

At their best, their participants are willing to concede that some of their deepest beliefs about God and truth are not or have not been fully proven. They admit their participation in historic injustices. (Mexicans who break laws by crossing our borders are returning to land stolen from Mexico.)

A pluralistic politics on the international scene may be equally vital, especially as walls between inside and outside become more porous. The World Social Forum (WSF) has a provocative motto, "another world is possible." The emphasis is on initiatives from the bottom up. The WSF rejects not only the corporate-dominated model but also the underlying assumption that the world can be united through one underlying ideology, philosophy, or worldview. Its only membership requirements are opposition to corporate domination, an international outlook, nonviolence, and open participation, terms whose meaning it continually reexamines.[22]

The WSF, the sister cities movements, and the recent global climate summit all recognize that justice among as well as within nations is central to both economic sustainability and to constructive alternatives to the forced population flows.

A Concluding Note on Climate Change

Part of any attempt to fuse concerns about immigration, joblessness, and the environment must be a more serious effort to address global climate change in ways that rely on more than apocalyptic scenarios. However accurate forecasts of doom, they run the risk of feeding the fears that play into the current concoction of fundamentalist economic and cultural politics. Addressing environmental concerns within a broader ambit of social justice issues and more diverse understandings of nature may be crucial.

The United States lags the world in its response to global climate change. *Guardian* columnist George Monbiot points out that as the consensus among climate scientists grows, public skepticism gains ground.[23]

Natural science is unlikely to control the outcome of this argument. Social and religious values, even core sense of identity, play at least as big a role as the natural sciences. Consider environmentalists' precautionary principle. Even if there is dispute as to the extent of man-made global warming, shouldn't we err on the side of caution by reducing carbon emissions?

All of us, however, understand threats in terms of some fundamental set of core values. If one is convinced that free-market-driven growth can solve any problem, that government invariably screws up and posits externalities where none exist or merely because of a quest for power and affluence by the regulators and if one has a core sense that he or she is a strong, self-reliant being, then taxes or regulation have disproportionate risk. The cautious course is not to intervene. As economic or environmental tragedy unfolds, many may cling all the more to the socially and economically conventional course. The Exxon Valdez oil spill brought us only double-hulled tankers to import even more oil safely.

Beyond concerns about the economic effects of global climate initiatives there are large moral issues as well. For much of mainstream culture, a quasi-religious perspective is part of core attitudes on these issues. Following sociologist Ernest Becker, Monbiot suggests: "the fear of death drives us to protect ourselves with 'vital lies' or 'the armour of character.' We defend ourselves from the ultimate terror by engaging in immortality projects, which boost our self-esteem and grant us meaning that extends beyond death."

In the United States, one popular immortality project has been a belief in a nature that can be fully understood in law-like terms and manipulated through free markets to serve growing individual prosperity. As noted earlier, both as symbol and contributor to that faith the auto has played a preeminent role, especially in a society that valorizes individual mobility.

This cultural and political background does not of course excuse BP of its responsibility to abide by accepted safety standards. Clear violations of law should be punished, but if our desire is to reduce corporate crime, we need to address the context in which both corporate and political terrorists or criminals regard themselves as above the law. In addition, we need to articulate positive alternatives to the culture of growth if environmentalists are to have much influence on a squeezed and insecure working class.

Today corporate crime and theoterrorism feed on each other. A rhetoric of international conspiracies undermining our freedoms strengthens the Cold War era national security state. That state has always fostered secretive dealings between government, the media, and supportive corporations. Corporations and governments have economic and political interests in pumping up the threat level. The atmosphere of imminent catastrophe creates a context in which CEOs and even substantial portions of the population can see corporations and political leaders as independent of any democratic political check and entitled to special support. This support in turn reinforces their power. A rhetoric of free markets and deregulation discourages public or worker checks on corporate power—though not substantial government beneficence toward the most powerful corporate interests. A social conservative evangelical discourse adds support to a black-and-white worldview and demeans the most vulnerable citizens, often scapegoating them for economic troubles, thus sidelining economic reform. This self-reinforcing mix may make us less safe. Though a minority even among Muslim radicals, theoterrorists receive and enjoy disproportionate media focus on them. They use such attention—and the excesses to which Western democratic governments go—as an occasion to gain recruits.

How would Americans feel if a foreign power, even one committed to uprooting acknowledged evil, frequently—albeit "accidentally"—killed thousands of civilians through high-tech assassinations? These are the questions that a dogmatic faith in our own values, ways of life, and policies often excludes. If there is a way out, it may require a renewed emphasis on decent jobs and social justice. We must also strive for more attentiveness to the selective use of concepts of crime and terrorism. These foster and reflect racist and religious divisions that impede all reform efforts. We must also challenge our more is better mindset. Progressives of all stripes need to question and challenge the conventional wisdom that ever-increasing amounts of consumer goods will make our lives happier. Growth may inflict social as well as environmental damage. Endless consumption may not be so much "human nature" as a process driven by corporate-controlled information, status anxieties fed by inegalitarian workplaces, long and involuntary working hours for those lucky enough to have full-time jobs, and the product choices of others. All of these are immunized from critique and reinforced by a countermodel portraying a group of radical terrorists out to undermine our freedoms.

At the philosophical level, following Jane Bennett's vibrant matter or Catherine Keller's process theology we might contemplate the possibility that nature itself is not designed to suit our purposes. Not only oil spills in deep and forbidding waters, but also volcanic eruptions and earthquakes may remind us that nature is not always fully predictable. But the nature that inflicts sporadic tragedy also gives us the unexpected splendor, from rainbows to the emergence of life itself. If we can reconcile ourselves to the possibility of untimely death and give ourselves more free time for interests and skills little developed, consider or reconsider what time with family and contemplation of our habitat brings us, we may develop more capacity to enjoy a pluralizing society and a pluripotential nature we need not conquer.

NOTES

Preface

1. James Carroll, "Hair Trigger Nation," http://www.commondreams.org/views05/1212–23.htm.
2. These remarks were conveyed to me in a personal e-mail from Dr. George McNeil.
3. Eckhart Tolle, *The Power of Now* (Navato: Namaste Publishing, 1999), 43–44; emphasis in the original.
4. See, for instance, George Lakoff, "The Policy Disaster for Health Care," *Huffington Post*, August 20, 2009, http://www.huffingtonpost.com/george-lakoff/the-policyspeak-disaster_b_264043.html.

Introduction: Listening to Talk Radio

1. See this *New York Times* portrait of Beck (last accessed April 6, 2011): http://topics.nytimes.com/top/reference/timestopics/people/b/glenn_beck/index.html?scp=1-spot&sq=Glenn%20Beck%20&st=cse.
2. For the CDs of the conference, please see www.socres.org/religioussecaldivide/.
3. The following discussion of differing Christian sensibilities draws on an unpublished paper by William Connolly, "The Spirit of Revenge."
4. James Carroll, "The End is Near," *Boston Globe*, July 20, 2009, http://www.boston.com/bostonglobe/editorial_opinion/oped/articles/2009/07/20/the_end_is_near/.
5. Quoted in William Connolly, *Capitalism and Christianity, American Style* (Durham: Duke University Press, 2008), 3.
6. See George Lakoff, "Empathy, Sotomayor, and Democracy: The Conservative Stealth Strategy," *Hiffington Post*, May 30, 2009 (last accessed May 2009), http://www.huffingtonpost.com/george-lakoff/empathy-sotomayor-and-dem_b_209406.html.
7. See Rom Coles discussion of King and Ella Baker on this point. Stanley Hauerway and Romand Coles, *Christianity, Democracy, and the Radical Ordinary: Conversations between a Radical Democrat and a Christian* (Eugene: Cascade Books, 2008), 55.
8. Ibid., 75.

One Evil and Identity

1. I Include among these thinkers William Connolly, Mark Blyth, Tom Dumm, Tom DeLuca, Bill Chaloupka, Bonnie Honig, Romand Coles, David Campbell, James Der Derian, Jane Bennett, Morton Schoolman, Michael Shapiro, and Kathy Ferguson. Since the boundaries of this school are almost by conviction ill defined, choices of whom to include and whom to leave out are exceedingly difficult. This list is not exhaustive. I draw most heavily on those who have inspired me and who seem to engage each other in an effort to develop such a deep pluralism.
2. Bonnie Honig, quoting William Connolly in "The Time of Rights," in David Campbell and Morton Schoolman, eds., *The New Pluralism: William Connolly and the Contemporary Global Condition* (Durham: Duke University Press, 2008), 86–87.
3. See James Der Derian, Global Security Manifesto (last updated March 2005): http://www.watsonblogs.org/globalsecurity/archives/2005/03/global _security_1.html.
4. See William Connolly, *Identity? Difference: Democratic Negotiations of Political Paradox* (Minneapolis: University of Minnesota Press, 2002), xiv.
5. William Connolly, *Political Theory and Modernity* (Ithaca: Cornell University Press, 1993), 138.
6. David Campbell, *Writing Security: United States Foreign Policy and the Politics of Identity* (Minneapolis: University of Minnesota Press, 1998), 2.
7. See ibid., 176–178.
8. James Der Derian, *Critical Practices in International Theory* (New York: Routledge, 2009), 149–150.
9. Ibid., 156–157; emphasis mine.
10. William Connolly, *Political Theory and Modernity* (Ithaca: Cornell University Press).
11. William Connolly, *Why I Am Not a Secularist* (Minneapolis: University of Minnesota Press, 1999), 158–159.
12. See interview with William Connolly in Campbell and Schoolman, eds., *The New Pluralism*, 314.
13. Ibid.; emphasis in the original.
14. William Connolly, *Pluralism* (Durham: Duke University Press, 2005), 61–64.
15. Connolly, *Why I Am Not a Secularist*, 154.
16. Campbell and Schoolman, eds., *The New Pluralism*, 314.
17. Connolly, *Pluralism*, 67.
18. This theme is developed in several ways in Bonnie Honig, *Emergency Politics: Paradox, Law, Democracy* (Princeton: Princeton University Press, 2009).
19. Honig, "The Time of Rights," 88.
20. Ibid.

Two Katrina, Rosa Parks, and the Color of Good and Evil

1. http://en.wikipedia.org/wiki/Criticism_of_government_response_to _Hurricane_Katrina (last accessed April 2011).

2. For a discussion of the two problems of evil, see William Connolly, *Identity /Difference: Democratic Negotiations of Political Paradox* (Minneapolis: University of Minnesota Press, 2002), pp. 1–15.

3. Jonathan Freedland, "The Levee Will Break," http://www.guardian.co.uk /world/2005/sep/07/hurricanekatrina.usa9 (last accessed September 7, 2005).

4. See, for instance, http://seattletimes.nwsource.com/html/nationworld /2002520986_katmyth26.html (last accessed September 25, 2005).

5. Jaime Yassin, "Demonizing the Victims of Katrina," http://www.fair.org /index.php?page=2793 (last accessed November/December 2005).

6. See Derrick Jackson, "Road Racism," *Boston Globe*, January 8, 2003.

7. This point and the subsequent discussion of slavery are indebted to Peter Kolchin's *American Slavery: 1619–1877* (New York: Hill and Wang, 2003).

8. Robert Marcus ed., *American Firsthand: Readings from Settlement to Reconstruction*, (New York City: Bedford/St. Martin's Press, 2004), p. 311.

9. James Morone, Hellfire Nation: *The Politics of Sin in American History* (New Haven: Yale University Press, 2004).

10. Ibid.

11. Ibid.

12. The classic statement on this is Reinhold Niebuhr, *The Nature and Destiny of Man* (New York: Charles Scribner's Sons, 1941, 1964), volume I.

13. Catherine Keller, *On the Mystery: Discerning Divinity in Process* (Minneapolis: Fortress Press, 2008), 82.

14. Ibid., 84.

15. Ibid., 12.

16. Ibid., 97.

17. Ibid., 99.

18. Ibid., 116.

19. Ibid., 120.

20. Ibid., 105.

21. Richard Fox, *Reinhold Niebuhr: A Biography* (New York: Pantheon, 1985), 212–213.

22. Reinhold Niebuhr, *The Children of Light and the Children of Darkness* (New York: Charles Scribner's Sons, 1944), xiii and 118.

23. E. J. Dionne, *Souled Out: Reclaiming Faith and Politics After the Religious Right* (Princeton: Princeton University Press, 2009), 185–186.

24. http://www.nytimes.com/2005/10/25/national/25parks.html?scp=2& sq=Rosa%20Parks&st=cse.

25. Cornel West, *Observer*, Sunday, September 11, 2005, http://www.guardian. co.uk/world/2005/sep/11/hurricanekatrina.comment.

Three   From the Model T to the Hummer: The Economics and Aesthetics of the American Automobile

1. *Briarpatch Magazine,* September 2001: .

2. See http://www.cnn.com/2006/POLITICS/01/31/bush.sotu/ (last accessed February 1, 2008).

3. http://krugman.blogs.nytimes.com/2009/05/29/same-as-they-ever-were/.

4. Bill McKibben, "Can 350.org Save the World?" http://www.commondreams. org/view/2009/05/17-4.

5. Gregory Mankiw, *Principles of Economics* (Boston: South-Western College Publishers, 2008).

6. See James Hansen at http://www.nybooks.com/articles/archives/2006/jul/13 /the-threat-to-the-planet/?page=2.

7. Michael Best and William Connolly, *The Politicized Economy* (Lexington: D. C. Heath and Co., 2nd edition, 1983).

8. Jeffrey Kaplan, "The Gospel of Consumption," http://www.orionmagazine. org/index.php/articles/article/2962/.

9. See especially Juliet Schor, *The Overspent American: Upscaling, Downshifting, and the New Consumer* (New York: Basic Books, 1998).

10. Schor's most recent work on children and consumption is *Born to Buy: The Commercialized Child and the New Consumer Culture* (New York: Scribner, 2005).

11. Keith Bradsher, "Domination, Submission, and the Chevy Suburban," *New York Times*, March 23, 1997, section 4.

12. Thomas Dumm, *A Politics of the Ordinary* (New York: New York University Press, 1999), 2.

13. See Cunniffe, "One for the Road," http://www.michigandaily.com/content /hummers-and-american-way.

14. For my discussion of Ryan, I draw on Benjamin Hunnicutt's superb study of the politics of shorter hours, *Work Without End* (Philadelphia: Temple University Press, 1988).

15. Catherine Keller, *On the Mystery: Discerning Divinity in Process* (Minneapolis: Fortress Press, 2008), 47–50.

16. Ibid., 62.

17. Ibid., 63.

18. See Stuart Kauffman, *Reinventing the Sacred: A New View of Science, Reason, and Religion* (New York: Basic Books, 2008), 131–143.

19. Jane Bennett, *Vibrant Matter: A Political Ecology of Things* (Durham: Duke University Press, 2009), 94–100.

20. Ibid., 122.

21. Ibid., 14.

22. Keller, *On the Mystery*, 76.

23. Quoted in William E. Connolly, *Why I Am Not a Secularist* (Minneapolis: University of Minnesota Press, 1999), 137.

24. See Bennett, *Vibrant Matter*, 36.

Four   The Immigrants are Coming!
The Immigrants are Coming!

1. See   http://www.splcenter.org/get-informed/intelligence-report/browse-all -issues/2009/spring/minority-meltdown (last accessed spring 2009).

2. Bonnie Honig, *Democracy and the Foreigner* (Princeton: Princeton University Press, 2001), 74–75.

3. Ibid., 75.

4. Jane Guskin and David L. Wilson, *The Politics of Immigration* (New York: Monthly Review Press, 2007), 65.
5. http://www.stwr.org/poverty-inequality/global-ruling-class-billionaires-and -how-they-made-it.html (last accessed March 2007).
6. Ibid.
7. For a socialist perspective on these raids, see Jim Lauverdure, "Let's Step It UP Against the ICE Raids," *Freedom Socialist*, December 2007, http://www. socialism.com/drupal-6.8/?q=node/469.
8. http://select.nytimes.com/2007/05/25/opinion/25krugman.html?_r=1.
9. For a review of Huntington, see http://bostonreview.net/BR30.1/lomnitz.html.
10. For discussion of these points, see Jane Guskin and David L. Wilson, *The Politics of Immigration* (New York: Monthly Review Press, 2007), 64 and 84.
11. Romand Coles, *Beyond Gated Politics: Reflections for the Possibility of Democracy* (Minneapolis: University of Minnesota Press 2005), 115.
12. Ibid., 116.
13. Ibid., 118–119.
14. Ibid., 121.
15. Ibid., 123.
16. Ibid., 136.
17. See William Connolly, *Capitalism and Christianity, American Style* (Durham: Duke University Press, 2008), 59–60.
18. I draw on Bonnie Honig, *Political Theory and the Displacement of Politics.* On immigration policy, Honig's metaphor for the perpetuation of politics verges on a literal recommendation. Immigration issues as they are debated and enacted in modern societies can enhance our understanding of politics and vice versa.
19. See economist Dean Baker's discussion of NLRB data on firing union orga- nizers: http://washingtonindependent.com/25398/economist-one-in-five-union -organizers-gets-canned.
20. Honig, *Democracy and the Foreigner*, 72.

Five   US Capitalism's Bumpy Ride: Where To From Here?

1. Chris Hedges, "The American Empire is Dead," http://www.commondreams. org/view/2009/06/15-0.
2. Mark Brenner and Jane Slaugher, "End of the Road," http://labornotes.org /node/254.
3. Robert Kuttner, *Everything for Sale: The Virtues and Limits of Markets* (Chicago: University of Chicago Press, 1999), 84.
4. See Thomas Sugrue, *The Origins of the Urban Crisis: Race and Inequality in Postwar Detroit* (Princeton: Princeton University Press, 1996), 36.
5. A concise, excellent summary of the dynamic leading to the bubble collapse is Dean Baker, *Blunder and Plunder* (Sausalito: Polipoint Press, 2009).
6. Robert Skidelski, *Keynes: The Return of the Master* (New York City: Public Affairs, 2009), 40–42.
7. Ibid., 97.
8. http://delong.typepad.com/sdj/2010/11/battered-but-not-beaten.html.
9. http://krugman.blogs.nytimes.com/2010/11/27/man-and-supermacro/.

10. Rawi Abdelal, Mark Blyth, and Craig Parsons, eds., *Constructing the International Economy* (Ithaca: Cornell University Press, 2010), 12.

11. I draw here extensively on William Connolly, *Neuropolitics: Thinking, Culture, Speed* (Minneapolis: University of Minnesota Press, 2002), chapters 3 and 4.

12. Conversation with Dave Feldman, professor of Physics, College of the Atlantic.

13. For discussion of these issues, see Wesley W. Widmaier, "Trade-Offs and Trinities," in Abdellal, Blyth, and Parsons, *Constructing the International Economy*.

14. Connolly, *Capitalism and Christianity, American Style* (Durham: Duke University Press, 2008), 76.

15. Dean Baker, "Was the Bank Bailout Necessary," *Guardian* May 16, 2010, http://www.guardian.co.uk/commentisfree/cifamerica/2009/may/18/us -economy-bank-bailout.

16. Timothy Canova, "The Legacy of the Clinton Bubble," http://www.dissent magazine.org/article/?article=1229.

17. Joanne Barkan, "Symposium on Affirmative Action," *Dissent*, Fall 1995, 463.

18. Tom DeLuca and I have commented on this in *The Progressive Populist*.

19. Martin J. Sklar's *The Corporate Reconstruction of US Capitalism* (Cambridge: Cambridge University Press, 1988) remains one of the seminal works on this theme.

20. See Baker, *The Conservative Nanny State: How the Wealthy Use the Government to Stay Rich and Get Richer* (New York: Lulu, 2006), for discussion of this theme

21. Naomi Klein and Avi Lewis, "The Cure for Layoffs: Fire the Boss," http: //www.naomiklein.org/articles/2009/05/cure-layoffs-fire-boss.

22. See Sugrue, op. cit., 153-177.

23. See http://www.truthout.org/033109A.

24. Thomas Dumm, *A Politics of the Ordinary* (New York: NYU Press, 1999), 5.

25. Romand Coles, *Christianity, Democracy and the Radical Ordinary* (Eugene: Cascade Books, 2008), 46.

26. Ibid., 62.

27. Ibid., 297 and 298.

28. See discussion of Jane Bennett, *Vibrant Matter: A Political Ecology of Things* (Durham: Duke University Press, 2009) in chapter three.

29. See Coles, *Christianity, Democracy*, 156.

30. I am presenting a slightly idealized version of occupational safety politics in Sweden as discussed in Robert Kuttner, *Everything for Sale*. I don't claim to have followed the course of this debate in Sweden since Kuttner's book was published, but their approach strikes me as suggestive for broader democratic theory.

31. See Elizabeth Warren's talk to Network Nation, http://www.alternet. org/economy/147699/elizabeth_warren:_my_mission_is_to_restore _america%27s_great_middle_class?page=entire.

32. Ibid., 165.

Six   National Security and Apocalypse

1. See, for instance, Charles W. Kegley, Jr and Shannon L. Blanton, *World Politics: Trend and Transformation* (Boston: Wadsworth, 2010), chapter 2.
2. See David Campbell, *Writing Security*, 144.
3. James Der Derian, *Critical Practices in International Theory* (New York: Routledge, 2009), 152.
4. Speech at West Point.
5. http://www.nytimes.com/2009/03/27/world/asia/27taliban.html?scp=1&sq=afghan%20and%20pakistani%20Taliban%20burying%20differences&st=cse (last accessed March 26, 2008).
6. Juan Cole, Friday, April 3, 2009, "Top Ten Ways the US is Turning Afghanistan into Iraq," Informed Consent Blog.
7. Ibid.
8. SSRC Home SSRC Blogs Blog Home " 'These Things are Old': Obama and the End of Exceptionalism," posted by Thomas L. Dumm.
9. http://georgewbush-whitehouse.archives.gov/news/releases/2007/02/20070214-2.html.
10. See Chris Hedges, "The Disease of Permanent War," http://www.alternet.org/news/140106/the_disease_of_permanent_war/.
11. "Actually, it was the Inept Empire," June 2004, http://pqasb.pqarchiver.com/latimes/access/648279351.html?dids=648279351:648279351&FMT=ABS&FMTS=ABS:FT&type=current&date=Jun+8%2C+2004&author=Andras+Szanto&pub=Los+Angeles+Times&edition=&startpage=B.13&desc=Commentary%3B+Actually%2C+It+Was+the+Inept+Empire.
12. "The Ism That Failed, The American Prospect," December 1, 2003. Interested readers can go to www.prospect.org and then go to archives.
13. William Blum, "The Myth of the Gipper: Reagan Didn't End the Cold War," *Counterpunch*, June 7, 2004, http://www.counterpunch.org/blum06072004.html.
14. "Still on Catastrophe's Edge," http://pqasb.pqarchiver.com/latimes/access/623920611.html?dids=623920611:623920611&FMT=ABS&FMTS=ABS:FT&type=current&date=Apr+26%2C+2004&author=Robert+McNamara+and+Helen+Caldicott&pub=Los+Angeles+Times&edition=&startpage=B.13&desc=Commentary%3B+Still+on+Catastrophe%27s+Edge%3B+In+a+flash%2C+U.S.+and+Russia+could+hurl+thousands+of+missiles+at+each+other.
15. http://dissidentvoice.org/Nov05/Blum1111.htm.
16. http://en.wikipedia.org/wiki/2007_(John_F._Kennedy_International_Airport_attack_plot).
17. See http://www.mindfully.org/Reform/2004/IISS-Iraq-Occupation26may04.htm.
18. http://www.getreallist.com/police-and-fbi-investigate-antiwar-protesters.html.
19. Jeff Milchen, "Security vs. Freedom: The False Choice," http://www.reclaimdemocracy.org/civil_rights/security_freedom_false_choice.html.
20. The Watson Institute for International Studies at Brown University, Global Security Manifesto, http://www.watsonblogs.org/globalsecurity/archives/2005/03/global_security_1.html.

21. "Private Prosperities, Public Breakdowns," http://pqasb.pqarchiver.com
/latimes/access/77030486.html?dids=77030486:77030486&FMT=ABS&
FMTS=ABS:FT&type=current&date=Aug+5%2C+2001&author=PETER
+G.+GOSSELIN&pub=Los+Angeles&edition=&startpage=A.1&desc=SU
NDAY+REPORT%3A+Private+Prosperities%2C+Public+Breakdowns%3B
+The+%2790s%3A+Private+Boom+Stingy+on+Public+Good%3B+As+indi
vidual+wealth+scaled+lofty+heights%2C+spending+on+America%27s+com
mon+needs+didn%27t+keep+up.+Series%3A+First+of+two+parts.

22. See George Will, "Congress's Unused War Powers," *Washington Post*,
November 4, 2007, http://www.washingtonpost.com/wp-dyn/content
/article/2007/11/02/AR2007110201785.html.

23. I have drawn on the commentary on this play in the edition, Aristophanes,
Acharnians, Lysistrata, Clouds, translated and introduced by Jeffrey
Henderson (Newburyport: Focius Classical Library, 1988).

24. See Jean Elshtain, *Women and War* (New York: Basic Books, 1986), concluding
chapter.

25. http://www.pbs.org/now/transcript/transcript_woodruff.html.

Conclusion: Addressing a World of Rhizomatic Crises

1. See William Connolly's discussion of arboreal and rhizomatic pluralism
in *The Ethos of Pluralization* (Minneapolis: University of Minnesota Press,
1995), 94–95. I find his discussion of the ways even rhizomatic pluralism can
become violent especially insightful.

2. See http://readersupportednews.com/off-site-news-section/49-49/2073-gulf-
oil-spill-is-public-health-risk-top-kill-effort-continues (last accessed May 28,
2010).

3. See http://www.democracynow.org/2010/5/27/expert_ecological_impact_of
_spill_could.

4. Quoted from Glenn Greenwald in Salon: http://www.salon.com/news/opin-
ion/glenn_greenwald/2010/05/24/wars/index.html.

5. Stephen Salisbury in CommonDreams: http://www.commondreams.org
/view/2010/05/24.

6. http://readersupportednews.org/off-site-opinion-section/57-57/2070-the
-truth-about-drones-they-are-inspiring-homegrown-terror.

7. http://www.commondreams.org/view/2010/05/25-0.

8. http://www.cnbc.com/id/15840232/?video=1504494372&play=1.

9. Full text and video: http://jalopnik.com/5397084/first-my-name-is-ram-ad-
my-tank-is-full.

10. Michael Klare, *Rising Powers, Shrinking Planet: The New Geopolitics of Energy*
(New York: Metropolitan Books, 2008), 36.

11. http://muse.jhu.edu/login?uri=/journals/american_quarterly
/v057/57.3campbell.html.

12. See Dean Baker, "Barack Obama's Big Stimulus," *Guardian*, January 19,
2009: http://www.guardian.co.uk/commentisfree/cifamerica/2009/jan/19/
barack-obama-economic-stimulus.

13. Dean Baker, "Attack Wall Street, Not Social Security," *Guardian*, April 12, 2010: http://www.guardian.co.uk/commentisfree/cifamerica/2010/apr/12/useconomy-obama-administration.

14. Quoted in Paul Krugman's blog: http://krugman.blogs.nytimes.com/2010/06/09/the-seductiveness-of-demands-for-pain/.

15. See David Streitfield, "Wealthy are the Biggest Defaulters on Mortgage Loans," *New York Times*, July 8, 2010: http://www.nytimes.com/2010/07/09/business/economy/09rich.html?_r=1&scp=1&sq=wealthy%20and%20mortgage%20defaults&st=cse.

16. See this blog comment of Reich's: "Recession Cause [*sic*] by Surgin Wealth Inequality," http://coyoteprime-runningcauseicantfly.blogspot.com/2010/07/robert-reich-recession-cause-by-surging.html.

17. For discussion of these issues, see Wesley W. Widmaier, "Trade-Offs and Trinities," in Rawi Abdellal, Mark Blyth, and Craig Parsons, eds., *Constructing the International Economy* (Ithaca: Cornell University Press, 2010).

18. Dean Baker, "Unemployment Solution: Pay People to Work Shorter Hours," *Huffington Post*, November 16, 2009: http://www.huffingtonpost.com/dean-baker/unemployment-solution-pay_b_359008.html.

19. Paul Krugman, "The Road to Dubai," *New York Times*, March 31, 2006.

20. Bonnie Honig, "Ruth, the Model Émigré," in David Campbell and Michael J. Shapiro, eds., *Moral Spaces: Rethinking Ethics and World Politics* (Minneapolis: University of Minnesota Press, 1999), 203.

21. See Campbell and Shapiro, eds., *Moral Spaces*.

22. For a discussion of its role in the left, see Boaventura De Sousa Santos: http://pas.sagepub.com/content/36/2/247.short.

23. See George Monbiot, "Death Denial," first posted in *Guardian*, November 2, 2009: http://www.monbiot.com/archives/2009/11/02/death-denial/.

BIBLIOGRAPHY

Books

Abdelal, Rawi, Mark Blyth, and Craig Parsons, eds., *Constructing the International Economy* (Ithaca: Cornell University Press, 2010).

Baker, Dean, *The Conservative Nanny State: How the Wealthy Use the Government to Stay Rich and Get Richer* (New York: Lulu, 2006).

————, *Blunder and Plunder: The Rise and Fall of the Bubble Economy* (Sausalito: Polipoint Press, 2009).

Bennett, Jane, *Unthinking Faith and Enlightenment: Nature and the State in a Post-Hegelian Era* (New York: New York University Press, 1987).

————, *The Enchantment of Modern Life* (Princeton: Princeton University Press, 2001).

————, *Vibrant Matter: A Political Ecology of Things* (Durham: Duke University Press, 2009), 94–100.

Best, Michael, and William Connolly, *The Politicized Economy* (Lexington: D. C. Heath and Co., second edition, 1983).

Blum, William, *Killing Hope: U.S. Military and CIA Interventions since World War II* (Monroe, Maine: Common Couage Press, 2008).

Campbell, David, *Writing Security: United States Foreign Policy and the Politics of Identity* (Minneapolis: University of Minnesota Press, 1998), 2.

Campbell, David, and Michael J. Shapiro, *Moral Spaces: Rethinking Ethics and World Politics* (Minneapolis: University of Minnesota Press, 1999).

Campbell, David, and Morton Schoolman, eds., *The New Pluralism: William Connolly and the Contemporary Global Condition* (Durham: Duke University Press, 2008).

Coles, Romand, *Beyond Gated Politics: Reflections for the Possibility of Democracy* (Minneapolis: University of Minnesota Press, 2005).

————, *Christianity, Democracy and the Radical Ordinary* (Eugene: Cascade Books, 2008).

Connolly, William, *Political Theory and Modernity* (Ithaca: Cornell University Press, 1993).

————, *The Ethos of Pluralization* (Minneapolis: University of Minnesota Press, 1995).

————, *Why I Am Not a Secularist* (Minneapolis: University of Minnesota Press, 1999).

————, *Identity/Difference: Democratic Negotiations of Political Paradox* (Minneapolis: University of Minnesota Press, 2002).

————, *Neuropolitics: Thinking, Culture, Speed* (Minneapolis: University of Minnesota Press, 2002).

Der Derian, James, *Critical Practices in International Theory* (New York: Routledge, 2009).

Dionne, E. J., *Souled Out: Reclaiming Faith and Politics after the Religious Right* (Princeton: Princeton University Press, 2009).

Dumm, Thomas, *A Politics of the Ordinary* (New York: New York University Press, 1999).

Elshtain, Jean, *Women and War* (New York: Basic Books, 1986).

Fox, Richard, *Reinhold Niebuhr: A Biography* (New York: Pantheon, 1985).

Galbraith, James, *The Predator State: How Conservatives Abandoned the Free Market and Why Liberals Should Too* (New York: Free Press, 2009).

Goldwater, Barry, *Conscience of a Conservative* (Victor Publishing Company, 1960).

Guskin, Jane, and David L. Wilson, *The Politics of Immigration* (New York: Monthly Review Press, 2007).

Hirsch, Fred, *The Social Limits to Economic Growth* (Lexington: D. C. Heath, 1981).

Honig, Bonnie, *Political Theory and the Displacement of Politics* (Ithaca: Cornell University Press, 1993).

————, *Democracy and the Foreigner* (Princeton: Princeton University Press, 2001).

————, *Emergency Politics: Paradox, Law, Democracy* (Princeton: Princeton University Press, 2009).

Hunnicutt, Benjamin Kline, *Work Without End* (Philadelphia: Temple University Press, 1988).

Kauffman, Stuart, *Reinventing the Sacred: A New View of Science, Reason, and Religion* (New York: Basic Books, 2008).

Kegley, Charles Jr., and Shannon L. Blanton, *World Politics: Trend and Transformation* (Boston: Wadsworth, 2010).

Keller, Catherine, *On the Mystery: Discerning Divinity in Process* (Minneapolis: Fortress Press, 2008).

Klein, Naomi, *The Shock Doctrine: The Rise of Disaster Capitalism* (Picador, 2008).

Kolchin, Peter, *American Slavery: 1619–1877* (New York: Hill and Wang, 2003).

Kuttner, Robert, *Everything for Sale: The Virtues and Limits of Markets* (Chicago: University of Chicago Press, 1999).

Mankiw, Gregory, *Principles of Economics* (South-Western College Publishers, 2008).

Marcus, Robert, ed., *American Firsthand: Readings from Settlement to Reconstruction* (New York City: Bedford/St. Martin's Press, 2004).

Morone, James, *Hellfire Nation: The Politics of Sin in American History* (New Haven: Yale University Press, 2004).

Niebuhr, Reinhold, *The Nature and Destiny of Man* (New York: Charles Scribner's Sons, 1941, 1964, Volume I).

————, *The Children of Light and the Children of Darkness* (New York: Charles Scribner's Sons, 1944).

Price, H. H., *Maine's Visible Black History: The First Chronicle of its People* (Maine: Tillbury House, Gardiner, 2006).

Rousseau, Jean-Jacques, *On the Social Contract: With Geneval Manuscript and Political Economy* (New York: St. Martins Press, 1978).

Sanders, John, *The God Who Risks: A Theology of Divine Providence* (IVP Books, 2007).

Schor, Juliet, *The Overspent American: Upscaling, Downshifting, and the New Consumer* (New York: Basic Books, 1998).

———, *Born to Buy: The Commercialized Child and the New Consumer Culture* (New York: Scribner, 2005).

Skidelski, Robert, *Keynes: The Return of the Master* (New York City: Public Affairs, 2009).

Sklar, Martin J., *The Corporate Reconstruction of US Capitalism* (Cambridge: Cambridge University Press, 1988).

Sugrue, Thomas, *The Origins of the Urban Crisis: Race and Inequality in Postwar Detroit* (Princeton: Princeton University Press, 1996).

Taylor, Charles, and William Connolly, *Capitalism and Christianity American Style* (Durham: Duke University Press, 2008).

Wagner, David, *The New Temperance: The American Obsession with Sin and Vice* (New York: Westview Press, 1997).

Woodruff, Paul, *Reverence: The Forgotten Virtue* (Oxford: Oxford University Press, 2003).

Articles

Bacon, David, "Up for Grabs: 10 Years of NAFTA and Mexico," http://www.thirdworldtraveler.com/NAFTA_FTAA/Mexico_NAFTA_TenYears.html.

Blum, William, "The Myth of the Gipper: Reagan Didn't End the Cold War," *Counterpunch*, June 7, 2004, http://www.counterpunch.org/blum06072004.html.

Bradsher, Keith, "Domination, Submission, and the Chevy Suburban," *New York Times*, March 23, 1997, section 4.

Carroll, James, "Hair Trigger Nation," http://www.commondreams.org/views05/1212-23.htm.

———, "The End is Near," *Boston Globe*, July 20, 2009, http://www.boston.com/bostonglobe/editorial_opinion/oped/articles/2009/07/20/the_end_is_near/.

Freedland, Jonathan, "The Levee Will Break," http://www.guardian.co.uk/world/2005/sep/07/hurricanekatrina.usa9.

George, Lakoff, "Empathy, Sotomayor, and Democracy: The Conservative Stealth Strategy," *Huffington Post*, May 30, 2009, http://www.huffingtonpost.com/george-lakoff/empathy-sotomayor-and-dem_b_209406.html.

Hansen, James, http://www.nybooks.com/articles/archives/2006/jul/13/the-threat-to-the-planet/?page=2.

Hedges, Chris, "The Disease of Permanent War," http://www.alternet.org/news/140106/the_disease_of_permanent_war.

———, "The American Empire is Dead," http://www.commondreams.org/view/2009/06/15-0.

Kaplan, Jeffrey, "The Gospel of Consumption," http://www.orionmagazine.org/index.php/articles/article/2962/.

Klein, Naomi, and Avi Lewis, "The Cure for Layoffs: Fire the Boss," http://www.naomiklein.org/articles/2009/05/cure-layoffs-fire-boss.

McKibben, Bill, "Can 350.org Save the World?" http://www.commondreams.org/view/2009/05/17-4.

Monbiot, George, "Death Denial," first posted in *Guardian* November 2, 2009, http://www.monbiot.com/archives/2009/11/02/death-denial/.

West, Cornel, "Exiles from a City and a Nation," *The Observer*, Sunday, September 11, 2005, http://www.guardian.co.uk/world/2005/sep/11/hurricanekatrina.comment.

Will, George, "Congress's Unused War Powers," *Washington Post*, November 4, 2007, http://www.washingtonpost.com/wp-dyn/content/article/2007/11/02/AR2007110201785.html.

Yassin, Jaime, "Demonizing the Victims of Katrina," http://www.fair.org/index.php?page=2793.

Blogs

Baker, Dean, "Beat the Press," http://www.cepr.net/index.php/beat-the-press/.

Cole, Juan, "Informed Comment," http://www.juancole.com/.

The Contemporary Condition, http://contemporarycondition.blogspot.com/.

Krugman, Paul, "Conscience of a Liberal," http://krugman.blogs.nytimes.com/.

Watson Institute, Global Security Blog, http://www.watsonblogs.org/globalsecurity/.

INDEX

advertising, 54–5, 60–1, 62, 124, 133
affirmative action, 43, 120
Afghanistan, 135, 138, 139–40, 151, 157
agape, 35–6, 39
  compare with Eros
antitrust law, 122
apocalypse, 4–7, 95, 103, 135, 165
  for the left, 127–33
  compare with existential anxiety
Arbatov, Georgi, 146
arboreal, 125, 165–6
  compare with rhizomatic
Aristophanes, 158–62
atheists, 13, 15, 18
automobiles, 47–74, 170–2
  addiction to, 48
  and mass transit, 52–3
  as a positional good, 53
  and religion, 60–2
  and social relations, 60–2
  sports utility vehicles, 55–6, 57
  see also public transit

Babel, 88
Baker, Dean, 118, 123, 131, 132, 172, 173
Baker, Ella, 126
bank bailout, 127
Barkan, Joanne, 119–20
Beck, Glenn, 1–2
Becker, Ernest, 180
Bell, Daniel, 96

Bennett, Jane, 23–4, 68–71, 74–5, 93, 129, 169, 182
Bennett, William, J., 28, 145
Best, Michael, 53
bin Laden, Osama, 146, 149, 151, 168
Blair, Tony, 148
Blum, William, 146, 148
Blyth, Mark, 110–11, 115–16
borders, 90–1, 136
Boyte, Harry, 127
Brennan, John, 168
BRICs, *see* developing countries
British Petroleum (BP), 166–7, 169, 170, 180
Bush, George W., 25, 43, 73, 81, 85, 100, 103–4, 110, 142–4, 147, 148, 150, 152, 157, 173

Caldicott, Helen, 146
Campbell, David, 13, 14, 24, 170–1
Canova, Timothy, 119
capitalism, 79, 95–133
  corporations, 121
  democratic, 128–9
  future of, 129
  see also free market
Carroll, James, 5–7
Carter, Jimmy, 99, 174
Catholicism, 62–4
causality, 115–16
cellular telephones, 58–9
Central Intelligence Agency (CIA), 169